Ansi C for Corporate Programmers

Ansi C for Corporate Programmers

A *No-nonsense Guide for Experienced Business Programmers*

Jim Inglis
Birkbeck College, University of London, UK

JOHN WILEY & SONS
Chichester • New York • Brisbane • Toronto • Singapore

Copyright © 1994 by John Wiley & Sons Ltd.
                          Baffins Lane, Chichester
                          West Sussex PO19 1UD, England

                          National Chichester (0243) 779777
                          International +44 243 779777

Other Wiley Editorial Offices

John Wiley & Sons, Inc., 605 Third Avenue,
New York, NY 10158-0012, USA

Jacaranda Wiley Ltd, 33 Park Road, Milton,
Queensland 4064, Australia

John Wiley & Sons (Canada) Ltd, 22 Worcester Road,
Rexdale, Ontario M9W 1L1, Canada

John Wiley & Sons (SEA) Pte Ltd, 37 Jalan Pemimpin #05-04,
Block B, Union Industrial Building, Singapore 2057

Library of Congress Cataloging-in-Publication Data

Inglis, Jim.
    C for corporate programmers : a no-nonsense guide for experienced
  business programmers / Jim Inglis.
        p. cm.
    Includes index.
    ISBN 0 471 93965 X
    1. C (Computer program language) 2. Business—Data processing.
  I. Title.
  QA76.73.C15I54 1994
  005. 13′3—dc20   93-45016
                                                           CIP

British Library Cataloguing in Publication Data

A catalogue record for this book is available from the British Library

ISBN 0 471 93965 X

Produced from CRC supplied by the author using Microsoft Word for Windows
Printed and bound in Finland by Bidecon Oy, Savonlinna

Contents

Preface

This book is addressed principally to application programmers in commercial and administrative data processing, and to others in that area who have a programming background.

You may very well be satisfied with the programming tools you use now, and with the way these tools are improving. Over a large range of application areas, as fourth-generation languages supersede Cobol, system development is becoming faster and more reliable, prototyping is a practical proposition, and system maintenance is easier. Cobol, much improved over the years, is still valuable for those applications which do not match 4GL paradigms.

Nevertheless, you cannot fail to be aware of the rapid growth of an alien culture. With the spread of Unix systems, C has emerged from a somewhat inward-looking world to become a much-used application language. Meanwhile, Cobol is losing its traditional application areas to 4GLs, and the demand for Cobol programmers is declining. In a few years' time, C (or C++, its object-oriented offspring) may replace Cobol as the most widely used third-generation language. It makes sense for commercial application programmers to learn C, both for use in their own organizations and to make themselves more marketable in the future. Any professional programmer today should have some knowledge of C.

It is one thing to be aware of this state of affairs, but another to find an introduction to C which is written for the experienced corporate programmer. C books fall into two broad categories - those which teach programming to beginners, and those which assume a knowledge of another programming language. Much of the space in books of the first category is taken up with material which you know already, and the material you need is consequently covered in less detail. Books of the second category are usually directed at programmers whose current languages have much in common with C and thus assume some familiarity with concepts like recursion and pointers which may be new to you. Neither kind of book has much to say about files and character-string handling, which are of primary interest to the corporate programmer. Reading one of these books is like walking in a strange land with a guide who does not speak your language and has no idea of what might interest you. What I have tried to do is to work from the familiar to the unfamiliar, explaining the latter in detail from first principles. I frequently relate features of C to those of 1985 Standard Cobol since Cobol is the language you are most likely to know; to enable Cobol programmers to locate quickly the corresponding parts of C, Appendix 4 indexes the Cobol features mentioned in the text. But a detailed knowledge of Cobol is not needed - you should have no problems if you are coming from another language.

Like Cobol, C is a victim of its own success. When a language is widely used, it cannot be redesigned from scratch to reflect changes in programming methodology or to extend its applicability. Early design decisions, however undesirable they appear with the benefit of hindsight, cannot be reversed; at best, new features can be grafted on as painlessly as possible, with minimum impact on existing programs. Both Cobol and C have suffered in this respect.

The version of C used throughout is the recent ANSI Standard, for which good inexpensive compilers are available. Use of an older, non-standard, compiler is a false economy and a recipe for grief. If you are purchasing a compiler, perhaps the best thing to buy is a C++ compiler, provided that it will also accept ANSI C programs. You will then be able later to learn about the object-oriented features of C++ without making any further software investment. Since C++ is virtually a superset of C, what you learn from this book will be needed if you later want to extend your knowledge to C++. (At present, most purchasers of C++ compilers seem to make little use of the object-oriented features; they write their programs in C. This situation is likely to change.) Most programs in the book have been tested with several compilers, and they have all been tested with Borland C++, version 3.0.

Do not imagine that, because C is fashionable, it is "better" than Cobol, or RPG, or whatever language you currently use. All languages have their strengths and their weaknesses; there are application areas in which they perform well and others for which they are unsuitable. No truly professional programmer will have unqualified enthusiasm for a single language to the exclusion of all others. Most C books do the language a disservice by claiming for C an excellence and a versatility which it does not possess. (C *is* very versatile, but only in the sense in which an assembly language is.) Reading these books is unnerving; because they praise the language and fail to acknowledge its weaknesses, they leave you questioning your understanding of what you have read. I hope that the following pages give an objective and comprehensive view of C, warts and all.

Acknowledgments

Over many a lunch-time discussion, I have had the benefit of Kevin Brunt's programming insight and C expertise; these have been invaluable at every level, from overall presentation to detailed examples. I have also profited greatly from observations and suggestions made by Keith Mannock, Nigel Martin, Roger Mitton and Ian Worthington. Each of these busy people has kindly found time to read the manuscript, at one stage or another of its development, carefully and critically. Peter King's observations on the final chapter were very helpful. In the end, of course, I have had to use my own judgment, and any faults are mine alone.

1

Introduction

The Preface has introduced C and indicated the scope and approach of this book. This short chapter explains how the material is presented. It tells you a little about C and its standard library, it explains the typographical conventions used in the program extracts, and it introduces three terms which will appear quite often in later chapters.

The version of C expounded here is the ANSI Standard, adopted and published by the International Organization for Standardization (ISO) in 1990. Unattributed quotations are from that Standard. The structure of the Standard reflects the way in which the C facilities are divided into modules. C's modularization is best explained by contrasting it with that of Cobol.

A programming language *standard* defines the language, and *implementors* provide compilers (or other language processors) in accordance with the standard's specifications. Cobol is a big language, which the 1985 Standard divides into functional modules, most of which may be implemented at one of two defined levels. When you buy a Cobol compiler, you accept the subset of the language which it provides. No Cobol program makes any reference whatever to the modularization of the language; a program simply uses the standard language, and the compiler will object to the use of any feature not present in the implementation. Most Cobol programmers are quite unaware of the fact that the Standard specifies modules and levels.

C, by contrast, is a small language, inconvenient for the vast majority of applications. It has to be supplemented by a *library* of functions and other things to make it more useful; all input and output, for instance, is done by calling library functions. In practice, therefore, C is the combination of the C language proper and its standard library. (Both of these are specified in the Standard.) It is in this sense that "C" is used in the rest of this book. When you buy a C compiler you receive also an implementation of the complete standard library. The standard library, like the Cobol language, is divided into functional units. Each unit has an associated *header*, which must be *included* in any program which uses any facility provided by that unit. Thus the C programmer, unlike the Cobol programmer, must know about the modularization of the language facilities. Before using any feature, the C programmer has to include in the program the appropriate header. (This nonsense may not last forever. With decreasing storage costs, the time is surely not far distant when programs can routinely include all the standard library headers.) For easy reference, Appendix 3 lists in alphabetical order all the facilities provided by the standard library and tells you, for each of them, which header your program must include.

For the benefit of readers who are familiar with Cobol, I often accompany descriptions of C features with examples of corresponding Cobol features, showing the similarities or pointing out the differences. When program extracts are used as illustrations, *Cobol code is enclosed in rectangular boxes to distinguish it from C code.* To older Cobol programmers the Cobol code may look peculiar, being in lower case (permitted since the 1985 Standard, and earlier by some compilers), with reserved words in bold type. I have for many years successfully used this very readable format in teaching Cobol.

In C's syntax, upper-case and lower-case letters are treated as distinct, and I use the usual C conventions (together with one or two of my own) in forming identifiers. I use bold type for reserved identifiers, including identifiers declared in the standard library (which are reserved when their headers are included in the program). Apart from making the program extracts more readable, this convention helps beginners by distinguishing identifiers defined in the language or the library from those declared by the programmer. Of course, in programs presented to a compiler, reserved identifiers are not typographically distinguished from the rest of the program text.

The C Standard defines the syntax, constraints and semantics of the language and the library facilities, but it does not fully specify all aspects of the language, its translation, or the run-time behaviour of programs; certain details are left to the implementor. There are three main kinds of implementor freedom. In specifying a particular aspect of C, the Standard may use one of the following terms (which are used with the same meanings throughout this book). Naturally, the examples given below may not make much sense to you yet; but, when you come back later to check what the terms mean, you will understand them.

undefined behaviour: *"behaviour, upon use of a non-portable or erroneous program construct, of erroneous data, or of indeterminately valued objects, for which this Standard imposes no requirements".* Here there is some error in the program or data, such as an error causing use of uninitialized data or causing integer overflow. When such things arise, the behaviour is undefined - depending on the situation and the implementor's whim, you may or may not get a compile-time warning, or a run-time message, the error may simply be ignored, or the program may terminate, or the complete system may crash. In effect, the implementor has *carte blanche* to let anything at all happen. Undefined behaviour occurs in situations where the Standard explicitly says it does, or where the Standard does not specify what happens.

implementation-defined behaviour: *"behaviour, for a correct program construct and correct data, that depends on the characteristics of the implementation and that* *each implementation shall document"*. In other words, where the Standard specifies implementation-defined behaviour, implementors may do what they like, but they must document the behaviour.

unspecified behaviour: *"behaviour, for a correct program and correct data, for which this Standard explicitly imposes no requirements"*. An example from the Standard is the order in which the arguments of a function are evaluated; perhaps your compiler always evaluates arguments in a specific order, but, if your program relies on that order, it will be non-portable.

Do not worry if the above explanations seem confusing at this stage. These terms will become more familiar in the chapters that follow.

2
Preliminaries

This chapter does not treat its material formally or exhaustively. Its purposes are to enable you to write and run little C programs and to tell you about the control structures you will use routinely in C programming. Many of the topics introduced here will be treated in greater detail in later chapters.

2.1. Variables

In the data division of a Cobol program, we *declare* an elementary data item by specifying a level-number, a name, and a picture (and possibly other things). A data item in Cobol is what C and other languages call a *variable*. However, C has no level-numbers and no pictures. Instead, a variable is declared as being of a particular *type*. For the present, we consider only one type - **int**.

An integer is a whole number; i.e. it is a number without any fractional part. A variable of type **int** is capable of assuming any integer value within a range specified by the implementor. The smallest range permitted by the standard is from −32767 to +32767; for many machines the range is much greater. The value is represented in storage in binary form (instead of character form), just as it is for some **computational** usages in Cobol.

        int count_1;

declares a variable named *count_1* and says that it is of type **int**. The declaration

        int count_1 = 0;

would also declare a variable named *count_1*, but would additionally assign to it the initial value zero. Ending a C declaration with

        = 0;

has the same effect as including in a Cobol declaration the clause "**value** 0". As in Cobol, the initial value may be any value of the appropriate type.

Multiple variables of the same type may be declared together, as in

> **int** x, y, z;

which declares three variables (*x, y* and *z*) as all being of type **int**.   Many C programmers, however, prefer to use a separate declaration for each variable (as is done in Cobol) to make program maintenance easier:

> **int** x;
> **int** y;
> **int** z;

2.2. Identifiers

In C, a name used to identify a variable (or almost anything else) is a sequence of one or more characters, each of which is a letter, a digit, or an underscore, except the first character of the name, which must be a letter or an underscore. This is rather like a Cobol word, with underscore (_) instead of hyphen (-), but C has these important differences:

- the first character must not be a digit;
- the first and/or last character may be an underscore;
- lower and upper case letters are distinct.

The last of these differences means that, for example, *fred*, *FRED* and *FrEd*, which would be the same identifier in Cobol, are different identifiers in C (though it would clearly be bad practice to use three such names in a program).

The Cobol Standard stipulates that the maximum length of a word is 30 characters and that all characters are significant. The C Standard imposes no maximum length, but only the first 31 characters are significant.

As in Cobol, certain identifiers are *reserved*. The notion of a reserved identifier is more complex in C than in Cobol. Appendix 2 explains the position, but you will not fully understand it until you have reached the end of chapter 11. For the time being, it will usually be enough to avoid declaring any identifier which

- appears in the list at the start of Appendix 2, or
- begins with an underscore.

(Library identifiers are reserved in certain limited contexts. This is unlikely to trouble you in your early programs; but, if you do have trouble, check that you have not used one of the identifiers listed alphabetically in the third column of Appendix 3.)

For future reference, note that additional restrictions may apply to identifiers which are visible outside the program source file - this point need not concern us at present.

2.3. **Program layout**

Cobol is not quite a free format language; certain syntactic units must start in Area A and others in Area B of a line. There are no such restrictions in C.

In C, commas and semicolons are important symbols. They must be used where the language syntax requires them, and they cannot be inserted at will anywhere else in a program.

In standard Cobol, spaces (or new-lines or tabs) are required as a separator, or as part of a separator, between syntax elements. In C also, spaces (or new-lines or tabs, both of which, for this purpose, are regarded as spaces) may be freely inserted between syntax elements; but in C they may be omitted altogether where the omission would not lead to misinterpretation. For example, these four declarations are equivalent:

```
          int    count_1=0 ;
          int  count_1    =0;
          int  count_1  = 0    ;
          int  count_1    =
     0;
```

but we could not write

```
     intcount_1  = 0;
```

because *intcount_1* would then be a single identifier. Nor could we write

```
     int  co  unt_1=0;
```

because, instead of *count_1*, there would be two identifiers, *co* and *unt_1*.

As in Cobol, the characters making up a multi-character operator must be contiguous. For instance, <= could not be written as < =.

2.4. **Assignment**

Because of its development history, Cobol contains a lot of redundancy. The functions of **move, compute, add, subtract, multiply** and **divide** statements are in most languages subsumed in a single concept, called *assignment*. In its simplest form, assignment in C resembles what would be written after the word **compute** in Cobol (but without any **size error** phrase). Assuming that *x, y* and *z* have been declared as of type **int**, here are examples of C assignment statements corresponding to some Cobol statements. (The alternative forms shown in square brackets are at this stage shown for interest only.)

	Cobol	*C*	
	move 0 **to** y	y = 0;	
	move x **to** y	y = x;	
	compute x = 2 * (y + 1)	x = 2 * (y+1);	
	add 1 **to** x	x = x+1;	[OR x++;]
	add y **to** x	x = x+y;	[OR x+=y;]
	add x, y **giving** z	z = x+y;	
	subtract y **from** x	x = x-y;	[OR x-=y;]

Note:

- Though C assignment resembles Cobol's **compute**, its use is not restricted to numeric data.
- A C assignment statement is terminated by a semicolon.

2.5. Simple output to your screen

This section contains only enough information to enable you to run little programs as you read this chapter. Output will be treated in detail in a later chapter.

Output of a character string is straightforward:

Cobol	*C*
display "Hello there" **no advancing**	**printf**("Hello there");
display "Hello there"	**printf**("Hello there\n");

In C, "\n" (pronounced "backslash en" or "escape en") stands for the new-line character.

In Cobol, if we want to get a sensible display of a signed or computational data item, we must first assign the value to an item with an editing picture, then display the latter item. In C, the editing is done by **printf** itself; to display the value of an **int** variable x, all we need is:

> **printf**("%d", x);

or, if we want to advance to the next line after displaying the value:

> **printf**("%d\n", x);

These particular C examples remove leading zeros, rather than replacing them by spaces.

The C approach has its drawbacks, but it has the advantage that, as well as displaying literals and the values of variables, we can directly display the values of expressions. In standard Cobol, if we want to display the value of the expression $x + y - 1$, we have to do something like

> **compute** z = x + y − 1
> **display** z

But, in C, all we need is

> **printf**("%d\n", x+y−1);

If x=3 and y=4, the characters output will be "6" and a new-line character. We can make our output more sensible by combining a piece of text with the value of the expression:

> **printf**("The result is %d\n", x+y−1);

If you are a Cobol programmer, you may already be feeling irritated by certain features of C. The use of silly names which are unmemorable and inappropriate, like **printf**, does not seem to worry C programmers, nor do the even less memorable symbols. "%d" means "insert a decimal number here". The quoted string in the last example above ("The result is %d\n") says: *display a character string consisting of "The result is ", followed by a number, followed by a new-line*; and the expression following the comma says that the number to be displayed is the value of the expression *x+y−1*. Unless you use C regularly, you will need a manual beside you when you write C programs.

2.6. The form of a complete program

For the present, all you need in order to make your C programs complete is:

```
#include <stdio.h>
main (void)
{
        return 0;
}
```

(This will all be explained later. With an older compiler, you may have to omit the word **void** but retain the parentheses.) Immediately before the statement "**return** 0", insert the program you want to try. For instance, a complete program for the last example in the preceding section might be:

```
#include <stdio.h>
main (void)
{
        int x = 3;
        int y = 4;
        printf("The result is %d\n", x+y−1);
        return 0;
}
```

or perhaps:

```
#include <stdio.h>
main (void)
{
      int x, y;

      x = 3;
      y = 4;
      printf("The result is %d\n", x+y-1);
      return 0;
}
```

All declarations must precede all executable statements. The first program above has two declarations and two executable statements (including **return** 0); the second program has one declaration (of two variables - **int** x, y;) and four executable statements. It is as though we had a data division followed by a procedure division, but with no explicit separation between them. It can be helpful to a reader of your program to separate them by a blank line, as in the second example above.

2.7. Compiling and running little programs

The processes of preparing a C program, compiling it and running it are much the same as those for a Cobol program. Using an editor, prepare your C source program and put it in a file; call the compiler to compile that file; perhaps, depending on your system, link the compiled code; the resulting file can then be run.

Examples:

(a) **In a Unix environment**, it is conventional to name your source file with the suffix *.c*; a source program in the file *test.c*, for instance, can be compiled by the command

          cc   test.c

There is no separate linking or loading step. If no errors are detected, the file *a.out* then contains the executable code, which can be run by the command

          a.out

If errors are detected, messages will appear on your screen, and you can edit the source file (*test.c*) and then try the *cc* command again.

The file *a.out* may, of course, be replaced by a new version whenever you use a *cc* command. If you want to retain the executable version of your program, you can assign it to another file, say *test.x*, instead of to *a.out*. To do this, include the name of the file in the *cc* command:

          cc   test.c   −o test.x

in which case you would run the program by saying

test.x

instead of *a.out.*

(b) **In a VMS environment**, you must first set up a reference to a link library by the command

define lnk$library sys$library:vaxcrtl.olb

This need be done only once at the start of each terminal session, rather than for every program.

Name your source file with the suffix *.c.* If you have named the source file *test.c*, then the command

cc test

compiles your program (*.c* is the default suffix for the input to *cc*) and, if successful, produces a file named *test.obj.* Then the command

link test

links your program (*.obj* is the default suffix for the input to *link*) and, if successful, produces a file named *test.exe.* Then the command

run test

runs your program (*.exe* is the default suffix for the input to *run*).

Errors can be corrected by editing *test.c* and restarting the above sequence. As with Cobol, if you use *cc/list* instead of *cc*, the compiler will additionally write a file named *test.lis* which will contain a listing of your program, with compiler-generated messages. The command

print test.lis

will print this file.

(c) **In a Windows environment on a PC, using Borland C++,** there is a simple development environment which enables you to edit source files in a window and provides menu options for compiling, running and many other functions.

If you have a C compiler available, you should now try compiling and running little programs using **int** declarations, assignment, and **printf**. In devising your own programs, note the following:

- Terminate each statement with a semicolon.
- Do not forget to declare all variables you use.
- As in Cobol, unless a variable is given an initial value, regard its value as initially undefined.

- Arithmetic expressions can be written as in Cobol, using the operators +, −, * and /, but *not* **. Operator precedence is the same as in Cobol, and parentheses can be used for sub-expressions. With type **int**, the division operator (/) gives only the integer part of the result (e.g. 15/4 = 3).
- There is a "modulus" operator, written as the percent sign, which gives the remainder after division (e.g. 23%8 = 7). For any values of *i* and *j*, except *j* = 0, the value of

    (i/j) *j + (i%j)

  is always that of *i*. (We have now met % in two different contexts - its meaning in an expression, as here, is quite different from its meaning in a string for *printf*.)
- Do not put leading zeros in front of a number (e.g. do not write 057 instead of 57). If you do, the number will be treated as octal.
- Where you put a unary minus sign after another operator, your compiler may object. If so, use parentheses. For instance, say *a*(−b)* instead of *a*−b*.

From this point on, you will find it helpful to write short programs to try out the various features as you learn about them.

2.8. Control structures

In Cobol, when we use an **if** or a **perform until** statement, we specify a conditional expression. When the statement is executed, the expression is evaluated to determine what action is to be taken. The C statements to be introduced in this section include similar expressions, and the operators provided are similar to those in Cobol. Here are the correspondences:

Cobol	C
<	<
not <	>=
<=	<=
=	==
not =	!=
>=	>=
>	>
not >	<=
not	!
and	&&
or	||

You will notice the unnaturalness and inconsistency of some of these C symbols. "!" is hardly a natural way to say "not". Though "==" means "is equal to", "<<" does *not* mean "is less than". (Indeed, it means something quite different.) And woe betide you if you write "&" instead of "&&" ("&" too means something different). Your C compiler will usually be unable to tell you that you have used a wrong operator, and your program will simply produce the wrong results or fail at run time. There is nothing for it but to memorize the symbols or to keep a manual beside you.

On the brighter side, operator precedence is the same as in Cobol, and sub-expressions can be parenthesized. It is safe practice to use redundant parentheses, as in

> (a **not** = b) **or** ((c **not** > d) **and** (e = f))

or, equivalently,

> (a!=b) || ((c<=d) && (e==f))

In both cases, the result of evaluating the expression would be unchanged if all the parentheses were omitted.

Another property that C shares with Cobol is that its **and** and **or** operators are what some people call *sequential* and others call *conditional*. This means that, at any precedence level, evaluation is from left to right and *ceases as soon as the truth value can be determined*. Thus, for example, the expression

> (i==0) || ((j/i)>10)

will not give rise to a runtime "division by zero" error if $i = 0$, for in that case the term ((j/i)>10) will not be evaluated. Similarly, if $i = 0$, evaluation of

> (i!=0) && ((j/i)>10)

will not give rise to division by zero, since the first term is false, and thus the whole expression is false; the second term is therefore not evaluated.

2.8.1. *if*

The Cobol statement

> **if** x < 5
>   **display** "x less than 5"
> **end-if**

is expressed in C as

> **if** (x<5)
>   **printf**("x less than 5\n") ;

Notice two differences between Cobol and C:

1. In C, the expression to be tested must be enclosed in parentheses.
2. When a Cobol statement contains other statements (as **if** always does), these statements are delimited by a scope terminator such as **else** or **end-if** (or, if you are still using ANSI 1974 style, a full stop). But, in C, only a *single* statement may be contained; there is therefore no need for a scope terminator.

In relation to the second of these points, a question naturally arises: what do we do if we want more than one statement within an **if**? How, for example, would we express the following code in C?

> **if** x < y
>   **display** "x is smaller"
>   **move** x **to** z
> **end-if**

The answer is that we place the statements in a *block*. A block is delimited by curly brackets ("{" and "}"); it may contain any number of statements - perhaps none at all - but, from the outside, a block is itself regarded as a single statement. Thus the above code would be expressed in C as:

```
if (x<y)
{      printf("x is smaller\n") ;
       z=x;
}
```

Usually, when a sequence of two or more statements is to be contained in another statement, these statements must be placed in a block. Notice the convention of placing the "}" on a line by itself, vertically aligned with the corresponding "{". This is not of course required by the language syntax, but it is useful in making programs more readable. For ease of maintenance, there is something to be said for also putting the "{" on a line by itself. Alternatively, for **if** and other statements, you can use the convention adopted in the rest of this book of placing the "{" on the same line as the condition.

As in Cobol, an **if** statement in C may have an **else** clause. The Cobol statement

> **if** x < y
>   **display** "x is smaller"
>   **move** x **to** z
> **else**
>   **display** "x is not smaller"
>   **move** y **to** z
> **end-if**

is expressed in C as

```
if (x<y) {
       printf("x is smaller\n");
       z=x;
}
else  {
       printf("x is not smaller\n");
       z=y;
}
```

As in Cobol, an **if** statement in C may contain other **if** statements; and, since a block may contain statements, a block may contain other blocks. (A block, remember, is a statement when viewed from outside.) For example, the Cobol statement

```
if  a < b
        move y to x
        if  z > 0
                compute  y  =  z  +  1
                move 0 to z
        end-if
else   add 1 to y
        move 0 to x
end-if
```

is expressed in C as

```
if (a<b) {
        x=y;
        if (z>0) {
                y=z+1;
                z=0;
        }
}
else  {
        y=y+1;
        x=0;
}
```

Since a *single* statement contained in an **if** does not need to be in a block, the following code, in which an **if** is contained in another **if**, is acceptable:

```
if (a<b)
        if (c<d)
                x=y;
else  printf("a not less than b");
```

But beware; this is equivalent to the Cobol statement

```
if  a < b
        if  c < d
                move y to x
        else  display "a not less than b"  no advancing
        end-if
end-if
```

and *not* what the indentation suggests:

```
if a < b
    if c < d
        move y to x
    end-if
else  display  "a not less than b"  no advancing
end-if
```

This is because, as happens in Cobol when we do not use an **end-if**, an **else** matches the latest unmatched **if**.   To correspond to this latter Cobol statement, the C statement should be:

```
if (a<b) {
    if (c<d)
        x=y;
}
else  printf("a not less than b");
```

C provides also a form of expression which yields one of two values, depending on a condition. A simple example is:

```
a < b  ?  i : j
```

If *a* is less than *b*, the value of this expression is that of *i*; otherwise it is that of *j*. This might, for instance, be used in an assignment statement:

```
smaller  =  a<b ? i : j;
```

which is equivalent to

```
if (a<b)
        smaller = i;
else   smaller = j;
```

We might instead display the selected value:

```
printf("%d\n", a<b ? i:j);
```

which we could achieve less neatly with

```
if (a<b)
        printf("%d\n", i);
else   printf("%d\n", j);
```

In general, the "?" is preceded by an expression, which is evaluated to determine which of the two *expressions* following the "?" is to be evaluated. There are many contexts in which this facility is useful, but it should not be used merely for brevity; the shortest program is not necessarily the best.

2.8.2. *switch*

The Cobol statement

> **evaluate** x + y − 1
>   **when** 0   **display** "zero"
>   **when** 1   **display** "one"
>   **move** 0 **to** d
>   **when other** **display** "wrong value"
> **end-evaluate**

is expressed in C as

> **switch** (x+y−1) {
>   **case** 0:   **printf**("zero\n");
>   **break**;
>   **case** 1:   **printf**("one\n");
>   d=0;
>   **break**;
>   **default**:   **printf**("wrong value\n");
> }

Notice that C requires the expression which is to be evaluated (the *switch expression*) to be in parentheses. (The **break** statements will be explained shortly.)

C's **switch** resembles Cobol's **evaluate** in these ways:

1. Multiple statements may be specified for a case. (They need not be in a block.)
2. The **default** part is optional. If no **default** is specified and the expression does not match any of the **case** values, nothing happens and control passes to the next statement in logical sequence.
3. If no statements are specified for a given **case**, the statements executed for that case are those for the next **case** (or **default**) for which statements are specified. For example, on execution of

> **switch** (i) {
>   **case** 1:
>   **case** 2:
>   **case** 3:   x=y;
>   **break**;
>   **case** 4:   x=z;
>   **break**;
>   **default**:   x=0;
> }

if $i = 1$ or $i = 2$ or $i = 3$, then $x=y$ is executed.

C's **switch** differs from Cobol's **evaluate** in these ways:

1. Consider these examples:

   ```
   evaluate  i
         when  0    move x to y
         when  1    move z to y
                    add 2 to z
         when other  move 0 to y
   end-evaluate
   ```

   and

   ```
   switch (i)  {
         case  0:    y=x;
         case  1:    y=z;
                     z=z+2;
         default:    y=0;
      }
   ```

   In the Cobol example, the executed statements are:

   If i=0:   **move x to y**

   If i=1:   **move z to y**
                   add 2 to z

   Otherwise: **move 0 to y**

   In the C example, the executed statements are:

   If i=0:   y=x;
                   y=z;
                   z=z+2;
                   y=0;

   If i=1:   y=z;
                   z=z+2;
                   y=0;

   Otherwise: y=0;

   In a **switch** statement, when a matching **case** value is found, the statements for *all cases* which follow (including the **default**, if appropriate) are executed in sequence. But at any point a **break** statement may be used to force immediate exit from the **switch** statement. If a **break** is placed at the end of each case (except the last, where it is unnecessary), the **switch** statement behaves like a Cobol **evaluate**.

2. In Cobol, any expression of the appropriate type may follow **when**. But in C, the expression following the word **case** must be a **constant expression**, which means that it must be evaluable at compile time, and therefore *must not include any variables*. Thus

   case 5*30−2:

is acceptable, but

   case line_length + 1:

is not, if *line_length* is a variable. (It is, however, acceptable if *line_length* is a constant. Constants will be introduced later.)

3. The constant expression following the word **case** must be of integral type. It may be a character constant (which is an integral type in C), but it cannot be a string. The **switch** statement cannot therefore be used, as **evaluate** commonly is in Cobol, to test the response of a terminal operator, e.g.:

> **evaluate** response
>   **when** "abandon" **perform** ....

4. The **switch** statement has no facility for specifying ranges of values (as, for example, in Cobol's **when** 0 **thru** 9).

5. Only a single expression may be tested by a **switch**. There is no equivalent for a Cobol **evaluate** beginning

> **evaluate** x + y **also** z **also true**

The **switch** statement is therefore a very poor relation of Cobol's **evaluate**. Because of the second limitation above, you cannot even use it to select one action from several on the basis of a number of different expressions (the familiar Cobol **evaluate true**); instead, you have to resort to using nested **if**s as Cobol programmers did when they had only the 1974 standard language.

2.8.3. *while*

The form of the **while** statement is:

   while (*expression*)
    statement

where the *statement*, of course, may be a block. For example

```
while (i<j) {
        printf("another 10\n");
        i = i+10;
}
```

is equivalent to

```
perform until  i  not < j
       display "another 10"
       add 10 to i
end-perform
```

In both cases, the test is made before each iteration. If *i* is not less than *j* initially, nothing is output and *i* is unchanged. Notice that **while** specifies the *continuation* condition instead of the *termination* condition; one is of course the complement of the other. Notice too that the expression giving the continuation condition must be in parentheses, and that the parentheses are not followed by a semicolon.

2.8.4. *do while*

The form of this statement is

> **do**
>> *statement*
> **while** (*expression*);

Again, the continuation condition is used, and again the expression must be in parentheses; note also the semicolon following the parentheses. For example, the statement

```
do  {
       printf("another 10\n");
       i = i+10;
}
while (i<j);
```

is equivalent to

```
perform with test after until  i not < j
       display "another 10"
       add 10 to i
end-perform
```

In both cases, the test is made after each iteration. Even if *i* is not less than *j* initially, output will occur and the value of *i* will be changed.

Notice that neither **while** nor **do while** provides an equivalent to Cobol's **perform** n **times**. Instead, C forces us to introduce another variable and make the counting explicit, as we would in Cobol with

```
perform varying i from 1 by 1 until i > n  ...
```

In C, this is done by a **for** statement.

2.8.5. *for*

The following Cobol statement, which displays the squares of integers 1 to 10 inclusive,

```
perform varying  i from 1 by 1 until  i  >  10
        compute  j  =  i  *  i
        display  j
end-perform
```

is equivalent (except for assignment to *j* and the format of the display) to the C statement

      for (i=1; i<=10; i=i+1)
          printf("%d\n", i*i);

(How much easier this is to write!) The general form of the **for** statement is

      for (*initialization; continuation-condition; increment*)
          statement

The *statement* may, of course, be a block. Cobol's **perform varying** and C's **for** have these features in common:

1. The initial value of the "control variable" (*i* in the above) and the value of the increment may be arbitrary values.
2. The continuation condition (or, in Cobol, the termination condition) may be an arbitrary expression, and need not include any reference to the control variable.
3. The continuation condition (or termination condition) is tested at the head of the loop, and incrementation occurs at the foot. The above example is equivalent to the more primitive C code:

          i=1;
     L1: **if** (i<=10) {
               printf("%d\n", i*i);
               i=i+1;
               goto L1;
          }

    (from which you will notice that C, like Cobol, has a **go to** statement; in C the single word **goto** is used). In both the Cobol and C examples, the value of *i* on exit from this loop is 11.

Standard Cobol, however, is much more restrictive than C. In Cobol the initial value and the increment must be written as identifiers or numeric literals. In C, they are expressions, so we might have

      for (i=(j*k)–2; i<=m+4; i=i+(8*n)) ...

Indeed, there is no need in C to have a control variable at all. The general form given above would be more appropriately expressed as:

> **for** (*expression1; continuation-condition; expression2*)
>   *statement*

where we can think of *expression1* and *expression2* for the present as each being one statement, or two or more statements separated by commas. (The relationship between expressions and statements will be explored later.)

In the **for** statement, *expression1* specifies what is to be done before the first entry to the loop, and *expression2* specifies what is to be done at the end of each iteration. The above formulation of **for** corresponds to:

> *expression1*;
> L1:   **if** (*continuation-condition*) {
>   *statement*
>   *expression2*;
>   **goto** L1;
>   }

We may omit *expression1*, in which case no initialization occurs. The fact that nothing appears before the first semicolon in the following indicates that *expression1* is null:

> **for** (; i<=10; i=i+1) ...

This statement is equivalent to

> | **perform varying** i **from** i **by** 1 **until** i > 10 ... |

If *expression2* is null (indicated by the absence of anything after the second semicolon), then nothing is done at the end of each iteration. So

> **for** (i=1; i<=10;) ...

has the same effect as

> | **perform varying** i **from** 1 **by** 0 **until** i > 10 ... |

(There may of course be statements in the loop that change *i*'s value.)

If we omit both *expression1* and *expression2*, the **for** is equivalent to a **while**:

> **for** (; i<=10;) ...

> **while** (i<=10) ...

The continuation-condition may be null, in which case we would appear to have an endless loop; exit from the loop would have to be achieved in some "irregular" way, such as with **go to** or **exit program** in Cobol. As we have seen, C too has a **goto** statement; it also has a **return** statement, which resembles **exit program**. But C also provides two neat additional methods of leaving a loop - **continue** (to leave the current iteration) and **break** (to leave the loop altogether).

2.8.6. *continue*

Both C and Cobol have **continue** statements, but their meanings are very different. In C, **continue** may appear anywhere in a loop, and is a means of jumping to *the end of the current iteration*. It can be used within **while**, **do while**, or **for**. For example, in the following **for**, *statements1* and *statements2* are executed for all values of *i* from 1 to 4 and from 7 to 10, but only *statements1* are executed for *i* = 5 and 6.

```
for (i=1; i<=10; i=i+1) {
    statements1
    if (i==5 || i==6) continue;
    statements2
}
```

In effect, **continue** is a **goto** with *expression2* (see section 2.8.5) as its destination.

2.8.7. *break*

We have seen the use of **break** in a **switch** statement. It may also be used anywhere in a **while, do while**, or **for** loop. The effect of **break** is to exit immediately to the statement logically following the loop (but see the exception at the end of this section).

Cobol, like many programming languages influenced by a fervour for "structured programming" in the nineteen-seventies, insists that exit from a loop be made at one point only - the head or the foot of the loop. In order to exit at some other point, we could of course use **go to**, which is forbidden by the tenets of structured programming, though not by the language. To avoid using **go to**, Cobol programmers sometimes introduce another data item to transmit the terminating condition from the body of the loop to the exit point. Consider the unnecessary complexity of these Cobol statements, which display a count of the number of records in file *f*:

```
open input f
perform with test after
        varying record-count from 0 by 1 until eof = "t"
        read f next
              at end    move "t" to eof
              not at end move "f" to eof
        end-read
end-perform
display record-count
```

If, like C, Cobol allowed us to omit the termination condition (eof = "t") and provided a **break** statement, the data item *eof* could be dispensed with, and we would write something like

```
open input f
perform with test after varying record-count from 0 by 1
      read f next;  at end  BREAK  end-read
end-perform
display record-count
```

In relation to **break** or **continue**, we speak of "the loop". What we mean, of course, is the nearest loop which encloses the **break** or **continue**. The following program fragment resembles Cobol's **perform varying ... after**, or nested **perform varying**s.

```
for (i=1; i<=2; i=i+1)
      for (j=1; j<=3; j=j+1)  {
            printf("A%d%d\n", i, j);
            if (i==1)  break;
            printf("B%d%d\n", i, j);
      }
```

It will display the following, each on a line: A11, A21, B21, A22, B22, A23, B23. The **break** causes exit from the inner loop, but not from the outer one. (Notice also the effect of placing more than one "%d" in the *printf* string. On the output, the values of the comma-separated expressions that follow the string are placed in the string in order, one in each "%d" position.)

However, there is one circumstance in which **break** does not cause exit from the nearest enclosing loop. You may recall that **break** also causes exit from a **switch**. What **break** actually causes is a jump to the statement logically following the nearest enclosing **switch, while, do while** or **for** statement. Here, for instance,

```
switch (.....)  {
      case  ...
      .....
      case ... : while (.....)  {
                  .....
                  if (.....)  break;
                  .....
                  .....
            }
            break;
      case ...
      .....
      .....
}
```

the **break** in the **if** causes a jump to the statement following the **while**, and the **break** at that point causes a jump out of the **switch**. Such behaviour is usually what we want in real programs (though not always); what can be more annoying is that there is no decent way, from within a **switch**, to exit from a loop that encloses it:

```
while (.....) {
        .....
        .....
        switch (d)  {
                case 0: .....
                case 1: .....
        }
        .....
        .....
}
```

If we wanted to exit from the **while** loop when d = 0, we could not use **break** within the **switch**, for that would merely cause a jump to the statement following the **switch**, which is reached also by the other case. The **break** in the following, however, would cause a jump to the statement following the **while**:

```
while (.....) {
        .....
        .....
        if (d==0) break;
        else  if (d==1)  .....
        .....
        .....
}
```

It is a pity that the correspondence which otherwise exists between a **switch** and nested **if**s does not extend to loop exits.

2.8.8. Summary

C provides the same kinds of control structures as Cobol and provides the additional facilities of the **break** and **continue** statements. While **switch** lacks the power of Cobol's **evaluate, for** is more powerful and flexible than Cobol's **perform**. But we have not so far used the C statements in an idiomatic C manner; we are still thinking in Cobol terms and expressing our thoughts in C. As we explore other aspects of C and learn to think in terms of the language, we will see many benefits which are not clear from the simple examples shown here.

2.9. Other assignment operators

There are two kinds of assignment to a variable - those in which it is assigned a value unrelated to its previous value, e.g.

a = b + c

compute a = b + c

and those in which its new value is derived in part from its previous value, e.g.

a = a + b

compute a = a + b

For this latter kind of assignment, both C and Cobol provide alternative forms, such as

a += b

add b **to** a

C's alternatives are less limited than Cobol's, because in C an *expression* can appear on the right of the assignment operator (+=).

The advantage of using these alternative forms is not clearly brought out by the simple examples above. Like those in Cobol, identifiers in C are not usually single letters, they may be qualified, and they may have complex subscripts. With the alternative forms, writing and keying are easier, and the likelihood of error is reduced.

The forms provided by C are:

a+=b	*means*	a=a+(b)
a-=b	*means*	a=a-(b)
a*=b	*means*	a=a*(b)
a/=b	*means*	a=a/(b)
a%=b	*means*	a=a%(b)

The longer forms are shown here with *b* in parentheses because *b* may be an expression, and all arithmetic operators have a higher precedence than any of these assignment operators, i.e. the arithmetic takes place before the assignment. As an illustration, suppose that *k*'s value is initially 3. Then

k *= 5+4

assigns 27 (i.e. 3*(5+4)) to *k*, since + has a higher precedence than *= ; but

k = k*5+4

assigns 19 to *k*, since * has a higher precedence than +.

C also provides special forms of assignment for the common operations of adding 1 and subtracting 1:

a++	or	++a	*means*	a+=1
a--	or	--a	*means*	a-=1

The difference between the two forms of double plus or double minus will be explained later. We will see a number of situations in which these forms are useful.

The assignment operators which have been introduced here are heavily used in C programs, and it is good practice to use them wherever appropriate. For instance, no C programmer would write, as I have done in this chapter,

>   **for** (i=1; i<=10; i=i+1) ...

The statement would be written instead as

>   **for** (i=1; i<=10; i++) ...

2.10. Characters

The only C type we have met so far is **int**, which corresponds to one of the **computational** usages in Cobol. We now look briefly at another type, **char**.

The declaration

>   **char** c;

declares a variable named *c* and says that it is of type **char**. We may assume for the present that the value of *c* at any time will be one character, so that the above declaration is like the Cobol declaration

> c **pic** x.

Unfortunately, C has no direct equivalent for **pic** xx, **pic** x(3), and so on. There is no standard C type corresponding to the most basic of Cobol types - a fixed-length string of characters. As we will see, to get the same thing in C, you will have to declare an array of characters; it is as though in Cobol, instead of saying

> 01 a **pic** x(4).

you had to say

> 01 a.
>   02 b **pic** x **occurs** 4.

and were then not allowed to use the name *a* (though we will see later that C has a means of specifying something like a Cobol record).

There is worse to come. If you are a Cobol programmer, you will be accustomed to being able to specify declaratively any character collating sequence for a program, as well as the character encoding used for any file. Your programs and data can thus be portable and the effect of running your programs always the same, regardless of the "native" encoding scheme of the system on which they are run.

In C, everything happens in terms of the encoding scheme of the environment in which you run the program. When you compare two characters, you are actually comparing the integers corresponding to the binary encodings that represent the two characters. Thus, in ASCII encoding, 'a' is greater than 'A'; but, in EBCDIC, 'a' is less than 'A'. Your program will not be portable from an environment using one encoding to an environment using another. This rarely worries C programmers, many of whom think exclusively in terms of ASCII; and nearly all implementations of C are for ASCII environments. But, even accepting this, it is unnecessarily difficult to order character strings on a collating sequence other than that of ASCII. C has at present no simple declarative means of defining or selecting a collating sequence. (The C Standard specifies a method of using a program-defined collating sequence in certain limited contexts - see section 13.16.)

C normally assumes that all input and output files use the environment's encoding scheme (usually ASCII). In C, there is no equivalent of Cobol's **code-set**. If a file uses a different encoding, you will have to supply your own functions to do the translation or, if you can, find a suitable C library function or a system utility.

A *character constant* (what Cobol calls a literal) is written as a character preceded and followed by single quotes. We can, for example, assign initial values, as in

> **char** c='A';
> **char** d='+';

and we can use **char** variables and character constants in expressions, as in

> **if** (c==d) ...

or

> **while** (c<='m') ...

In C, 'X' is a character constant, but "X" is a *string literal* which consists of just one character; the two are quite distinct, as we will see in chapter 4. We have already used string literals in connection with **printf**.

Another feature of C that we met in using **printf** was the *escape sequence* \n, which denoted a new-line character. (Backslash is sometimes pronounced "escape" in this context.) New-line is one of several characters which have no convenient graphical representation (the kind of character for which the Cobol **symbolic character** is commonly used). A general method of specifying such characters as character constants is to specify their representations in octal or hexadecimal notation, but the C standard gives the more portable alternative of escape sequences for certain commonly-used characters:

> \a   alert (i.e. bell)
> \b   backspace
> \f   form feed (i.e. page throw)
> \n   new-line

     \r   carriage return
     \t   horizontal tab
     \v   vertical tab

Escape sequences are used in character constants and string literals. Other escape sequences provided, for reasons which should be obvious from the syntax of character constants and string literals, are: \' for a single quote; \" for a double quote; and \\ (two backslashes) for \. For a reason which will not be obvious at present, \? can stand for a question mark character. There is also the null character, always represented by zero and written as \0. Though written as two characters, each of the above represents, and is stored as, a single character. So, for example, we could initialize a **char** variable named *tab* to be the horizontal tab character:

     char tab = '\t';

and we could then determine whether a **char** variable *c* had a tab character as its value by

     c == tab

as well as by

     c == '\t'

Values of **char** type may be displayed by **printf**, using %c to denote insertion of a character. Execution of

     char k='A';
     printf("The character is %c\n", k);

would display "The character is A" followed by a new line. Now look at what happens here:

     int j=66;
     char k='A';
     printf("%c,%d$%c,%d", j, j, k, k);

You will see that this displays the value of *j* first as a character then as an integer, followed by the value of *k* first as a character then as an integer. When executed in an ASCII environment, this little program displays "B,66$A,65". (In ASCII, 'A' is encoded as binary 1000001 (65 in decimal) and 'B' as binary 1000010 (66 in decimal).) The following would give the same display:

     int j='B';
     char k=65;
     printf("%c,%d$%c,%d", j, j, k, k);

From these examples you will see that C is not a "strongly-typed" language. In C, many operations on a character are treated as operations on the integer corresponding to its representation. The two types **char** and **int** can be freely mixed in expressions; **int**s can be assigned to **char**s, and **char**s to **int**s. (Implicit type conversion takes place, but that is a subject for a much later chapter.) A character constant is of type **int**. C even has the absurd notions of signed and unsigned characters! The distinction can cause subtle errors, particularly when programs are transferred from one environment to another. Of course, though every character corresponds to a unique integer, not all integers correspond to characters. The result of using an inappropriate integer in a context where a character is required varies from one implementation to another. (It depends on whether the implementation regards **char** as signed or unsigned.)

Since C sees characters as integers, it is possible to perform arithmetic on characters. What do you think the following nonsense code does?

```
char  j='s';
char  k='A';
printf("%d*%c\n", j-k, j-k);
```

Run in an ASCII environment, it displays "50*2" followed by a new line. Subtracting 'A' from 's' is, in C, subtracting 65 from 115, giving 50, which is the integer corresponding to the character '2'. Just occasionally, arithmetic operations on characters make sense (as when we want to establish how far apart two characters are in the collating sequence, or when we use the encodings for encryption purposes), but for most applications they are to be sedulously avoided. A character is *not* a number; do not think of it as a number unless you have to.

A Cobol programmer would think that last piece of advice unnecessary. But more than one C textbook gives the following method for converting the value of *ch* from lower case to upper case:

```
char  ch;
   ....

   ....
ch += 'A' - 'a';
```

This code has a misleading appearance of portability; in fact it makes certain assumptions about the underlying character representations. We will see later that there are standard functions which enable case conversion to be done safely.

Your attention has been drawn to character arithmetic not because it is an important facility, but to caution you. Unlike a Cobol compiler, your C compiler will not give you an error message if you inadvertently apply an arithmetic operator to a character constant or variable. The information given here should help you to make sense of output produced by a program containing an error of this kind.

2.11. A debugging checklist

A fault in your program may be detected at compile time or it may cause a run-time error. Implementations differ in the amount of information you get on detection of an error; for example, there are still C compilers which respond to most syntax errors by simply reporting "syntax error". To help you find errors in your early programs, here are some of the commoner mistakes made by programmers coming to C from another language:

1. Using the wrong operator, in particular "=" instead of "==". Take care also with && and ||.
2. Omission of parentheses round the expression following **if** or **while**.
3. Incorrect insertion of a semicolon immediately after the bracketed continuation condition of a **while** statement. This often results in an endless loop.
4. Incorrect use of single and double quotes, or failure to terminate a quoted item.
5. Omission of a *#include* line.
6. Incorrect insertion of a semicolon at the end of a line beginning with "#".
7. Incorrect matching (or omission) of parentheses or brackets.
8. Use of "-" instead of underscore in an identifier. The "-" will be interpreted as a minus sign.
9. Failure to declare a variable.

As in Cobol, errors can cascade; so always start checking at the first message.

2.12. Summary

You now know about C's control structures and about manipulating objects of types **int** and **char**; you can (and are encouraged to) write and run very simple C programs. You will still be using a Cobol-like approach, and you will be severely limited by the absence of any treatment so far of data input and the manipulation of character strings. In order to understand these topics, you must first learn about other general features of C. These will be introduced in the next chapter, which will also help you to develop a more characteristic approach to writing C programs.

3

Basic Concepts

This chapter looks in more detail at expressions and their evaluation and introduces functions and pointers. Much detail is still omitted; the object is to get you quickly to a stage at which you can write substantial C programs. If you have programmed only in Cobol, some of the concepts will be new to you. Be patient - an understanding of this chapter will be needed for the treatments of character strings, input-output and files in later chapters, where you will be back on more familiar ground.

3.1. Expressions

When an expression is evaluated at run time, the value it returns is of a predetermined type. In Cobol, an arithmetic expression returns a number and a conditional expression returns a truth value. At a superficial level, the same is true of C - and C, like Cobol, lacks the boolean type found in the strongly Algol-based languages. But in C a conditional expression returns a truth value that is represented as a number. An expression like

$$i > 10$$

actually returns the value 1 if i is greater than 10, and returns 0 otherwise. As long as your program is correctly written, you need not usually be aware of this fact. But, as with characters, you have to be cautioned that a C compiler will give you no error warning if you apply arithmetic operators to what we normally think of as truth values. It will actually be applying the operators to values 0 and 1 (or, more generally, zero and non-zero), so again you have to be told about the numeric representations so that you can understand errors in a program's output.

Occasionally, the numeric representation of truth values can be useful, as in determining how many of a number of conditions are true. For example, in a program dealing with responses to a questionnaire, **char** variables a, b and c might be responses to three different questions; then the expression

$$(a == 'y') + (b \mathrel{!=} 'y') + (c \mathrel{!=} 'n')$$

would give a count of how many of the three questions were answered in the specified ways.

As with characters, not only is a truth value a number, but a number is also a truth value. Zero corresponds to *false* and any non-zero number corresponds to *true*. You will remember that && means *and*, and that || means *or*. The expression

    125 && 0

is permissible, and its value is 0, representing *false*; the value of the expression

    125 && (0 || 8)

is 1, representing *true*. Once again, you are not advised to do such stupid things; but you have to know about them, otherwise you would not understand the effects of your errors. If we omitted the parentheses in our questionnaire example, we would have

    a == 'y' + b != 'y' + c != 'n'

Because the + operator has a higher precedence than the equality and inequality operators, this expression would be interpreted as

    a == ('y' + b) != ('y' + c) != 'n'

Now let us see how this expression would be evaluated in an ASCII environment when a = 'y', b = 'y' and c = '-' (in which case our original parenthesized expression would return the value 2). The ASCII encodings of 'y', 'n' and '-' are 121, 110 and 45 respectively. The sub-expression ('y' + b) would return 242, and ('y' + c) would return 166. The expression would then be

    a == 242 != 166 != 'n'

which gives

    121 == 242 != 166 != 110

The operators == and != have the same precedence and are evaluated left to right, so the effect is

    ((121 == 242) != 166) != 110

giving

    (0 != 166) != 110

then

    1 != 110

giving the final result 1.

Now that we have met a large number of C operators (and there are many more!) and seen an example of expression evaluation, it is time to review the operator precedence levels. For the operators already introduced, these are summarized in Table 3.1; a full precedence table is given in Appendix 1. Operators on each line of the table (i.e. on each level) have the same precedence as each other. The lines are ordered with the highest precedence at the top and the lowest at the bottom. The higher the precedence of an operator, the earlier it is applied during expression evaluation. For instance, looking at the top three lines, we see that the expression a * –b + c is equivalent to (a * (–b)) + c; first the unary minus is applied to *b*, then the * is applied, and finally the +.

```
- (unary)  ++  --  !
*  /  %
+  -
<  <=  >  >=
==  !=
&&
||
? :
=  *=  /=  %=  +=  -=
```

Table 3.1: Precedence table for the operators introduced in Chapter 2.

Cobol programmers will notice that those operations that are common to Cobol and C have the same precedence ordering in both languages, with the exception of what C calls the *relational operators* (<, <=, >, >=) and the *equality operators* (==, !=). In Cobol, the corresponding operators are all on a single level, but the relative position of both sets with respect to all the other operators is the same as in C. Notice that all the operators in the top line of the table are *unary* (i.e. they are applied to only one operand); that the *conditional operator* (? :) is applied to three operands - one before the question mark, one between the question mark and the colon, and one after the colon; and that the remaining operators are placed between the two operands to which they are applied. *The operands to which operators are applied are expressions.*

Let us look in more detail at what we mean by an *expression*. In its simplest form, an expression is a character constant (e.g. 'X') or a numeric constant (e.g. 512) or an identifier (or other things, which need not concern us at this stage). Thus

> a + 7

consists of the operator + and the two expressions to which it is applied (*a* and 7). *a* + 7 is itself an expression, which may be an operand of another operator, and so on. The precise manner in which a given expression is *parsed* (i.e. decomposed into sub-expressions for the purpose of evaluation) is implied by operator precedence and associativity (i.e. left-to-right or right-to-left evaluation). Any sub-expression may be enclosed in parentheses, which may confirm the implied parsing, as in

> a + (b * c)

or override it, as in

(a + b) * c

Every expression returns a value. In the second of these examples, the expressions "a" and "b" return the values of variables *a* and *b* respectively. These values determine the value returned by the expression "a + b". This value and the value returned by the expression "c" determine the value returned by the expression "(a + b) * c".

None of this, of course, is peculiar to C; expressions in other languages are written and evaluated in the same way. In most other languages, programmers manage to write expressions correctly in a natural and almost intuitive way - you have probably never had any great trouble with expressions in Cobol. But C has many more operators; and, as we have seen, characters and truth values are treated as numbers. Expressions require greater care in C, and it is advisable to include redundant parentheses to guard against possible misunderstandings on your part or that of the person who later has to maintain your program.

Where C differs from many other languages is in *regarding assignment as an expression*. (You will have noticed that the assignment operators are included in Table 3.1.) Since assignment is an expression, assignment *returns a value*, as any other expression does. The difference between an assignment operator and the other operators in Table 3.1 (except ++ and --) is that assignment affects the value of a variable. In a program, the assignment operators on the bottom line of Table 3.1 are placed between two expressions. In the simplest and commonest case, the expression on the left is an identifier of a variable. The value of the whole expression is the value assigned to the variable.

Let us look at the implications. The expression

x = 1

does not only assign 1 to *x*; it also returns the value 1. This means that we could (unless prudence deterred us) write expressions like

y = (x = 1) + 2

which assigns 1 to *x*, assigns 3 to *y*, and returns 3. Without the parentheses, the expression is

y = x = 1 + 2

Since + has a higher precedence than =, and since = associates from right to left, this is equivalent to

y = (x = (1 + 2))

The value returned is 3, as is the value assigned to *y*; but this time 3 (instead of 1) is assigned to *x*.

Now we can appreciate one of the absurdities of C. Any multi-lingual programmer using C is liable to make the mistake of writing

if (x = 1) ...

in order to test whether x's value is 1. But C's inexplicable use of "=" as an assignment operator and consequent adoption of "==" to test for equality means that

    x = 1

is always true, whatever the value of x. (The expression x=1 assigns 1 to x and returns 1. Interpreted as a truth value, this means *true*, as does any non-zero value.)

Since an assignment expression returns the value assigned, it is possible to get an effect similar to that of a Cobol multiple assignment. If all the variables are of type **int**, statements like the following pairs are equivalent:

> | **move** a **to** b, c, d |
> | :--- |

    b = c = d = a;

> | **compute** w, x, y = z + 1 |
> | :--- |

    w = x = y = z + 1;

Because of operator precedence and the right-to-left associativity of the assignment operator, the second C statement shown above is parsed as

    w = (x = (y = (z + 1)))

which means that the value returned by $z+1$ is assigned to y and is returned by the expression $y=(z+1)$; this returned value is then assigned to x, becoming the value returned by the expression $x=(y=(z+1))$, which is then assigned to w. Notice how this differs from the way in which Cobol treats multiple destinations. The difference can be important when variables of different types are involved.

3.2. Expressions and statements

Assignment expressions can be useful in many contexts. Here, for instance, is a program to display all squares (of integers) which are less than 1000:

```
int sq;
int i=1;
while ((sq = i*i) < 1000) {
    printf("%d\n", sq);
    i++;
}
```

In the third line, a new value is assigned to sq, and that new value is tested. Note, incidentally, the use of the ++ operator to increment i.

We make an expression into a statement when we append a semicolon.

x = y + z

is an expression; but

x = y + z;

is a statement. When we do this, we discard the value returned by the expression. We use a *statement* purely for the things it does (e.g. changing the value of a variable, controlling the flow of program execution, or sending data to an output device). We use an *expression* both for the things it does and for the value it returns.

Not always, however. *Commas* have the effect of combining several expressions so that they are regarded from the outside as a single expression (in much the same way as statements may be placed in a block and regarded as a single statement). If three expressions *E1, E2* and *E3* are combined into a single expression by commas:

E1, E2, E3

then the three sub-expressions are evaluated successively in left-to-right order, but the values of *E1* and *E2* are discarded. The value returned by *E3* (or, in general, by the rightmost sub-expression) is also returned by the expression (*E1, E2, E3*) as a whole. *These rules do NOT apply to the commas within multiple declarations such as*

int a, b, c;

nor to commas within the parentheses following a function name, e.g.:

printf ("%d%d", x, y)

Using the comma facility, we could rewrite the above squares program as:

```
int sq;
int i=0;
while ((i++, sq = i*i) < 1000)
        printf("%d\n", sq);
```

The expression

i++, sq = i*i

consists of two sub-expressions. When it is evaluated, first *i* is incremented and the value of the sub-expression *i++* is discarded, then a value is assigned to *sq* and also becomes the value of the whole expression. This value is then compared with 1000. Regarded as an operator, the comma has lower precedence than any other operator. The inner parentheses of the **while** are therefore necessary.

printf can display the values of expressions. Here too assignment expressions may be used. The following program displays the factorials of the integers 1 to 7. (The *factorial* of a positive integer n, denoted by $n!$, is the product of all integers from 1 to n; $2! = 1 \times 2$, $3! = 1 \times 2 \times 3$, etc.) Notice how this program uses assignment expressions in **for**'s initialization expression as well as for **printf**. On each iteration, **printf** displays both *i*'s value and that of the expression that assigns a new value to *fact* (which is, of course, the new value of *fact* itself). This does not necessarily produce the clearest code.

```
int  i, fact;
for (i = fact = 1;  i <= 7;  i++)
        printf("%d! = %d\n", i, fact *= i);
```

A **for** statement requires a single expression for its initialization;   as was explained above, two or more expressions will be regarded as a single expression if they are separated by commas. So another way of writing the above program is:

```
int  i, fact;
for (i = 1, fact = 1;  i <= 7; i++)
        printf("%d! = %d\n", i, fact *= i);
```

In this case, no use is made of the value returned by the expression

```
i = 1,  fact = 1
```

You may have noticed that in Table 3.1 the operators ++ and --, like other operators which have a single operand, have very high precedence, while the other assignment operators have very low precedence. The advantage of this arrangement will become clear as we go on. For the moment, let us examine the difference between ++i and i++. Though both add 1 to *i* (i.e. they *increment i*), the value returned by ++i is the value *after* incrementation, but i++ returns the value *before* incrementation. (A similar rule applies to the *decrement* operator --)

```
int  x = 3;
printf("%d", x++ * 2);
```

displays "6", but

```
int x = 3;
printf("%d", ++x * 2);
```

displays "8". Both the following programs display the integers 1 to 10:

```
int  i = 0;                     int  i = 1;
while (i<10)                    while (i<=10)
        printf("%d\n", ++i);            printf("%d\n", i++);
```

Now refer back to the second of our two programs to display the squares less than 1000. You may feel that instead of

```
while ((i++, sq = i*i) < 1000)  ...
```

we could write

```
while ((sq = ++i * i) < 1000)  ...
```

though it is not clear what you would hope to gain by doing so. It would make the program text a bit shorter (or "more concise", as people who believe that to be a virtue like to say); but, when we choose how to express an algorithm, what we ought to be aiming for is ease and security in program maintenance - the program should be understood readily by someone reading it. The expression $++i * i$ causes unnecessary subtleties of interpretation; and, though it may give the result you want with your C compiler, it may not be portable to other environments, because the C Standard does not guarantee that the two operands of * will be evaluated in a particular order. To make your programs safe and portable, adopt this general rule: *Within an expression, never change the value of any operand whose value is used elsewhere in the expression.* (Clearly this rule can be disregarded when the whole expression is an assignment like

   x = y / x

because the expression *y / x* is guaranteed to be evaluated before the new value is assigned to *x*.) For this purpose, regard expressions separated by commas as different expressions, rather than as one expression. C's ability to change the value of a variable within an expression is a frequent source of confusion.

Finally, a word about the role of commas in relation to **printf**. **printf** is not a language statement; it is a *function*. When a function is invoked, its *arguments* are written as expressions in parentheses after the function name. The arguments are separated by commas, but that does not mean that the sequence of expressions is regarded as a single expression; nor are the values of any expressions discarded; nor are the expressions evaluated from left to right - *the sequence of evaluation is unspecified, which means that they are evaluated in an unpredictable order.* For example, the code

   int i = 99;
   printf ("%d,%d\n", i, ++i);

produces the output "100,100" on at least two implementations.

This use of commas for separating arguments is quite different from their use in forming a multiple expression, as described earlier. If a multiple expression is to be used as an argument, it must be enclosed in parentheses, as in

   printf("%d\n", (i++, sq=i*i));

where the first comma separates the two expressions that act as arguments, and the second argument is in the inner parentheses. Functions are the subject of the next section.

3.3. Using functions

Let us leave C for a moment and look generally at expressions. Conventionally, we place a unary operator before its operand, as with the operator "-" in "-1", or the operator "not" in "not(a or b)"; these are *prefix* operators. We place a binary (i.e. dyadic) operator between its operands, as with the operator "+" in "a+b", or the operator "or" in "a or b"; these are *infix* operators. This conventional arrangement cannot be extended easily to operators with more than two operands.

An alternative scheme is to use prefix operators throughout. Unary operators like "-" and "not" precede their operands as before, but instead of "a+b" we would write "+a b", and, instead of "a or b", "or a b". This scheme extends naturally to any operator which has a fixed number of operands. (But notice that we would have to use different symbols for unary "+" and "-" from those used for binary "+" and "-" in order to know whether one or two operands should follow.) Compare these simple examples, illustrating the two schemes:

Infix	*Prefix*
a + b	+ a b
a * b	* a b
a + b * c	+ a * b c
(a + b) * c	* + a b c
a * b + c	+ * a b c

In the third example, + is applied to the two operands following it; these are *a* and ** b c*. In the fourth example, * is applied to the two operands + *a b* and c. Prefix expressions like those above are unambiguous, and there is no need for precedence or associativity rules, since the order of evaluation is determined by the expression itself.

But sometimes we want to use an operator which may have a variable number of operands. Suppose we had a *max* operator which returned the maximum of the values of however many operands were supplied; for instance, *max a b* would return the maximum of the two values *a* and *b*, and *max a b c* would return the maximum of *a, b* and *c*. An easy way to deal with this is to use parentheses to enclose the operands, so that we can see how many there are. We would write *max(a,b)*, *max(a,b,c)*, and so on. Extending this idea to all operators (and inserting commas), the prefix expressions above become easier to read:

+(a, b)
*(a, b)
+(a, *(b, c))
*(+(a, b), c)
+(*(a, b), c)

This is called *functional notation*. Each operator is now called a *function*, and its operands are called *arguments*. Each of the above examples is still an *expression*. A *function returns a value, and an expression still returns a value.*

The trouble with using symbols like + and * is that, if you want to design a powerful language, you quickly run out of symbols, or at least you soon start having to use symbols whose appearance is unrelated to what they actually mean. So we usually represent the functions (i.e. the operators) by natural-language names. For instance, instead of saying +(a, b), we might say *add(a, b)*, just as we said *max(a, b)* earlier.

Functional notation can be extended to encompass control structures, and then it can be used to write complete programs;   this is the basis of functional programming languages. But most languages, including C, retain conventional arithmetic and logical expressions, while also supplying functions for other things and giving the programmer a means of specifying other functions that may be needed.

We now look briefly at two of C's predefined functions, and then go on to learn how to specify our own functions. One predefined function, supplied with C, is **isprint**, pronounced "is print", not "eye sprint". The function **isprint** takes one argument of type **int**, and returns a value of type **int**, representing a truth value - an unspecified non-zero value represents *true*, and zero represents *false*. The function tests whether its argument corresponds to the encoding for a printable character. The space character is regarded as a printable character. (If you want to try a program using **isprint** - or **tolower**, which we'll use in a moment - you should add this extra line at the start of your program, before or after the *#include <stdio.h>* line:

        #include <ctype.h>

This will be explained shortly.) You might use the function like this:

        int k;
        ....
        ....
        if (**isprint**(k))
                printf("%c", k);
        else **printf**("unprintable character");
        ....

Equivalently, the **if** statement could be replaced by

        printf((**isprint**(k) ? "%c" : "unprintable character"), k);

(Note that, since the second option contains no % symbol, the value of k is printed only if the first option is chosen.)

Another standard function, named **tolower**, takes one **int** argument and returns an **int** value:

• If the argument is an integer which represents an upper-case letter, the return value is the integer representing the corresponding lower-case letter.
• Otherwise, the value returned is that of the argument.

We might amend the above call of **printf** so that it also replaces an upper-case letter by its lower-case equivalent:

        printf((**isprint**(k) ? "%c" : "unprintable character"), **tolower**(k));

making the reasonable assumption that every upper-case letter has a printable lower-case equivalent. But there is nothing to prevent us saying

        printf((**isprint**(**tolower**(k)) ? "%c" : "unprintable character"), **tolower**(k));

In these examples, we are *using* the functions (i.e. *invoking* them, or *calling* them). The last **printf** example illustrates three obvious, but essential, points:

- In general, an argument is written as an *expression*.
- A function call (i.e. invocation) is an expression. It can therefore be used as an argument, or as a term of an argument, for another function call (even of the same function). The first **tolower***(k)* is the argument for **isprint**; the second **tolower***(k)* is the second argument for **printf**.
- If an argument is specified in the form of a variable, the value of that variable is unchanged by the function call. The function call **tolower***(k)* cannot change the value of *k*. (This is not true of a **call** statement in Cobol, where parameters are by default passed by reference.)

In order to use **isprint** and **tolower**, we had to insert some gobbledygook at the start of the program. You probably found this and the other gobbledygook on the first few program lines more mystifying than the functions themselves. The gobbledygook now has to be explained.

3.4. The standard library

The Cobol language aims to provide all the basic facilities likely to be needed in writing programs. It also allows the programmer to place programs in libraries for use as sub-programs by other programs.

By contrast, nobody is expected to write programs in the C language alone. It contains no facilities for input, output, character-string manipulation, files, or common mathematical functions. Like Cobol, C provides a library facility, and programmers may store their own function definitions for use by their programs. C libraries contain function definitions. The major difference from Cobol is that a standard library is supplied along with the language. In that standard library are function definitions for the commonly-needed facilities which the language itself lacks. For example, all file-handling in C is done by calling library functions. Unfortunately, the functions defined in the standard library cannot just be invoked by your program; your program must also include appropriate *headers*. You need not be too concerned at present with what a header is. It is enough to know that the standard library functions are arranged in groups, with one header corresponding to each group. For example, there is a particular header which a program should include if it is to use string-handling functions, and another if it is to use mathematical functions.

This makes things complicated for the newcomer to C. In order to use a function, you have to know

- the name of the function, what it does, and what type of value it returns;
- the number and types of arguments required.

These are fair enough. If there were a **read** statement in C, rather than a function in a library, you would still have to know that the statement is called "read", you'd have to know what it does, and what information has to be supplied to it (e.g. a file name). But, for a C function, you have to know also

- the name of the header appropriate to that function.

Before we could use **isprint** in our example, we had to know that the appropriate header is <*ctype.h*>, and we therefore wrote

>   #include <ctype.h>

at the head of the program. The meanings of the musical sharp (pronounced "hash") and the angled brackets need not concern us at this stage. The line has the effect of placing at the head of our program everything needed to enable the program to call safely the functions concerned with character handling.

We have seen that **printf**, which we have been using in our examples, is a function. It required the header <*stdio.h*> (C's way of saying "standard input-output header"). That is why our programs started with the line

>   #include <stdio.h>

The header <*stdio.h*> enables us to call standard functions for input, output and file manipulation.

So that you will not have to remember at this stage which headers are appropriate to which functions, you should from this point on put at the start of all the programs you run:

>   #include <stdio.h>
>   #include <ctype.h>
>   #include <assert.h>
>   #include <string.h>

These will be adequate for all the standard functions introduced in the next few chapters, so you can forget about headers for the time being. In the full programs given in the text, only the relevant headers are included.

Appendix 3 lists all the standard library functions and tells you which header is required for each function.

3.4.1. The value returned by *printf*

A few functions return **void**, which means that they do not return any value, and are invoked only for the actions they perform; their invocation would normally appear as a statement rather than as an expression. Most functions, however, do return a value.

The **printf** function returns a value, but we have always so far discarded that value by writing **printf** calls as statements. What **printf** returns is a count of the number of characters it displayed. Since the number of characters displayed using %d varies according to the sign and the number of significant digits, it may be useful to keep track of the position reached on the current display line. In displaying a succession of integers separated by colons, we may want to start a new line whenever we are within 10 character widths of the end of the current line. (Assume that one or more numbers have already been displayed before the **while** is executed.)

```
const int  line_length=80;
int  position;
int  num;
....
position = ....
....
while (....)  {
      ....
      ....
      num = ....
      if (position < line_length - 10)
            position += printf(":%d", num);
      else  {
            printf(":\n");
            position = printf("%d", num) ;
      }
      ....
}
....
```

(**const** in the declaration of *line_length* means that the program will not change the value of *line_length*.) Alternatively, the **if** statement could be replaced by

```
position = (position < line_length - 10 ?
            position + printf(":%d", num) :
            (printf(":\n"), printf("%d", num))
            );
```

Notice how the style of both of these versions distorts our perception of the program by making the display of a number look like an adjunct of tracking the position on the output line.

3.5. Defining functions

A C program contains a sequence of function definitions. The form of the programs we are writing at present is

```
#include  <stdio.h>
#include  <ctype.h>
#include  <assert.h>
#include  <string.h>
main (void)
{
      ....
      ....
          return  0;
}
```

Before the compiler begins its main job, each *#include* line is replaced by the appropriate header. What we write between the curly brackets (i.e. our program) is in fact the body of a function whose name is *main*. Everything from and including the line

          main (**void**)

to the end is a definition of the function *main*. The name *main* is special: when we "run a program" what we are doing is calling the function *main*, as it is defined in that program. Here, **void** indicates that *main* has no arguments. Most functions are given arguments when they are invoked, and they return values.

The easiest way to understand function definitions and use is to look at a simple example. Here is a definition of a function named *max_of_3* which takes three parameters of type **int** and returns a value of type **int**.

```
int  max_of_3 (int x, int y, int z)
{     if ((x>=y) && (x>=z))
          return  x;
      else  return ((y>=z) ? y: z);
}
```

or, equivalently:

```
int  max_of_3 (int x, int y, int z)
{     return ((x>=y && x>=z) ? x : (y>=z ? y : z));
}
```


The first line resembles a declaration of an **int** variable, with these differences:

- the name following **int** is itself followed by parentheses (the opening parenthesis may be preceded by zero or more spaces);
- there is no semicolon at the end.

This line says that

- the function being defined returns a value of type **int**;
- the name of the function being defined is *max_of_3*;

- there are three *parameters*, named *x, y* and *z*. These names stand for the first, second and third arguments respectively; all three are of type **int**. So, when the function is invoked, there must be three arguments of type **int**.

The remainder of the definition is a block, consisting of the realization, or **body**, of the function. Even when the realization is by a single statement, as above, it must be in a block. Within the block (and *only* there), the names *x, y* and *z* stand for the values of the first, second and third arguments respectively. (This over-simplification will be corrected later.) The **return** statement does two things:

- it causes an exit from the function block back to the point of call;
- it specifies, as an expression, the value to be returned by the function.

Any block may contain declarations, as well as executable statements. All declarations must be at the start of the block. As an illustration, here is an alternative definition of *max_of_3*:

```
int  max_of_3 (int x, int y, int z)
{
      int  max;

      max = (x>=y ? x : y);
      return (z>max ? z : max);
}
```

Any declaration in a block is local to that block, so that *max*, like *x, y* and *z*, has no significance outside the block. Other functions in the program may, of course, declare things of their own called by these names; there is no relationship at all between an *x* defined within one function definition and an *x* defined within another. (Similarly, in Cobol, if two nested programs both define data items named *x*, there is no relationship between the *x*'s.)

Here is an example to illustrate the last point and to show how a program consisting of more than one function is written. It also shows how comments are written in C: they are enclosed between the symbols /* and */, may begin or end anywhere on a line, and may extend over several lines. Comments cannot of course be written within strings or character constants. From the compiler's point of view, a comment is equivalent to one space character.

```
#include  <stdio.h>
int  max_of_3(int x, int y, int z)
        /* returns the maximum value from x, y, z. */
{       int max;

        max = (x>y ? x : y);
        return (z>max ? z : max);
}
```

```
main (void)
{
      int max;  /* this is quite different from the max
                    declared in max_of_3 */
      int a=1;
      int b=2;
      int c=3;

      max = max_of_3(7, 4, 8);
      printf("%d\n", max);                          /* displays "8" */
      printf("%d\n", max_of_3(a+3, c, -1));          /* displays "4" */
      printf("%d\n", max_of_3(b*c,  max_of_3(4, 5, 2),  b*a));
                                                     /* displays "6" */
      return  0;
}
```

Notice that *max_of_3* is defined before *main*. For the present, define a function before defining another function that invokes it. This point will be considered in detail later.

In the definition of a function which has no arguments, no parameters appear in the definition; the parentheses following the function name contain the word **void**, as in *main* above. Empty parentheses follow the function name when such a function is invoked. For instance, in the case of an argumentless function which returns a random number, the function definition might begin

```
int  random (void)
{     ....
```

and the function would be invoked by the expression

```
random ( )
```

A function which does not return a value is said to return **void**, and is spoken of as a "void function". The definition of such a function, named *clean_up*, would begin

```
void  clean_up ( ...
{      ...
```

Invocation of a void function would normally be a statement rather than an expression. A **return** statement in the body of a void function has no expression; it is written

```
return;
```

Exit from a void function may also be implicit; implicit exit occurs when control reaches the end of the definition body.

You may have noticed that, in the definition of *main*, no type identifier precedes the function name. For the moment, regard *main* as a special case; for every other function you define, a type (perhaps **void**) should be specified.

3.6. Storage classes

Let us return to Cobol for a moment. Apart from **external** data items, all data items declared in a program's data division are local to that program; they are inaccessible by other programs. The first time a program is **call**ed by another program in a run-unit, the initial value of each data item is:

- the value specified by the **value** clause, if there is one;
- undefined, if there is no **value** clause.

On later **call**s in the run-unit, the initial value of every data item is:

- the value of the data item at the time when the program was last quitted (by an **exit program** statement).

In general, data items like these, whose values are remembered between one call and the next, are described as **static** variables. Local data items in Cobol are usually static, but there is one exception. When a program is described in Cobol as **initial**, then *every* time it is called, the initial value of each data item is:

- the value specified by the **value** clause, if there is one;
- undefined, if there is no **value** clause.

A Cobol **initial** program has no memory of its earlier invocations. All the data items are, in C terminology, automatic (**auto**) variables; they are reinitialized by their value clauses, or their values are undefined, on each call of the program. In Cobol, we choose for each program whether that program's variables are to be static or automatic.

In general, automatic variables are needed for recursion (though not in Cobol, where recursive calls are forbidden); static variables are needed to give a (Cobol) program or a (C) function a memory of its earlier invocations. C, like many other languages, allows us to decide, for each variable individually, whether it is to be static or automatic. *In C, the variables declared in a function are* **auto** *by default*; if we want a variable to be **static**, we have to say so, as in

    static char ch = 'x';

which also initializes variable *ch*'s value. The initial value of a **static** variable must be specified as a constant expression (i.e. an expression evaluable at compile time).

All the variables we have used so far have been automatic. If they were not initialized by their declarations, their initial values were undefined. But a static variable is by default initialized to zero. If the above definition had been

    static char ch;

then the initial value of *ch* would be the character whose encoding is zero. Nevertheless, to help those who read your program, it is good practice, when the program relies on zero initialization, to make the initialization explicit by saying

    static char ch = 0;

To illustrate the difference between automatic and static variables, here is the definition of a function with one integer argument, which returns the maximum integer it has so far received as an argument. The argument value is expected to be positive.

```
int  max_so_far (int i)
{       static int max = 0;

        return (i>max ? max=i : max);
}
main (void)
{
    ....
    ....
    while (....)  {
        ....
        n = ....
        if (n>0)
                printf("%d", max_so_far(n));
        ....
        ....
    }
    return  0;
}
```

Since *max* is static, its value remains unchanged from one invocation to the next. If the word **static** were omitted from the declaration of *max*, then *max* would be initialized to zero on every invocation, and *max_so_far* would always return the value of its (positive) argument *i*.

Remember that variables may be declared at the start of *any* block, not just the outer block of a function. The same rules regarding automatic and static variables apply to all blocks. The value of a variable local to a block is retained between successive executions of the block only if the variable is declared as **static**.

3.7. Assertions

You will have noticed that *max_so_far* does not check that the integer passed to it as an argument is positive. One way in which it could do so would be to include an *assertion*:

```
int  max_so_far (int i)
{       static  int  max = 0;

        assert (i>0);
        return (i>max ? max=i : max);
}
```

(**assert** is actually a macro, not a function; but that need not concern us at present.) The definition of **assert** is in the standard library, and the appropriate header is *<assert.h>*. So it is necessary to include that header in the program:

    #include <assert.h>

The effect of **assert** is drastic. If *i>0* is false, a run-time message identifying the failed assertion will be displayed and execution aborted. So, if there were a real possibility of a non-positive value being passed to the function as an argument (as, for instance, when the argument value comes direct from input), it would be better in that event to return a specified value indicating the error. The normal uses of **assert** are for debugging, as a means of detecting unlikely events like hardware errors, and as an insurance against errors in the program logic.

3.8. Pointers

Neither Cobol nor C operates on abstract data items. In using either language, we think of a variable name as corresponding to an address in computer storage. In C, unlike Cobol, it is possible to obtain the address corresponding to a named variable. In most programs there would be little point in printing or displaying it, but the addresses of data are important in C programming. We will use the phrase "address of *i*" to mean "the address corresponding to the name *i*", or, more loosely, "where *i* is stored". Assuming the declarations

    int   m=5;
    char ch='x';

the expressions

    &m   *and*   &ch

return the addresses of *m* and *ch* respectively.

So far the two types we have used are **int** and **char**. We now examine types of another kind - pointers. A pointer value is an address, so the two expressions above will each return a pointer value, just as the expression *m* returns an **int** value and the expression *ch* returns a **char** value. A pointer to an **int** is a different type from a pointer to a **char**. (Though we are here regarding pointers as addresses, it would be wrong to equate them with hardware storage addresses.) The declarations

    int*   pm;
    char* pc;

declare *pm* as being of the type "pointer to an **int**" and *pc* as being of the type "pointer to a **char**". The effect of the assignment expression

    pm = &m

is to assign the address of *m* to *pm*, so that *pm* then "points to" *m:*

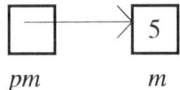

pm   *m*

Similarly, *pc* can be made to point to *ch* by

      pc = &ch

giving:

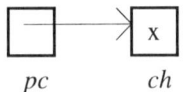

    pc   *ch*

When a variable name (or, in general, an expression) is preceded by a star, the star means "the value of the thing pointed to by". So, after evaluation of the above two assignment expressions, the expressions

      *pm == 5   *and*   *pc == 'x'

are both true, and the expression

      printf("%d%c", *pm, *pc)

displays the string "5x". The expressions

      *&ch   *and*   ch

return the same value, since the first of them returns the value of the thing pointed to by the address of *ch*, which of course is the value of *ch* ('x' in the above example).

In expressions, both * and & can be used with other meanings. The expression

      a *b

is *not* interpreted as "*a* followed by the thing pointed to by *b*", but as "*a* multiplied by *b*". The language syntax ensures that the uses of * are never confused. But it is a good convention to help those who read your programs by writing

      a * b

(i.e. with embedded spaces) for multiplication, and writing

      *b

(without embedded spaces) when you mean "the thing pointed to by *b*".

Pointer variables, like variables of other types, may be initialized on declaration. If we declared

      char   c = '+';
      char* p = &c;

then *p* would be initialized as pointing to *c*. The value of **p* would be '+', and the value of *p* would be the address of *c*. As with other types of variable, if a pointer variable is not initialized, then, unless it is **static** (see section 3.6), its value is undefined until a value is assigned to it. There is, however, a special value, **NULL**, which can be assigned to a variable of any pointer type, either on declaration or later. A **NULL** value means that the variable is not pointing to anything, which is very different from its value being undefined. If **NULL** is to be used with its standard meaning, the header *<stdio.h>* (or another header containing **NULL**'s definition) must be included. Naturally, pointer variables can be tested for the **NULL** value, as in

    if (p == **NULL**) ....

A pointer can point to a pointer. As a result of the declarations

    int s = 6;
    int* p = &s;
    int** q = &p;

s is declared as an **int** and initialized to 6; *p* is declared as a pointer to an **int** and initialized to the address of *s*; *q* is declared as a pointer to a pointer to an **int**, and initialized to the address of *p:*

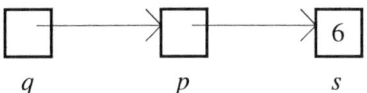

      q   *p*   *s*

Following the above declarations, the values returned by some expressions are:

&s	the address of *s*
s	6
&p	the address of *p*
p	the address of *s*
*p	6
&q	the address of *q*
q	the address of *p*
*q	the address of *s*
**q	6
*p == s	1 (true)
p == &s	1 (true)
*q == **NULL**	0 (false)

The three declarations declare the items to be of different types. The type of a pointer is characterized by both the number of levels of pointer involved (1 for *p*, 2 for *q*) and the type of the non-pointer object ultimately pointed to. Thus **int*** is a different type from **int****, and is also a different type from **char***. We cannot assign a value from one of these types to another.

Pointers may be regarded as unsigned integers. Certain limited forms of arithmetic can be performed on them. Where *p* and *r* represent expressions returning pointer values, and *i* is an expression returning an integer, the following forms of expression are permitted:

> p + i
> i + p
> p – i
> p – r

The first three of these return pointer values of the same type as *p*, and the last an integer. The last form produces a sensible result only when the two pointers concerned point to the same array; indeed, all pointer arithmetic is, for practical application programming, restricted to operands pointing to arrays. Nevertheless, your curiosity may lead you at this stage to try little programs which display pointer values and the values returned by pointer arithmetic. If so, you should use %u, instead of %d, in the first argument of **printf**; this will interpret a pointer value as an unsigned integer. You may be surprised by the results of pointer arithmetic. These will be explained in the next section.

The **NULL** value may be assigned to a pointer variable of any type. The value of a pointer variable (or an expression returning a pointer value) may be assigned to a pointer variable *of the same type as itself*. Pointer variables (or expressions) of the same type may be compared, using the relational, equality and "?" operators in the usual way.

3.8.1. Layout problems

If you look at other people's C programs, you will probably see that instead of

> **int*** pm;
> **char*** pc;

they write

> **int** *pm;
> **char** *pc;

The only difference is in the position of the embedded spaces, which does not affect the meaning of the declarations. I prefer the first version because it reads naturally as: "variable *pm* is of type *pointer to* **int**", whereas the second version reads awkwardly: "the type of thing pointed to by *pm* is **int**". Even worse,

> **int** **pz;

reads as: "the type of thing pointed to by the thing (pointer) pointed to by *pz* is **int**"; but

> **int**** pz;

reads more simply: "*pz* is of type *pointer to pointer to* **int**".

My preferred style involves having only one object declared in each declaration. (This also makes for easier maintenance.) If I used multiple declarations, I would have to be careful. The declaration

      int* pm, pn;

does *not* mean that *pm* and *pn* are both of type *pointer to* **int**. It is in fact equivalent to

      int* pm;
      int pn;

To get the equivalent of

      int* pm;
      int* pn;

we would have to write

      int* pm, *pn;

We are more likely to wrongly omit the star preceding *pn* in this multiple declaration than if we affixed the star to each identifier:

      int *pm, *pn;

Multiple declarations are best avoided, especially in relation to pointer variables.

Another observation applies to constructions like

      a=*b

which quite unambiguously means "assign to *a* the value of the thing pointed to by *b*". It is better to ensure that there is a space between the assignment operator and the star:

      a = *b

or to use parentheses:

      a =(*b)

This makes the meaning clearer and also avoids the possibility of getting warning messages from some compilers, since =* was once the operator now written as *=.

3.9. Arrays

An array is what would be called a "table" in Cobol. The C declaration

      char a [10];

is similar to the Cobol declarations

      01 aa.
          02 a **pic** x, **occurs** 10.

C and Cobol arrays have these features in common:

- As declared above, the array has 10 elements, each of which is one character.
- An element is identified by the name *a*, followed by a subscript.
- The elements of the array are stored contiguously.
- The elements have a uniform type. The type may be "elementary", like (in C's case) **int** or **char** or a pointer type, or it may be an aggregate type such as another array. (For the present, we consider only one-dimensional arrays.)

But there are these significant differences:

- The number of elements must be specified in Cobol as an integer; in C, a *constant expression* (see section 2.8.2) may be used, and in certain circumstances the square brackets in the declaration may be empty.
- C subscripting starts at 0, Cobol subscripting at 1. Thus the elements of the C array declared above are *a[0], a[1], a[2], ... , a[9]*. The last element in a C array has a subscript one less than the size of the array.
- Subscripts are written in *square* brackets in C.
- The form of a Cobol subscript is severely limited (in standard Cobol); in C a subscript may be an expression of arbitrary complexity.
- C has no method of operating on the array as a whole (unless it is a **struct** - see chapter 10). Any operation is effected as a set of operations on the elements one by one.

The values of C array elements are initially undefined, unless

- the array declaration itself initializes them, or, failing that:
- the array is declared as **static** (see section 3.6), in which case they are initialized to zero, or to the value of their type corresponding to zero.

C provides no simple declarative means of initializing all the elements of an array to the same value, unless that value is zero. In Cobol, **value** clauses may be used, as in

```
01  jj.
      02  j  pic s99,  occurs 5,  value  -1.
```

To get the effect of a **value** clause, we have to say, for example:

> **int** j[5]={-1, -1, -1, -1, -1};

This technique is wearisome and error-prone for arrays of realistic size; so, in C, such initialization is not usually done in the declarations. Instead, a **for** loop is used to initialize array elements to uniform values, as in

> **for** (i=0; i<5; i++)
>   j[i] = -1;

Initialization to non-uniform values, which we might do declaratively in Cobol by a **value**d redefinition, is done in C for arrays of realistic size by a sequence of assignments to the individual elements. For small arrays, the above method can be used, as in

> **int** odds[3]={1,3,5};

which initializes *odds*[0] to 1, *odds*[1] to 3, and *odds*[2] to 5. Indeed, the declaration could be equivalently written as

> **int** odds[ ]={1,3,5};

in which case the number of elements is implied by the number of listed values. For a **char** array, we might say

> **char** k[ ]={'K', 'a', 't', 'e'};

which is equivalent to the same declaration with 4 in the square brackets. A simpler way to initialize a **char** array is to use a string literal, as in

> **char** k[4]="Kate";

but, surprisingly, this is not equivalent to

> **char** k[ ]="Kate";

because a string is assumed to have the null character '\0' at the end. This character is placed in the array following the last character of the string, unless there is no space for it. The last declaration above is therefore equivalent to

> **char** k[5]="Kate";

The general rules for initialization with a string literal are illustrated by the examples that follow. The declaration

> **char** w[7]="William";

declares the array as having 7 elements, initialized w[0]='W', w[1]='i', ... , w[6]='m'. The declaration

> **char** w[8]="William";

declares the array as having 8 elements, initialized w[0]='W', w[1]='i', ... , w[6]='m', w[7]='\0', as does the declaration

> **char** w[ ]="William";

The declaration

> **char** w[10]="William";

declares the array as having 10 elements, initialized w[0]='W', w[1]='i', ... , w[6]='m', w[7]='\0', with the values of w[8] and w[9] undefined. But the declaration

> **char** w[10]={'W','i','l','l','i','a','m'}

also initializes w[8] and w[9] to '\0' because, when braces (curly brackets) are used, all excess elements are initialized to zero, which is the representation of the null character '\0'. (Check that your compiler does this properly. If it does not, see chapter 4 for the **memset** function.) The declaration

> **char** w[3]="";

which initializes to an empty string, results in w[0] being initialized to '\0' (to terminate the empty string), and the values of the remaining elements being undefined. The declaration

char w[3]="William";

will probably result in a warning message and the array having three elements, initialized w[0]='W', w[1]='i', w[2]='l'.

Arrays are closely associated with pointers. Suppose that we have this declaration:

int ax[5];

When we use the identifier *ax* with a subscript in the range 0 to 4, we are of course referring to one of the **int**s in the array. It is possible, however, to use the identifier *ax* without a subscript. What it (nearly always) means then is "the address of *ax*[0]", i.e. it is equivalent to &*ax*[0]. Similarly, **ax* is equivalent to *ax*[0]. In other words, *ax* is a pointer to the first element of the array, and its type is "pointer to an **int**". Now, if you have been puzzled by pointer arithmetic, here is the explanation. When we add 1 to, or subtract 1 from, a pointer of a given type, what is actually added or subtracted is not necessarily 1, but the number of addressable storage units occupied by an object of the type that that pointer points to. An **int** might occupy four bytes, so adding 1 to a pointer to an **int** would actually add 4. The importance of this in relation to arrays is that the expression *ax* + *n* (where *n* is an integer expression) returns the address of *ax[n]*; and, generally, adding 1 to a pointer to an element will give us a pointer to the next element, if there is one. If we simply wanted the address of *ax[n]*, we would usually say &*ax[n]* rather than *ax* + *n*.

To use an array as an argument in a call of a function, what we pass to the function is the address of the first element, which acts as a pointer to the array. We often do not want a function to be restricted to operating on an array of a particular size, so we will often pass to the function as another argument the number of elements in the array. For example, we might define a function, *sum*, whose arguments were a pointer to an array of **int**s and the size of the array (i.e. the number of elements in it); the value returned by *sum* would be the sum of the element values. The function definition might begin

int sum (**int*** p, **int** size)

and then, given the above declaration of *ax*, the call

sum(ax,5)

would return the sum of the elements of *ax*. The function definition might be:

```
int  sum (int* p,  int size)
{     int* limit = p + size;
      int total = 0;

      while (p<limit)
            total += *(p++);
      return total;

}
```

Within this definition, there is no explicit reference to an array. Instead, pointer incrementation (*p++*) is used to step from one array element to the next. At the second line the pointer variable *limit* is initialized to point to one step beyond the last element. (The Standard says that this is always safe.) Because *size* is being added to *p* (a variable of type "pointer to an **int**"), *size* is interpreted as the product of its value and the size of an **int**. Finally, look at the expression **(p++)*: *p* is incremented; since it is a pointer to an **int**, the effect is that it points to the next element of the array, or one step beyond the last element. Since ++ appears after *p*, the value of *p++* is *p*'s value *before* incrementation. The * thus causes a reference to the element pointed to by *p* before *p* was incremented. The parentheses around *p++* are unnecessary, since the * and ++ operators have the same precedence and associate right to left; they are inserted to eliminate any possible misunderstanding. This kind of expression is so common in C programs that programmers rarely use parentheses; from this point on, we too will omit them. (Remember that there is a full precedence table in Appendix 1.)

The parameters of a function are treated in the function as local variables whose values are implicitly initialized to those of the corresponding arguments supplied by the call. Thus for the call

sum (ax, 5)

the first things that happen are that *ax* is evaluated and the value is assigned to *p*, and the value 5 is assigned to *size*. Thereafter, the function body may assign new values to *p* (as it does in the above example) and to *size*, without affecting anything outside the function. However, when a pointer value is passed as an argument, there is nothing to prevent the function using that pointer to change the values of outside objects. Indeed, the purpose of many functions is to do just that - functions to modify arrays are very common. Our *sum* function is not intended to change the array in any way, and it would be good to ensure that it did not do so inadvertently.

Some degree of security can be achieved by changing the heading of *sum*'s definition to

sum (**const int*** p, **int** size)

so that *p* now points to a "constant integer", i.e. *sum* will not change the thing pointed to by *p* (though it may change the value of *p* itself). At the very least, our compiler should then warn us of any assignment to the thing pointed to by *p*, or any assignment from *p* to another pointer variable which was not also a pointer to a constant integer.

(So the declaration of *limit* also should be changed to **const int***.) This is the only effect of using **const** in the parameter declaration. When *sum* is called, the argument corresponding to *p* is required to be of type **int***. The argument may or may not be qualified by **const** in the calling function.

For a final example, we return to Cobol. The declarations

> a **pic** x(3).
> b **pic** x(5).

would be realized in C by

> **char** a[3];
> **char** b[5];

A Cobol **move** between two alphanumeric items is such that space-filling or truncation, if appropriate, occurs on the right. We now define a C function which gives the effect of an alphanumeric **move**. The function, *alpha_move*, is specified in such a way that, for instance, the Cobol statement

> **move** a **to** b

is simulated by the C call

> alpha_move (a, 3, b, 5)

(We will see later a tidier way of simulating such a **move**.) The function returns **void**; it is called for what it does, not for what it returns. Here is a possible definition:

```
void alpha_move(const char* x, int xsize, char* y, int ysize)
{    const int common = xsize<ysize ? xsize : ysize;
     int i=0;

     for (; i<common; i++)
          *y++ = *x++;
     for (; i<ysize; i++)
          *y++ = ' ';
}
```

This example gives you some idea of why it has been necessary in this chapter to introduce so many concepts before dealing with what any Cobol programmer would regard as basic operations - character-string handling, input, output and file handling. Only now are we in a position to examine how C performs these operations. But, in writing C programs, we should not try to mimic Cobol by providing functions for the common Cobol operations; we should rather accept C on its own terms and try to match our programs to the C model. This is the approach taken in the remaining chapters.

4

Character Strings

4.1. Character string representation

The forms of reference to character data in a C program are, as we have seen:

- character constants, each consisting of a pair of single quotes within which there is one character or an escape sequence representing one character. Surprisingly, these are constants of type **int**.
- variables of type **char**. The value of a **char** variable is one character.
- string literals, each consisting of a pair of double quotes within which is a sequence of characters. A character may be represented by an escape sequence. Several string literals written one after the other are concatenated to form a single string literal (e.g. "ab" "c" is equivalent to "abc".) A string literal is of type "pointer to a **char**", and may be written as an argument where that type is appropriate. For instance, the first argument of the standard **printf** function is required to be of type "pointer to a **char**", and we have so far always written it as a string literal. A string literal cannot be continued onto another line of the program, but this causes no problem since two successive string literals will be concatenated, whether or not they are on the same line.

Thus, though the language has string literals, it has no "string" type. Language users, however, have a *convention* for the storage representation of strings. A string is stored in a **char** array, starting usually at the first array element and with a null character ('\0') following the last character of the string. This convention is reflected in the way string literals are stored. For instance, if *pc* is of type **char***, the assignment

        pc = "Ned"

results in *pc* pointing to the first character in an otherwise undeclared array whose elements are 'N', 'e', 'd' and '\0'. The convention is similarly reflected in C's provision for initializing an array by specifying a string literal (see section 3.9). Strings which are represented in this way are, of course, variable in length, since the end of a string is denoted by the null character. Such strings, as well as fixed-length sequences of characters, can be manipulated by standard library functions, particularly those made available by the headers *<stdio.h>* and *<string.h>*. We look first at some of the *<string.h>* functions; to use them, you need a line:

        #include <string.h>

4.2. Finding the length of a string

The function **strlen** returns the number of characters in a string, excluding the terminating null character. Its single argument is of type "pointer to a **char**" and points to the first character of the string. Thus, given the declaration

>   **char** a1[10];

the call

>   **strlen**(a1)

returns the length of the string stored in array *a1*. (Remember that the identifier *a1*, when unsubscripted, is a pointer to the first element of the array.) If the array contains, as its first four characters, 'R', 'a', 'y', '\0', then, regardless of what the remaining characters are, the above call returns the value 3. If the first character of the array (a[0]) is null ('\0'), the call returns 0. If no character in the array is null, the function does *not* return 10; it continues searching through store beyond the end of the array until a null character is found, and thus may cause a run-time error or return some meaningless value.

4.3. Suggested conventions for strings

The example we have just looked at illustrates an important principle. An argument passed to a string-handling function is normally a pointer to an element of an array (usually the first element). The function, of course, sees the argument value simply as a storage address and knows nothing about the size of the array. If an array is used as a source of data, the function may well overrun the end of the array and access data from storage allocated to some other objects. Even more alarming is the fact that a function can overrun an array which is the *destination* of data; in this case, a function may well overwrite storage allocated to other objects. C programs are insecure because it is virtually impossible to do anything substantial without using pointers, and errors in the use of pointers can in C lead to far-reaching and often mystifying effects. The best we can do is try to minimize the risk.

The following conventions make string handling more secure and programming slightly easier. If a **char** array is to be used for storage of a string:

* for a string whose length (you hope) will never exceed *c* characters, declare an array of size *c* + 1.
* ensure that the extra character (the last in the array) is set to null before using the array. If no initialization would otherwise be needed, initialize the array to {'\0'}, which automatically sets all characters of the array to null (see section 3.9).
* always manipulate the array as though its size were *c*.

For example, suppose that the maximum expected length of a surname is 20 characters. An array intended for storage of a surname value as a string would be declared like this:

>   **char** surname [21] = {'\0'};

Remember that this initializes *surname* [0]. All remaining elements of *surname* are initialized to null, and would be so even if *surname* [0] had been initialized to some other value. Thereafter the program should take care to change only the first twenty elements of *surname* (i.e. *surname* [0] through *surname* [19]), leaving *surname* [20] always null.

C has a **sizeof** operator (*not* a function) which, applied to any object, returns the number of bytes occupied by that object. Bearing in mind that the name of an array usually denotes a pointer to the first element, you would expect the value of

>   **sizeof** surname

to be the number of bytes occupied by a pointer. But it isn't - when applied to an array identifier, it is the number of bytes occupied by the array. Since one character occupies one byte of storage, the **sizeof** a **char** array is the number of elements in it. So the value of the above expression is 21. Consistent use of "**sizeof** surname", instead of "21", makes the program easy to amend in the event of the number of elements in *surname* being changed. But there is a trap: within a function such as one whose definition begins

>   **void** X (**char*** ax)

the value of

>   **sizeof** ax

is always *the size of a pointer*, so if *X* is called by

>   X (surname)

the **sizeof** operator cannot be used within the function to get the size of the array. If the function needs to know the size of the array, its definition should begin:

>   **void** X (**char*** ax, **int** s_ax)

The function could then be called by

>   X (surname, **sizeof** surname)

Nevertheless, we will use **sizeof** extensively in the sections that follow.

Let us now see how these conventions apply in relation to other string-handling functions. In doing so, assume the following declarations:

```
char  a1 [11] = {'\0'};
char  a2 [9] = {'\0'};
char  a3 [4] = {'\0'};
char  a4 [11] = {'\0'};
```

4.4. Copying strings

The function **strncpy** (this is not a misprint; you have to get used to these peculiar names) copies a string from one place in storage to another. The call

strncpy (a2, a1, (**sizeof** a2)−1)

copies a string from *a1* to *a2*. The third argument ((**sizeof** a2)−1) specifies the maximum number of characters to be copied; this helps us to prevent the function, or a later use of *a2* as a source of data, from over-running into any storage area beyond the end of array *a2*. (There is another function, **strcpy**, for which no maximum is specified; its use is best avoided.) The function returns the value of its first argument, a pointer to the destination array - in this case *a2*.

Here are some examples, which assume the above declarations:

	a1											**a2** after **strncpy**(a2,a1,(**sizeof** a2)−1)								
	0	*1*	*2*	*3*	*4*	*5*	*6*	*7*	*8*	*9*	*10*	*0*	*1*	*2*	*3*	*4*	*5*	*6*	*7*	*8*
(1)	K	a	t	\0	b	a	r	\0	x	1	\0	K	a	t	\0	\0	\0	\0	\0	\0
(2)	K	a	t	a	r	i	n	\0	*	y	\0	K	a	t	a	r	i	n	\0	\0
(3)	K	a	t	a	r	i	n	a	\0	y	\0	K	a	t	a	r	i	n	a	\0
(4)	K	a	t	a	r	i	n	a	s	\0	\0	K	a	t	a	r	i	n	a	\0

Because the value of the third argument is 8, copying can never extend beyond *a1*[7] or *a2*[7]. In all cases, the null in *a2*[8] is the result of *a2*'s declaration, not of the function call. Think of copying proceeding from left to right through the arrays. In (1), copying ceases after *a1*[3] has been copied, because that character is null; the next four elements of *a2* (*a2*[4] to *a2*[7]) are set to null, making 8 characters in all written to *a2* by **strncpy** (since 8 is the value of the third argument). In (2), the first null detected (at *a1*[7]) coincides with the eighth character. In (3) and (4), copying ends when 8 characters have been copied, no null having been found. Thanks to our conventions and the use of (**sizeof** a2)−1 as the third argument, we ensure that, even if no null character is copied to array *a2*, there is always a null character at the end of *a2*. So, if *a2* is subsequently used in another string operation, there will always be a null to prevent overrun.

Now consider the call

      strncpy(a2, a3, (**sizeof** a2)–1)

As before, the effect of the third argument value is to avoid any unwitting overrun of array *a2*. These examples

	a3				**a2** after **strncpy**(a2,a3,(**sizeof** a2)–1)								
	0	*1*	*2*	*3*	*0*	*1*	*2*	*3*	*4*	*5*	*6*	*7*	*8*
(5)	T	\0	x	\0	T	\0	\0	\0	\0	\0	\0	\0	\0
(6)	T	o	m	\0	T	o	m	\0	\0	\0	\0	\0	\0

introduce nothing new, but notice in (6) how the presence of a null at the end of *a3* prevents characters from beyond *a3* being copied to *a2*.

Since a string literal is treated as a constant pointer to the start of a stored string, a string literal may be used as the second argument of **strncpy**. The call

      strncpy(a2, "Danger!", (**sizeof** a2)–1)

assigns the string "Danger!" to array *a2*. The string literal is treated as though it were an array containing that string with a terminating null appended.

To set all characters of an array to a given value, the void function **memset** is used. The call

      memset(a1, ' ', (**sizeof** a1)–1)

sets all the characters in *a1* (except *a1*[10]) to spaces, and

      memset(&a1[6], 'x', (**sizeof** a1)–7)

sets *a1*[6] through *a1*[9] to 'x'. The third argument is the number of characters to be set. In both cases, we have ensured that the "buffer" element, *a1*[10], is left unchanged. The call

      memset(a1, '\0', **sizeof** a1)

sets all the characters in *a1* (including *a1*[10]) to null.

There are two functions which copy a sequence of characters of a specified length, and which do not treat nulls as being any different from other characters. The call

      memcpy(p2, p1, s)

copies *s* characters from the address specified by *p1* to the address specified by *p2*. For example

      memcpy(&a2[5], a1, 4)

copies *a1*[0] to *a2*[5], *a1*[1] to *a2*[6], *a1*[2] to *a2*[7] and *a1*[3] to *a2*[8]. This function can be useful for copying a complete array (including the final character) to another of the same size, as in

> **memcpy**(a4, a1, **sizeof** a4)

If the third argument is in error, the function may copy beyond the ends of the arrays. It is advisable to derive the third argument value from the size of the destination array (*a4* here), rather than that of the source array; then, if there is a program error and *a1* is the larger array, other data in store are less likely to be corrupted. **memcpy** gives unpredictable results if the source and destination areas of store overlap, as in

> **memcpy**(&a1[4], &a1[2], 5)

which is intended to copy the characters at *a1*[2] through *a1*[6] into *a1*[4] through *a1*[8]. If the areas do overlap, there is a possibly less efficient function, **memmove**, which guarantees the intended result:

> **memmove**(&a1[4], &a1[2], 5)

(The **memmove** function may not be available in older libraries.)

As an example of the use of **memset** and **memcpy**, suppose that we want to output a fixed-length line in which a variable-length message is to appear in the centre of the line, surrounded by asterisks. The message is stored as a string in an array (*m1*) and is to be centred in another array (*m2*). The following function returns the value of its first argument. If the message string is null or too long, *m2* is filled with asterisks. The third argument is the size of *m2*. (If the argument corresponding to *m2* is an array which follows our convention of having a null character at the end, the third argument of the *star_centre* call should, of course, be one less than the size of the array.)

```
char* star_centre (char* m2, const char* m1, int s_m2)
{
        memset (m2, '*', s_m2);
        if ( (strlen(m1) > 0) && (strlen(m1) <= s_m2) )
               memcpy ( &m2[(s_m2 - strlen(m1)) / 2], m1, strlen(m1) );
        return (m2);
}
```

For instance, the call

> star_centre (a2, "Fred", 8)

returns a pointer to array *a2*, whose first 8 characters will be "**Fred**".

4.5. Concatenating strings

The function **strncat** appends one string to another. The string appended is subject to a specified maximum size. For example, if *a1*, as declared earlier in the chapter, contains as its first four characters 'd', 'i', 's', '\0' and *a2* contains as its first six characters 'c', 'o', 'v', 'e', 'r', '\0', then the call

> **strncat**(a1, a2, (**sizeof** a1) − 1 − **strlen**(a1))

results in *a1* containing, as its first nine characters, 'd', 'i', 's', 'c', 'o', 'v', 'e', 'r', '\0'. The null that terminated the original string in *a1* is overwritten, and a null is always appended to the concatenated string. The function returns its first argument. The third argument specifies the maximum number of characters to be appended, *excluding* the terminating null. The expression used in the above call demonstrates the best way to specify the maximum, given that we retain our earlier conventions for the declaration and manipulation of arrays and their sizes. The value of the third argument for our "discover" example is $11-1-3 = 7$; this is the number of elements following "dis" in the array into which characters can be placed without overrun. If seven characters are appended, our additional null at the end of the array is simply overwritten by the null written by the function. This would happen when, for instance, the string in *a2* was "covered" or "coveries". In the latter case, the 's' would not be copied to *a2*.

Using **strncat** in C is like using **string** in a very simple way in Cobol, but with the danger of overrunning the destination area. The conventions used in this chapter reduce the danger.

4.6. Comparing strings

We have seen that comparison of characters in C is a comparison of the numeric values of their representations. Comparison of strings in C resembles comparison of alphanumeric items in Cobol, but in C the lengths of the strings are determined by the null characters that terminate them. For comparison purposes, the terminating null is regarded as part of a string.

As in Cobol, if two strings consist of the same sequence of characters (including the terminating nulls) they are equal. Otherwise, the first corresponding pair of characters in which the strings differ determines the result; the first string is greater or less than the second string depending on whether the character in the first string is greater or less than the character in the second string. The string "Danger!" is less than the string "David" because 'n' is less than 'v'. Since the null character is represented by zero, it is less than any other character; in C, therefore, "Dan" is always less than "Danger". (In Cobol, the result of that comparison depends on the relative positions of 'g' and the space character in the program collating sequence.) Notice that "Dan" is always less than "Dan   " in C, but that they are always equal in Cobol.

The function which compares two strings is **strcmp**. The strings in arrays *a1* and *a2* are compared by the call

   strcmp(a1, a2)

which returns 0 if the strings are equal, an unspecified negative integer value if the string in *a1* is less than that in *a2*, and an unspecified positive integer value if it is greater. Thus the expression

   strcmp(a1, a2) >= 0

tests whether or not the string in *a1* is greater than or equal to the string in *a2*; and

> **strcmp**(a1, "Danger!") == 0

tests whether the string in *a1* is "Danger!".

4.7. Searching arrays

The value returned by the call

> **strchr** (s, i)

is a pointer to the first occurrence of the character corresponding to the value of *i* in the string pointed to by *s*. The second parameter is of type **int**, but the second argument in a call can be of type **char**, since automatic conversion to **int** takes place on entry to the function. So **strchr** is commonly used as in these examples:

> **strchr** (a1, '+')

returns a pointer to the first occurrence of '+' in the string in array *a1*.

> **strchr** (a1, c)

gives the same result if *c* is a **char** variable whose value is '+'. The null character which terminates the string is regarded for this purpose as part of the string, so the call

> **strchr** (a1, '\0')

returns a pointer to the terminating null. If the character specified by the second argument is not found in the string, a null pointer is returned.

A similar function, **strrchr** (note the double 'r') does the same, except that it returns a pointer to the *last* occurrence of the character in the string, or a null pointer if the character is not found.

The function **strstr** returns a pointer to the first occurrence within a string of a given substring. For example, the call

> **strstr** (a1, "xyz")

returns a pointer to the 'x' in the first occurrence of the sequence 'x', 'y', 'z' within the string in array *a1*. If that sequence is not found in the string, a null pointer is returned.

> **strstr** (a1, a2)

gives the same result if the first four characters of array *a2* are 'x', 'y', 'z', '\0'. (The terminating null character is not regarded as part of the string.)

A number of other useful searching functions are available in the standard library (see Appendix 3). If you have an application requiring more sophisticated string searching, have a look at the specifications of **memchr**, **strcspn**, **strpbrk**, **strspn** and **strtok** in your implementor's manual. Most of the remaining *string.h* functions enable us to do the kinds of things done by the Cobol **unstring** statement. But we have now learned enough to enable us, at last, to look at C's input, output and file-handling facilities.

4.8. Style

When you have learned the names of the various functions, string-handling operations are simple and useful. They are also dangerous, and you are strongly advised to use the conventions described in section 4.3.

You will have to make your own decisions on matters of style. Would you write

```
    if    (strcmp   (strncat   (strncat (a2, a1, (sizeof a2) – 1 – strlen(a2)),
                                    "?",
                                 (sizeof a2) – 1 – strlen(a2)
                                 ),
                         strncpy (a3, a4, (sizeof a3)–1)
                       )
              <= 0
       ) ....
```

or would you write

```
    strncat(a2, a1, (sizeof a2) – 1 – strlen(a2));
    strncat(a2, "?", (sizeof a2) – 1 – strlen(a2));
    strncpy(a3, a4, (sizeof a3)–1);
    if (strcmp(a2, a3) <= 0) ...
```

to do the same thing? The first form is attractive to those who like functional programming languages; the changes to array *a2* and *a3* are seen as side-effects of function evaluation. The first example above illustrates the pitfalls of its style, for it is not really equivalent to the second example. Can you see why?

Coming from Cobol, you probably prefer the second form, which treats the functions **strncat** and **strncpy** as though they were procedures. Even so, it is worth spending some time finding the error in the first example, for it is often useful to nest function calls.

> *Read this when you have studied the first example above.* The order of evaluation of a function's arguments is unspecified (see the end of section 3.2). Look at the outer call of **strncat**. If **strlen** in the third argument is to return the intended value, the first argument (i.e. the inner call of **strncat**) must have been evaluated first. But C gives no guarantee that any argument is evaluated before any other.

5

Text Files

5.1. Files

All file handling, including input and output involving terminals and printers, is done by calls to standard library functions; the header is *<stdio.h>*. You can rightly assume from your experience with string handling that these functions will not be as easy to use as Cobol statements like **read** and **write**, and that the functions will not have such straightforward names. But there is worse news to come: the only file organization for which standard functions are available is sequential. Even with its standard library, C knows nothing of relative or indexed organization. Your implementor may provide access from C programs to such files through system calls; but then of course your programs using these files will not be portable.

But in one respect C is vastly superior. Most programming languages, including C and Cobol, expect programs to refer to a file by a name which is local to the program, thus enabling a program to be used on different occasions to manipulate different files without requiring changes to be made throughout the program. During program execution, therefore, a file has two names - the name by which it is known in the program (its *local name*), and the name by which it is known to the operating system (its *system name*). The difference between Cobol and C is in how the correspondence between these names is established. In Cobol, the names are equated declaratively by a **select** sentence in the program's environment division and/or by an operating system command - the two names must be equated before the start of program execution. C has a much better arrangement - the names are not equated until the file is opened. One consequence is that a local name can be equated to a system name on the basis of data read in from some other file by the program itself, or perhaps as a result of a dialogue with a user at a terminal. Another is that system names of files can be treated as strings and they can be passed as arguments between functions, even when the functions are separately compiled.

In C, the local name of a file is the name of a variable whose type is **FILE*** (remember that C is case-sensitive - do not write *file**) - a pointer to "an object which controls a

71

file". We can think of **FILE** as just "a file", and the name of a variable of type **FILE***
as identifying that file. The name of a variable of type **FILE*** is C's equivalent of the
name which follows **fd** in a Cobol data division. Since it denotes a variable, it too can
be passed as an argument between functions. The declaration

> **FILE*** f1;

says that the program will use a file which it will identify by the name *f1*. The identity
of the actual file corresponding to *f1* (in Cobol terms, the name to which it is **assign**ed)
will be determined if and when the file is opened. The name by which the actual file is
known to the operating system is treated as a character string.

The standard library provides for two kinds of sequential files:
* **text files**, which contain only character data;
* **binary files**, in which objects of any C types may be stored.
This chapter describes text files and shows how they are used.

5.2. Text files

A text file either is empty or consists of a sequence of lines, each *line* being a sequence
of zero or more characters followed by a new-line character. (The new-line character
will typically be physically stored in a text file as two characters - carriage return and
line feed - but this does not concern the C program, which consistently sees it as a
single new-line character on reading and writing.) Most implementations probably
conform to this simple and orderly definition; but unfortunately the definition is vitiated
by the Standard's concessions to implementors:

* An implementor may decide that an empty text file does not exist. In a Cobol
  program, if you open a stored output file, write nothing to it, and then close it, you
  will have created an empty file, which you can then open on a later occasion as an
  extend or i-o or input file. If you do the equivalent with a C text file, you have no
  guarantee that the empty file will exist, and you cannot rely on its being present on
  a later occasion.
* It is left to the implementor to decide whether the last character of a text file must
  be a new-line character. This makes some sense for, as we will see, the new-line
  characters are explicitly written by a program that creates a file. A text file may
  therefore be simply a sequence of characters including no new-lines at all; in other
  words, it may consist of just one line with no new-line character at the end.
* What you read from a text file is not necessarily identical to what you earlier wrote
  to it, if:
  (a) it contains any unprintable characters other than new-line and horizontal
  tab. (Remember that the space character is a printable character.)
  (b) a new-line is immediately preceded by a space character. (An implementor
  is allowed to remove any sequence of spaces at the end of a line.)
  (c) the last character in the file is not a new-line.

These limitations may well not apply to the implementation you use, but keep them in mind if you want your programs and files to be portable.

A text file resembles a Cobol sequential file of variable-length records, with a *line* corresponding to a Cobol *record* in which all items are of **display** usage (i.e. containing no **binary**, **computational**, **index** or **packed decimal** items and no signed numeric items in which the sign is not **separate**). The major differences are:

- In Cobol, the unit of transfer to or from a file is one record. In C, any sequence of characters may be written; for instance, the sequence may be part of a line, or it may be several lines.
- A Cobol program is not concerned with how the operating system software marks or recognizes the ends of records. A C program explicitly writes the new-line character which terminates a line; and, when a line is read from a file, the terminating new-line is read with it. As with writing, a C program need not read one line at a time; for instance, it may read part of a line or several lines in one read operation.

There are three text files which are automatically open when a C program starts to run. They are an input file, **stdin** (pronounced "standard input"), and two output files, **stdout** and **stderr** (pronounced "standard output" and "standard error" respectively). These names are of type **FILE***. It is to **stderr** that the system sends its run-time messages, but there is nothing to prevent the program itself writing to **stderr**. All these files are normally assigned by default to your terminal. So, if a program writes to **stdout** (as **printf** does), what it writes will appear on your terminal display; if it reads from **stdin**, the input will come from your terminal. All other files must be explicitly opened by the program.

5.3. Opening and closing text files

A file is opened by the function **fopen**, which returns a pointer to the file. Its arguments are a pointer to a string which is the system name of the file, and the mode in which it is to be opened. As an example, consider the following:

> **FILE*** f1;
> ....
> ....
> f1 = **fopen** ("cd1.dat", "r");

This is similar to Cobol's:

> **select** f1 **assign to** "cd1.dat".
> ....
> ....
> **open input** f1

The second argument of the call of **fopen** specifies the open mode. Translated into Cobol terms, "r" (read) means input, "w" (write) means output (the creation of a new file to which data may be written), and "a" (append) means extend. Opening in input-output mode will be considered later.

As an equivalent of the C extract above, we could have:

> **FILE*** f1;
> **char** sysf1 [] = "cd1.dat";
>   ....
>
>   ....
> f1 = **fopen** (sysf1, "r");

or, more usefully:

> **FILE*** f1;
> **char** sysf1 [31] = {'\0'};
>   ....
>
>   ....
> f1 = **fopen** (sysf1, "r");

in which case we would ensure that the system name of the file was assigned to *sysf1* before execution of the assignment to *f1*. The name could, for instance, be supplied by a user at a terminal.

Remember that, within a string literal, the backslash character acts as an escape character (see section 2.10). So, if you wanted to open the file c:\x, the program would specify its name by the string literal "c:\\x".

If the open operation fails (for example when an input file cannot be found), **fopen** returns a null pointer.

A file is closed by the **fclose** function. To close the above file, the call is

> **fclose** (f1)

The function returns zero if the file is successfully closed. As in Cobol, exit from the program automatically closes all open files.

5.4. Character input and output

With text files, it is possible to write or read on a character-by-character basis, using the function **fputc** or **fgetc** respectively. **fputc** takes two arguments, the integer which represents the character to be written and a file pointer. For instance, given

> **FILE*** f1;
> **char** ch;

and assuming a prior assignment

        f1 = **fopen**(.... , "w")   *or*   f1 = **fopen**(.... , "a")

the calls

        fputc (ch, f1)   *and*   **fputc** ('+', f1)

write respectively the value of *ch* and the character '+' to file *f1*, returning the character written, or, if a write error occurs, **EOF**. (**EOF** is defined in *<stdio.h>* as a negative integer, and is thus distinguishable from any encoding of a character.)

The function **fgetc** returns either one character or **EOF**. Because **EOF** is a negative integer, the value returned by **fgetc** should be assigned to a variable of type **int** rather than of type **char**. If we declare

        FILE* f1;
        int ch;

and use the assignment

        f1 = **fopen** (.... , "r")

then the call

        fgetc (f1)

returns the integer representing the next character from file *f1*. We can think of this as simply returning the character itself, but typically we would assign the returned value to an **int** variable, as in

        ch = **fgetc** (f1)

and subsequently use it as a character. If there is no next character in *f1* (i.e. when the end of the file is reached) or if a read error occurs, the function returns **EOF**. To process all the characters in file *f1* one by one, the controlling **while** statement might be

        while ((ch = **fgetc**(f1)) != **EOF**) {*process one character*}

(Remember that the value of the assignment expression is the value assigned to *ch*, which of course is the value returned by the function.) On exit from the **while** loop, the functions **feof** and **ferror** (to be described at the end of section 5.6) can be called to determine the reason for **fgetc** returning **EOF**.

From this point on, we will concentrate on the functions which enable us to read and write sequences of characters rather than single characters.

5.5. String output to a text file

As with a Cobol sequential file, the normal pattern is to open the file, write successive records (lines), then close the file. Writing is done by the function **fputs**, whose arguments are a pointer to a **char** (often the name of an array of **char**) and a pointer to a file. The function writes to the file the string pointed to by the first argument; it does not write the terminating null of the string. It returns **EOF** if a write error occurs; otherwise it returns an unspecified non-negative value.

If the string written does not end with a new-line, then the next string written will be a continuation of the same line in the file. For example, given the declarations

> **FILE*** f2;
> **char** a[81] = {'\0'};
> **char** b[81] = {'\0'};

if the following calls were made in the order shown

> **strncpy**(a, "Danger! ", (**sizeof** a)-1);
> **strncpy**(b, "Men at Work\n", (**sizeof** b)-1);
> **fputs**(a, f2);
> **fputs**(b, f2);

or simply

> **fputs** ("Danger! ", f2);
> **fputs** ("Men at Work\n", f2);

then a single line would be written to *f2*: "Danger! Men at Work\n".

But it is a useful convention to think of lines as the equivalent of Cobol records, and to write one line to the file with each call of **fputs**. To do so, we must first assemble the line in an array as a string, the last character of which (i.e. the character before the terminating null) is a new-line. If the string has been assembled in array *a*, but *without* the new-line, the line may be written by the call

> **fputs**(**strncat**(a, "\n", (**sizeof** a) − 1 − **strlen**(a)), f2)

but, in the event of the string already being (**sizeof** *a*)-1 characters in length, the written string will have no new-line character. It would be better, therefore, to say

> **if** (**strlen**(a) < (**sizeof** a)-1)
>   { **fputs**(a, f2); **fputc**('\n', f2); }
> **else** /*display a message saying string is too long ... */

on the assumption that we have decided that the maximum line length for the file, including the new-line, is to be one less than the size of *a*. The typical pattern for writing an output file in C is therefore to call **fopen** with its second argument value "w", then to write successive lines using **fputs**, then to close the file.

5.6. String input from a text file

Similarly, the pattern for reading from an input text file is to call **fopen** with its second argument value "r", then to read successive lines using **fgets**, then to close the file. The function **fgets** takes three arguments:

- a pointer to a **char**, indicating where characters from the file are to be read to;
- an integer one greater than the maximum number of characters to be read;
- a file pointer.

The first argument is usually the name of a **char** array. (Remember that the array name is a pointer to the first element of the array.) The second argument allows for the fact that, after reading characters, **fgets** always appends a null character. The following call reads a sequence of characters into array a:

    fgets (a, **sizeof** a, f2)

If the maximum number of characters ((**sizeof** a)-1) is read, the function overwrites the null in $a[($**sizeof** $a)-1]$ by another null.

The main feature of **fgets** is that it is intended as a means of reading one line from a file. The array into which the characters are read should therefore be large enough to accommodate the longest possible line in the file. The function transfers successive characters from the file into the array until it has transferred a new-line character, or until end of file is reached, or until it has transferred one fewer than the number of characters specified by the second argument, whichever occurs first. It then appends a null character.

It is interesting here to compare the approaches of C and Cobol to reading variable-length lines (records) from a file. Both languages require the program to specify a maximum line (record) length - in Cobol, this is done as part of the file description, and in C it is done by the second argument of each call of **fgets**. With operating systems which have the capability, the maximum length specified in a Cobol file description can be checked against the actual file characteristics when the file is opened; in any event, every **read** statement accesses a different record. In C, each call of **fgets** (except the first) starts reading at the character following the last character read by the previous call of an input function for that file. Thus, if a line cannot be completely read by **fgets**, the unread portion can be read by subsequent calls.

If it reads successfully, **fgets** returns the value of its first argument. If a read error occurs, or if end of file is encountered before any characters have been read, it returns a null pointer. To distinguish between the two situations, there are two functions, **ferror** and **feof**. Associated with each file are an "end-of-file indicator" and an "error indicator", each of which may be set by functions which access the file. The call

    ferror(f1)

returns zero if the error indicator for $f1$ is not set, and a non-zero integer if it is. Similarly, the call

    feof (f1)

returns zero if the end-of-file indicator for $f1$ is not set, and a non-zero integer if it is. Both indicators for $f1$ are cleared by the call **clearerr** *(f1)*.

5.7. Direct input and output

(*Warning*: The meaning of "direct" in C is very different from its meaning in "direct access" in non-C contexts.)

A Cobol file containing fixed-length records may of course be simulated by a C text file in which all lines are the same length. The lines can be written and read as strings, in the way described in the preceding section.

Alternatively, such a file, when open in "w" or "a" mode, may be written to by use of the *fwrite* function; when open in "r" mode, it may be read by the *fread* function. *fwrite* writes a specified number of array elements and *fread* reads into a specified number of array elements. *These two functions do not treat new-line or null as having any special significance.* With a declaration, say, of

> **char** a[20];

the call

> **fwrite**(a, 1, **sizeof** a, f1)

writes the complete array *a* to file *f1*. The second argument gives the size of one array element (for a **char** array this will always be 1), and the third argument gives the number of elements to be written. Since the first argument is a pointer, it is possible, for example, to say

> **fwrite**(&a[5], 1, (**sizeof** a)−5, f1)

which writes all but the first five characters of *a*, or

> **fwrite**(&a[8], 1, 1, f1)

which writes only *a*[8]. The function returns the number of elements successfully written, which will be less than the value of the third argument only if a write error occurs. To a Cobol programmer, the obvious use of **fwrite** in relation to a text file is to assemble a "record" in an array, then use **fwrite** to write it.

A file written with a sequence of calls in the form

> **fwrite**(a, 1, **sizeof** a, f1)

may be read back, "record by record", by a sequence of calls in the form

> **fread**(a, 1, **sizeof** a, f1)

Each such call reads the next (**sizeof** *a*) characters from *f1* into array *a*, starting at *a*[0]. **fread** is similar to **fwrite** in that, for instance, the call

> **fread**(&a[4], 1, 2, f1)

reads the next two characters from *f1* into *a*[4] and *a*[5]. The **fread** function returns the number of elements successfully read, which will be less than the value of its third argument if a read error occurs or if the end of the file is reached. The two cases can be distinguished by use of the functions **ferror** and **feof**.

Remember that the only structure which C functions recognize in a text file is its division into lines. Since **fwrite** and **fread** treat new-line as just another character, they ignore this structure. The units in which a file is written are not reflected in the file structure, as they would be in Cobol. A file written in units of 20 characters each may be read in units of 14 characters each, for example. Nevertheless, it is for many reasons a useful convention to make each "record" end with a new-line (either by including the new-line character in the array written by **fwrite**, or by following each call of **fwrite** by a call of **fputc** to write a new-line character) and to ensure that, when the file is read, the new-line is included in the count of characters to be read by **fread**.

You do not have to write a complete file character-by-character or string-by-string or entirely by **fwrite** calls; a single text file may be created by any combination of **fputc**, **fputs** and **fwrite** calls. But it is usually good practice to think in Cobol terms, regarding lines as Cobol records, and to read a file consistently with the way it was written.

5.8. Some simple examples

This section illustrates how the facilities introduced so far may be used. They are all concerned with copying from one file to another. It is unlikely that, with system utilities available, you will very often want to write programs for straightforward file copying, but programs of this kind serve to illustrate both input and output techniques without being cluttered up with irrelevant details.

5.8.1. Copying from one stored file to another

We will look at various ways of defining a function *copyfile*, which receives as arguments the system names of a source file, *name1*, and a destination file, *name2*. The function will copy the source file to the destination file and return an integer value:

    0: Copying successfully completed.
    1: Source file cannot be opened.
    2: Destination file cannot be opened.

The name of the destination file is the *first* argument, and that of the source file is the *second* argument. This arrangement may seem unnatural, but it reflects the convention used in the standard string-handling functions, which in turn reflects the order of operands in an assignment.

We are clearly going to need *<stdio.h>* and *<string.h>* functions. Also, since C has no equivalent of Cobol's **declarative** procedures, we will assume for simplicity that the function *copyfile* deals summarily with read and write errors by using assertions to abort execution (see section 3.7). So the program might begin:

```
#include <stdio.h>
#include <string.h>
#include <assert.h>
```

The program might then define the function, beginning with the line

int copyfile (**const char*** name2, **const char*** name1)

Here is one way in which the function might be used. The function is called in the switch expression, and the comments on the left refer to the notes below.

```
/*1*/ const int  s_name = 21;
            char  N1[22];
            char  N2[22];
            ....

            ....
/*2*/ fputs ("Name of file to be copied: ", stdout);
         fgets (N1, s_name, stdin);
/*3*/ N1[strlen(N1)-1] = '\0';
         fputs ("Name of new file: ", stdout);
         fgets (N2, s_name, stdin);
         N2[strlen(N2)-1] = '\0';
/*4*/ switch (copyfile (N2, N1) ) {
            case 0:    fputs("Copied successfully\n", stdout);
                       break;
            case 1:    fputs("Source file cannot be opened\n", stdout);
                       break;
            case 2:    fputs("Destination file cannot be opened\n", stdout);
/*5*/                  break;
         }
         ....
```

Notes.
1. Assume that the maximum length of the system name of a file is 20 characters. The declaration of *s_name* allows for a terminating new-line when a name is input from a terminal. Ideally, we would specify the sizes of *N1* and *N2* as *s_name+1*, which would be acceptable to some compilers, though the Standard forbids it. A better way of dealing with constant values is introduced in a later chapter.
2. The files **stdin** and **stdout** are automatically opened, and both are by default assigned to your terminal. The call of **fputs** prompts for a file name, and **fgets** reads the line typed at the terminal. Notice that we are now using **fputs** to display a simple string at the terminal, as an alternative to **printf**, which we have used so far.
3. Removes the terminating new-line from the string obtained by **fgets**.
4. Notice again how this functional style of programming regards what a function does as a side-effect of obtaining its return value.

5.   Placing a **break** at the end of the last case of a **switch**, though unnecessary, means that, if we later add another case at the end, we do not have to remember to insert the **break** statement.

Using character input and output, *copyfile* could be defined as shown below. If you open an output file with the name of a file which already exists, the existing file will be lost. The function *copyfile* therefore attempts to open the file with *name2* as an input file. If that attempt succeeds, the newly-opened file is closed and the value 2 is returned. If the attempt fails, the output file is opened. It is still possible, however, that opening for output will be unsuccessful, for instance where there is no space or when the name is not a syntactically valid file name for the system.

```
int copyfile (const char* name2,  const char* name1)
{
        FILE*  file1;
        FILE*  file2;
        int  ch;

        if ( (file1 = fopen (name1, "r") ) ==NULL)
                return (1);
        if ( ( file2 = fopen (name2, "r")) != NULL ) {
                fclose (file1);  fclose (file2);
                return (2);
        }
        if ( (file2 = fopen (name2, "w")) == NULL) {
                fclose (file1);
                return (2);
        }
        while ( ( ch = fgetc (file1) ) != EOF)
                fputc (ch, file2);
        fclose (file1);
        fclose (file2);
        return (0);
}
```

In the fifth line from the end, the function **fputc** treats the value of the **int** variable *ch* as a character.

Since *file1* and *file2* are local variables, their values are lost on return from the function; but, if the function did not close the files, the files might remain open until exit from the program as a whole. For tidiness and safety, it is best to close a file as soon as its use is complete.

The above definition of *copyfile* is probably close to what many C programmers would write. But bear in mind that C has no declarative procedures to trap other possible errors:

- read or write failure;
- failure to close the files successfully.

Such errors can be detected by the function and appropriate action taken. But, accepting that these errors are unlikely to occur, we may handle them by assertions, which at least will produce messages that make sense in terms of our program:

```
int copyfile (const char* name2, const char* name1)
{
        FILE* file1;
        FILE* file2;
        int ch;

        if ( (file1 = fopen (name1, "r")) == NULL)
                return (1);
        if ( ( file2 = fopen (name2, "r")) != NULL) {
                assert ( fclose (file1) == 0 && fclose (file2) == 0 );
                return (2);
        }
        if ( (file2 = fopen (name2, "w")) == NULL) {
                assert ( fclose(file1) == 0 );
                return (2);
        }
        while ( (ch = fgetc(file1)) != EOF)
/*1*/           assert ( (fputc(ch, file2)) >= 0);
/*2*/   assert (feof(file1));
/*3*/   assert ( fclose(file1) == 0 && fclose(file2) == 0 );
        return (0);
}
```

Notes.

1. The assertion fails if **fputc** returns a negative value, indicating a write error.
2. This statement is reached when **fgetc** returns **EOF**. But that may be the result of a read error rather than end of file being reached (as described for **fgets** in section 5.6). The assertion checks that end of file has been reached.
3. Closes both files, and checks that they were closed successfully.

If they are to be robust, programs ought to handle the kinds of situation covered by the above assertions, and these situations ought to be handled in a more orderly and less drastic way than by using assertions. Unlike Cobol, C has no facilities for hiding exception-handling in declarative procedures; to avoid cluttering up the application logic with tests for unlikely situations, we would have to build our own file manipulation functions on top of those supplied by the standard library. But our purpose here is to learn about the basic facilities provided by the standard functions; so, to keep the exposition clear from this point on, we will adopt the common but lamentable practice of assuming that these inconvenient situations do not arise, or that they can be dealt with summarily by assertions. This does not, however, mean that you should do the same when you write real working programs.

Another way to copy a file is to use direct input and output, reading and writing in fixed-length units. The following definition of *copyfile* reads and writes in units of 2000 characters. The final read will retrieve fewer than 2000 characters (0 if the number of characters in the file is a multiple of 2000). Since **fread** returns the number of elements read, a returned value less than 2000 indicates either end of file or a read error.

```
int copyfile (const char* name2,  const char* name1)
{
        FILE*  file1;
        FILE*  file2;
        char  a[2000];
        int  n;

        if ( ( file1 = fopen(name1, "r") ) ==NULL)
              return (1);
        if ( ( file2 = fopen (name2, "r")) != NULL)  {
              assert ( fclose (file1) == 0  &&  fclose (file2) == 0 )
              return (2);
        }
        if ( ( file2 = fopen (name2, "w")) == NULL)  {
              assert ( fclose(file1) == 0 );
              return (2);
        }
/**/    while ( (n = fread(a, 1, sizeof a, file1)) > 0 )
/**/          if ( fwrite (a, 1, n, file2) < sizeof a )  break;
/**/    assert ( feof(file1) && ! ferror(file2) );
        assert ( fclose(file1) == 0  &&  fclose(file2) == 0 );
        return (0);
}
```

Only the lines marked by the null comments (/**/) differ from what we have seen before. It would probably be acceptable to call **fwrite** to write no characters, but the function here avoids doing so. The variable *n* stores the number of characters read; it is used to determine the number of characters to be written by the **fwrite** call. The **break** will be the usual exit from the **while** loop; exit occurs when fewer than 2000 characters are read or written. The assertion checks for the end of the input file and detects any write error. For a better diagnosis, separate assertions could be specified. Since *n* and the array *a* are used only within the first two marked statements, these statements may be put in a block, and *a* and *n* can be declared for the block instead of for the function as a whole:

```
{      char a[2000];
       int n;
       while ( (n = fread(a, 1, sizeof a, file1)) > 0 )
              if ( fwrite (a, 1, n, file2) < sizeof a )  break;
}
```

Alternatively, *n* could be dispensed with and the first two marked lines replaced by

```
while ( fwrite (a, 1, fread(a, 1, sizeof a, file1), file2) == sizeof a )
       ;
```

This style of programming is not recommended, but examination of the statement may reinforce your understanding. This is the first **while** we have seen which controls a null statement - the continuation condition is immediately followed by the semicolon that terminates the **while**. (In Cobol, the corresponding structure is a **continue** statement within a **perform until**.) Everything that has to be done on each iteration (the reading and writing) is done during evaluation of the continuation condition. Since the semicolon is so important, it is a good habit to put it on a separate line in such cases.

Remember that, when a function is called, the first thing that happens is that the arguments are evaluated. The **fwrite** call in the above **while** statement correctly does not depend on any particular order of evaluation. Evaluation of the first argument (*a*) yields a pointer to the array. Evaluation of the third argument causes a call of **fread** to place any data read from *file1* into the same array and return the number of characters read. That number of characters is written after all arguments are evaluated. **fwrite** returns the number of characters successfully written, and this number is tested. When the test fails and we are not at the end of *file1* or a write error has occurred, the assertion will cause abortion of execution.

5.8.2. Creating a file from terminal input

The next program creates a text file named "cd1" by accepting successive lines of input from **stdin** and writing them to the file. The maximum line length for the file is 50 characters, excluding the terminating new-line. The person typing the input enters "end" on a line by itself to indicate that there is no more input. The "end" line is not written to the file.

The program illustrates the use of **fgets** and **fputs**. Remember that **fgets** reads up to a maximum number of characters (one less than the second argument value), or up to a new-line (which is retained), or up to end of file, whichever comes first; in any event, it appends a null character, thus making the line into a string. Remember also that **fputs** writes a string, excluding the terminating null. For the sake of clarity, detection of open, close, read and write errors is not considered.

3

```
#include <stdio.h>
#include <string.h>
main (void)
{
     FILE* outfile;
     char filename[] = "cd1";
     char a[52] = {'\0'};

     outfile = fopen ( filename, "w" );
     while ( strcmp ( fgets(a, sizeof a, stdin), "end\n" ) != 0 ) {
         if ( a[strlen(a)-1] == '\n' )
                fputs (a, outfile);
         else {
                while ( fgets(a, sizeof a, stdin),  a[strlen(a)-1] != '\n')
                ;
                fputs ("**Line too long; please try again\n", stdout);
         }
     }
     fclose (outfile);
     return 0;
}
```

Notes.

- In the continuation condition of the outer **while**, the pointer returned by **fgets** is used by **strcmp** to determine whether the sequence of characters read by **fgets** is the "end" line.
- The maximum number of characters read by **fgets** is 51, to allow for a line of 50 characters plus a new-line. In such a case, **fgets** overwrites the null in $a[51]$ by another null. (Remember that the second argument of **fgets** is a number one greater than the maximum number of characters to be read, thus allowing also for the null character appended by **fgets**.)
- Since read errors are not considered, the program logic assumes that, if **fgets** retrieves a sequence of characters not ending with new-line, the sequence is 51 characters in length. To make this clearer, we may change the **if** statement so that it begins

     if (**strlen**(a) < (**sizeof** a)−1
        || (**strlen**(a) == (**sizeof** a)−1 && a[**strlen**(a)−1] == '\n'))

- The inner **while** (which controls a null statement) reads successive sequences of characters until a new-line is found; in effect, it ensures that the current line is discarded when the line exceeds the maximum length. The continuation condition is a multiple expression: the next sequence is read from input and then its last character is tested for new-line. Notice the use of the comma operator (described in section 3.2).

5.8.3. Displaying a text file

Now consider a function to copy a stored text file to a device which has a fixed maximum line length. The lines in the stored file may be arbitrarily long and so may exceed the device's maximum line length. The original lines may therefore have to be split into a number of smaller lines, and a blank line inserted after each of the original lines so that these retain their identity. The name of the function is *displayfile*. Let us assume that the device is standard output (**stdout**) so that the result is displayed on your terminal. If the 'erminal has a maximum line length of 80 characters, and the system name of the stored file is *ex1.dat*, the function call will be

> displayfile ("ex1.dat", 80)

Assume that the last line in the stored file is terminated by a new-line and that the program includes *<stdio.h>*.

Using **fgetc** and **fputc**, the function definition could be

```
void displayfile (const char* file,  const int line_length)
{
        FILE*  f1;
        int  c;
        int  i;

        f1 = fopen (file, "r");
        while ( (c = fgetc(f1)) != EOF ) {
            while (c != '\n') {
                for (i=0;  c!='\n' && i<line_length; i++) {
                    fputc (c, stdout);
                    c = fgetc (f1);
                }
                fputc ('\n', stdout);
            }
            fputc ('\n', stdout);
        }
        fclose (f1);
}
```

Making the same assumptions, a function definition using **fgets** and **fputs** is slightly more complex:

```
void displayfile (const char* file,  const int line_length)
{
    FILE* f1;
    char  a[200];

    f1 = fopen (file, "r");
    while ( fgets(a, line_length + 1, f1) != NULL ) {
        if ( a[strlen(a)-1] == '\n' )
            fputs (a, stdout);
        else {
            while ( a[strlen(a)-1] != '\n' ) {
                fputs (a, stdout);
                fputc ('\n', stdout);
                fgets (a, line_length + 1, f1);
            }
                            /*No output if only new-line remains*/
            if ( strlen(a) != 1 )
                fputs (a, stdout);
        }
        fputc ('\n', stdout);                /*output blank line*/
    }
    fclose (f1);
}
```

(Notice the arbitrary size of array *a*. Ideally, the declaration of *a* would be

> **char** a[line_length + 1];

but the Standard forbids the use of a **const** object in a constant expression - see section 7.3.)

Remember that these functions do not test for errors in opening, closing, reading or writing. They are therefore a little simpler than they would be if intended for practical use.

6
Converting Text Data

An integer will be represented in a text file by a sequence of numeric digits, possibly preceded by a plus sign or a minus sign. Unlike Cobol, C does not allow you to perform numeric operations (like numeric comparisons and arithmetic) on numbers represented in this way. You will constantly have the additional chores of converting numbers in both directions between character-string representation and internal representations (such as **int**) on which numeric operations can be performed. We have already seen an example of number conversion with **printf**, when we used %d to convert an **int** to a sequence of characters.

C provides facilities, as in **printf**, for conversion to be done during output or input of data. While **printf** served its purpose in enabling you to write little programs at an early stage, the approach taken in this book is to follow the Cobol model for input and output. On output, first assemble a complete "record", then write it to a file using either **fputs** or **fwrite**. On input, first read a complete "record" from a file using either **fgets** or **fread**, then do any required conversion. **printf** will still be used occasionally in contexts where Cobol **display** statements would be appropriate.

In reading this chapter, remember that the null character, though shown as \0, is a single character in store.

6.1. Conversion for output

We now look at the **sprintf** function (which requires inclusion of *<stdio.h>*). Its actions are identical to those of **printf**, except that the character sequence it produces is placed in an array instead of being sent to standard output. It has an additional argument, in the form of a pointer to a **char** (which of course may be an array name) specifying the destination of the converted data. For the examples that follow, assume these declarations:

```
char  a[200];
char  b[10] = {'x', 'y', 'z'};   /*b[3] through b[9] initialized to null*/
char  c = '#';
int  d = -45;
```

The call

    sprintf (a, "X%dY", d+3)

places the sequence "X-42Y\0" in $a[0]$ through $a[5]$ and returns a count of the number of characters "written", which is 5. (This is what the Standard says is returned; but some older compilers return a pointer to the generated string, in which case **strlen** has to be used to obtain the number of characters written.) Notice that a null (\0) is appended but is not included in the count. %d generates as many characters as are necessary for representation of the value, including a leading minus if the value is negative.

    sprintf (&a[5], "%c%d%%%c", 'k', d-100, b[1])

places the sequence "k-145%y\0" in $a[5]$ through $a[12]$ and returns 7. Notice that, to generate a percent character, we specify "%%".

Strings may be incorporated by use of %s:

    sprintf (a, "%s", b)

places "xyz\0" in $a[0]$ through $a[3]$ and returns 3.

    sprintf (a, "%s%s", &b[1], b)

places "yzxyz\0" in $a[0]$ through $a[5]$ and returns 5. Notice that the terminating nulls in the strings are not copied to array a. A null is always appended to the complete sequence generated by **sprintf**; hence the null in $a[5]$.

To obtain something like fixed-length representation of individual values, a minimum *field width* may precede the letter c or d or s in the second argument. Values are then right-justified and the appropriate number of spaces, if any, are generated on the left. If a value requires more characters than the field width, truncation does *not* occur; the number of characters generated is then the minimum necessary to express the value and thus will exceed the field width. To obtain left-justification, write a '-' after the %. To obtain a '+' for positive values as well as a '-' for negatives, write a '+' after the %. If both left-justification and a positive sign are required, the '+' and '-' may be written in either order. If leading zeros are required with %d, write a dot followed by the minimum number of digits to be generated; this is called *precision* (misleadingly in this context), and must appear after the field width. If precision is specified with %s, no more than the specified number of characters are taken from the string. In the examples that follow, space characters in the results are denoted by ∇, so that you can count the spaces generated; the null appended by **sprintf** is not shown.

call	*returns*	*generates* (starting at a[0])
sprintf (a, "%d", d)	3	–45
sprintf (a, "%6d", d)	6	∇∇∇–45
sprintf (a, "%–6d", d)	6	–45∇∇∇
sprintf (a, "%2d", d)	3	–45
sprintf (a, "%c", c)	1	#
sprintf (a, "%4c", c)	4	∇∇∇#
sprintf (a, "%–4c", c)	4	#∇∇∇
sprintf (a, "%s", b)	3	xyz
sprintf (a, "%5s", b)	5	∇∇xyz
sprintf (a, "%2s", b)	3	xyz
sprintf (a, "%.2s", b)	2	xy
sprintf (a, "%3.2s", b)	3	∇xy
sprintf (a, "%–5s", b)	5	xyz∇∇
sprintf (a, "%+d", d)	3	–45
sprintf (a, "%d", d+100)	2	55
sprintf (a, "%+d", d+100)	3	+55
sprintf (a, "%+4d", d+100)	4	∇+55
sprintf (a, "%–+4d", d+100)	4	+55∇
sprintf (a, "%6.4d", d)	6	∇–0045
sprintf (a, "%–7.4d", d)	7	–0045∇∇

The second argument of **sprintf** is known as the *format string*. In relation to stored files, we can regard the sequence of characters generated by each % item in the format string as a field; the remaining characters in the format string are characters which will appear before, after or between fields.

For an example of an **sprintf** call which generates several fields, assume the variable declarations

```
char weekday[10];
char month[10];
int day, hour, min;
char a[200];
```

and that the values of *weekday* and *month* are terminated by nulls. Then the call

```
sprintf (&a[4], "%s, %d %s, %.2d:%.2d\n",
         weekday, day, month, hour, min)
```

places in array *a*, starting at *a*[4], something like

    Thursday, 5 April, 09:31

followed by a new-line and a null. It also returns the number of characters placed in the array, excluding the terminating null. Just as we define the format of a record declaratively in Cobol, we can define a format in C by an array declaration with initialization:

>   **const char** time_format[] = "%s, %d %s, %.2d:%.2d\n";

and then use it in calls of **sprintf**:

>   **sprintf** (&a[4], time_format,
>   weekday, day, month, hour, min)

Along with others which will be considered later, these facilities enable us to build fixed or variable length "records" (lines) for writing to text files, and to use fixed or variable length fields within the records.

All the formatting facilities described here are available with **printf** as well as with **sprintf**.

6.2. Conversion of input

The function **sscanf** provides the complementary facilities for decomposing and converting lines read from text files. Like **sprintf**, it requires inclusion of *<stdio.h>*. Here is a simple example of its use:

```
char  in[82] = {'\0'};        /*input string*/
char  name[82] = {'\0'};
int  age;
int  inchars;         /*count of characters of in consumed*/
int  incount;         /*count of assignments made*/
.... ....
incount = sscanf ( in, "%s%d%n", name, &age, &inchars );
```

A call of **sscanf** looks rather like a call of **sprintf**. The first argument is a pointer to a **char** (usually an array name), treated as a pointer to the first character of a string, referred to as the *input string*. The second argument is a *format string*, and the remaining arguments correspond, left to right, to % items in the format string. The basic action of **sscanf** is to scan through the input string, isolating the fields and assigning their values (converted as necessary) to the variables pointed to by the remaining arguments. Notice that the third and later arguments are pointers to (i.e. addresses of) variables. This is because, when the arguments are evaluated, **sscanf** does not want the current values of these variables - it wants their addresses, so that it can deposit data at these addresses; in other words, it wants to assign to the variables. In the example above, ampersand (&) precedes *age* and *inchars*, but not *name*, because *name*, being the identifier of an array, is already a pointer to the first element of the array. If we wanted the assignment to begin at the sixth element of *name*, we would specify *&name[5]*.

White space is any character sequence which contains only characters from the set: space, new-line, form-feed, carriage-return, horizontal tab and vertical tab. White space can act as a separator between fields in the input string.

The above example decomposes the string in array *in*, which is meant to consist of someone's surname, then white space, then a number representing that person's age. The complete string is, of course, terminated by a null character. (For simplicity, we assume for the present that there are no spaces in a surname; e.g. we do not provide for a surname like "Van Basten".) **sscanf** works from left to right through *in*, under control of the format string. The first item in the format string (%s) causes **sscanf** to pass over any white space at the start of *in*; then characters are transferred from *in* to *name* until white space is found. At that point a null character is appended in *name*, so that the sequence of non-white-space characters is stored there as a string. The next item in the format string (%d) passes over white space in *in* and treats the characters following as a representation of a number, which is converted to **int** form and stored as the value of *age*. For example, if *in* contained the string

AirdrieᐁᐁV25\0

(∇ represents one space character) the first eight characters of *name* would become "Airdrie\0" and the value of *age* would become 25. The last item in the format string (%n) causes the number of characters consumed from *in* to be stored as the value of *inchars*; %n does not cause any scanning of *in*. In this case, the value would be 11, because the null following "25" has not been "consumed", though it has served to signal the end of the number. In general, the character which signals the end of a field is the one at which scanning starts for the following field. Finally, **sscanf** returns the number of assignments successfully made, *excluding* any assignments made by %n. In this example, the value assigned to *incount* is 2, the successful assignments being to *name* and *age*.

The value returned enables the calling function to analyse any error which may have occurred. If the value is negative, no suitable characters have been found in the input string - for example, when the string is null or consists entirely of white space. If some non-negative value *n*, less than that expected, is returned, a matching failure has occurred on the (*n*+1)th item.

The following examples show what happens to *incount*, *name*, *age* and *inchars* if the statement

incount = **sscanf** (in, "%s%d%n", name, &age, &inchars);

is executed when the input string in *in* has the values shown in the first column. The terminating nulls in *in* and *name* are not shown; ⇒ stands for a tab character; "(u)" means that the value is unchanged; as before, ∇ stands for one space character. The value of *inchars* will be changed only when *name* and *age* are found by the scan; otherwise the %n in the format string is not reached.

in	incount	name	age	inchars
Ayr∇12	2	Ayr	12	6
Brechin∇∇–5	2	Brechin	–5	11
Dundee⇒+1	2	Dundee	1	9
Dundee⇒⇒⇒+1	2	Dundee	1	11
∇⇒Falkirk∇5	2	Falkirk	5	11
East∇Fife	1	East	(u)	(u)
Cowdenbeath	1	Cowdenbeath	(u)	(u)
∇Forfar60	1	Forfar60	(u)	(u)
∇∇	–x	(u)	(u)	(u)
(null string)	–x	(u)	(u)	(u)

All the cases of failure assign a value less than 2 to *incount*. The value of *inchars* is useful either as a check that the complete input string has been consumed or for indicating the position at which a later call of **sscanf** should start if there is further data in the input string.

In the event of an error, the value of *incount* tells us, in effect, the field at which matching failed. As a further aid to error analysis, it can be useful to know what position in the input string the scanning process had reached when it tried to match the field (including any preceding white space). This information can be obtained by inserting %n before each %d, %s or %c in the format string, and ensuring that appropriate arguments are added. For example, if the above statement is changed to

    incount = **sscanf** (in, "%n%s%n%d%n",
                      &inchars, name, &inchars, &age, &inchars);

the results of the last five cases above will be changed to:

in	incount	name	age	inchars
East∇Fife	1	East	(u)	4
Cowdenbeath	1	Cowdenbeath	(u)	11
∇Forfar60	1	Forfar60	(u)	9
∇∇	–x	(u)	(u)	0
(null string)	–x	(u)	(u)	0

and the results of the first five cases will be unchanged. The value of *inchars* can be used in determining the position in the input string at which to begin searching for the error.

Fields need not always be separated by white space. Assuming that no surname begins with a digit, a person's age and surname might be presented in the input string with the age preceding the surname. Then the end of the first field would be recognized by detection of a non-digit. The statement incount = **sscanf** (in, "%d%s%n", &age, name, &inchars);

would have the following effects:

in	incount	name	age	inchars
12Ayr	2	Ayr	12	5
12∇Ayr	2	Ayr	12	6
–5∇∇∇Brechin	2	Brechin	–5	12
+1⇒Dundee	2	Dundee	1	9
∇5Falkirk∇	2	Falkirk	5	9
East∇Fife	0	(u)	(u)	(u)

Notice that in two cases there is no white space between the age and the surname in the input string. This is acceptable because the first character of the surname, being a non-digit, signals the end of the number; the scan then resumes at that character.

Sometimes an input field may contain white space. Suppose that a person's full name, instead of just the surname, is to be in the input string. Now there will be spaces between the parts of the name, and so white space cannot be used to terminate the *name* field in the input string. We must choose as the field terminator some character which cannot occur as part of a person's name. Suppose we choose the exclamation mark (!). Then, instead of using %s in the format string, we use %[^!]. In general, a number of characters appear between '[' and ']'; %[/q] matches a sequence of characters, every one of which is either '/' or 'q', in the input string. But, if the first character in the square brackets is a circumflex (^), then what is matched is a sequence of characters *not* including the characters between the circumflex and ']'. For example, %[^/q] matches all characters up to, but not including, the next '/' or 'q' (or, if there are none, up to the end of the string). So, if we use '!' to terminate a name, %[^!] will match the name. Scanning, of course, thereafter resumes at the '!' character in the input string. To accommodate people's names, rather than just surnames, we would amend the statement in our first example to:

incount = **sscanf** (in, "%[^!]!%d%n", name, &age, &inchars);

A few examples of the effect of this statement are:

in	incount	name	age	inchars
Jim∇Bell!25	2	Jim∇Bell	25	11
Joe∇E.∇Brown!76	2	Joe∇E.∇Brown	76	15
∇∇Alex∇∇Crewe!18	2	∇∇Alex∇∇Crewe	18	16
Tom∇Fox15	1	Tom∇Fox15	(u)	(u)

Unlike %s, this will include any initial white space in *in* as part of the *name* field. A method of skipping over the leading white space is shown at the end of the next paragraph.

A character in the format string which is not part of a % item is matched against itself. The second '!' follows the % item %[^!] and so is matched against the exclamation mark in the input string at which scanning resumes after the *name* field has been matched. An input string expected to be in the form exemplified by

    name=Ian Bell; age=20

would be handled by the statement

    incount = **sscanf** (in, "name=%[^;]; age=%d%n",
                    name, &age, &inchars);

where the sequences "name=", ";", and "age=" are to be matched precisely (but, not being part of % items, are not assigned to any variables). The space (or spaces) between ";" and "age=" will match *any* white space which appears between ";" and "age=" in the input string. In general, any white space in the format string consumes any white space that may be at the appropriate position in the input string. So, going back to the penultimate example, a way to avoid including initial white space in the *name* value is to include one or more spaces at the start of the format string:

    incount = **sscanf** (in, " %[^!]!%d%n",
                    name, &age, &inchars);

Fixed-length fields are matched and their values assigned to variables using %c. If the input string were expected to consist of a four-character sales code followed by a number the call of **sscanf** might be

    sscanf (in, "%4c%d", sales_code, &qty)

A program which is interested only in certain selected fields of a record may scan and recognize other fields without assigning their values to variables. The first example in this section extracted values for *name* and *age* from the string *in*:

    incount = **sscanf** (in, "%s%d%n", name, &age, &inchars)

but if a program processes only people's ages and is not concerned with their names, it may instead use

    incount = **sscanf** (in, "%*s%d%n", &age, &inchars)

which differs from the previous version by the omission of *name* from the argument list and by the insertion of '*', known as the "assignment suppressing character", before 's' in the format string. The effect is that the *name* field is scanned over but not assigned. The '*' must precede width and precision if these are present; for instance, the effect of "%*4c" in a format string is to skip over the next four characters of the input string.

Regardless of what programming language is used, it is common practice to distinguish between reading raw input data and reading data which a program has previously stored in a file. When reading raw input data, a program should apply rigorous format and value checks; the method of handling failures of these checks should be part of the program specification. But a program should have more confidence in data it reads from a stored file. With such a file, the reading and writing programs should use a common file description (for instance, by copying it from a Cobol library) and common access procedures for that file, though this will not necessarily ensure that the reading program can rely on the writing program having done its job correctly. We have not yet learned enough about C to understand how these matters may be arranged; let us for the present assume that any checks we apply to a stored file can be in the form of assertions.

To illustrate the difference in approach between reading raw input and reading stored files, and as an introduction to the use of **sscanf**, we look at how two programs might handle files containing very simple records, each consisting of a person's surname and age. The first program reads records entered at a terminal and writes them to a file. In this file, named *persons.d*, there is one line for each person, with a '!' separating the surname from the age. The maximum length of a surname is 20 characters, and any age should be in the range 0 to 100. The records will be variable-length, each one terminated by a new-line. The maximum record length in *persons.d* is therefore 25 characters, including the terminating new-line character.

```
/*          PROGRAM A        */

#include <stdio.h>
#include <string.h>

main (void)
{       const char  separator = '!';
        FILE* persons;
        char  in[82] = {'\0'}; /* max input line 80 chars and new-line */
        char  out[26] = {'\0'};
        char  name[82] = {'\0'};
        int  age;
        int  inchars;
        int  incount;

        persons = fopen ("persons.d", "w");
        fputs ("For each person, type (on one line):\n", stdout);
        fputs ("    surname\n", stdout);
        fputs ("    at least one space\n", stdout);
        fputs ("    age\n", stdout);
        fputs ("then press RETURN\n", stdout);
        fputs ("To finish, type \"end\" then press RETURN\n", stdout);
```

```
            while ( strcmp (fgets (in, sizeof in, stdin), "end\n") != 0 )  {
                if ( in[strlen(in) - 1] != '\n')  {
                    while (fgets (in, sizeof in, stdin),  in[strlen(in) - 1] != '\n' )
                    ;
                    fputs ("**Line too long\n", stdout);
                }
                else  {
                    incount = sscanf (in, "%s%d%n", name, &age, &inchars) ;
                    if (incount < 0)
                    { fputs ("???\n", stdout);  continue; }
                    if (incount == 0)
                    { fputs ("**Failed to find name\n", stdout);  continue; }
                    if (incount == 1)
                    { fputs ("**Failed to find age\n", stdout);  continue; }
                    if (inchars != strlen(in) - 1)
                    { fputs ("**Extra characters at end\n", stdout);  continue; }
                    if (strlen(name) > 20)
                    { fputs ("**Name exceeds 20 characters\n", stdout);
                                                      continue;}
                    if ( strchr (name, separator) != NULL )  {
                        fputs ("**Name includes \"", stdout);
                        fputc (separator, stdout);
                        fputs ("\"\n", stdout);  continue;
                    }
                    if (age < 0 || age > 100)
                    { fputs ("**Age not in range 0 to 100\n", stdout);  continue;}
                    sprintf ( out, "%s%c%d\n", name, separator, age );
                    fputs ( out, persons );
                }
            }
            fclose (persons);
            return  0;
        }
```

(Notice that this program ensures that no '!' occurs within a *name*, because '!' is to be used as the terminator of *name* in the output records.)

The second program puts each line from the *persons.d* file into a line in *printfile.d*. Ages are right-justified in the first column and surnames are left-justified in the second column; the columns are separated by two spaces. On the assumption that the *persons.d* file is correct, the program deals with errors by assertions.

```
/*          PROGRAM B        */

#include <stdio.h>
#include <string.h>
#include <assert.h>

main (void)
{
     FILE* persons;
     FILE* printfile;
     char  in[26] = {'\0'};
     char  out[26] = {'\0'};
     char  name[26] = {'\0'};
     int  age;

     persons = fopen ("persons.d", "r");
     printfile = fopen ("printfile.d", "w");
     fputs ("Contents of persons file\n", printfile);
     fputs ("\nAGE  SURNAME\n", printfile);
     while ( fgets (in, sizeof in, persons) != NULL ) {
          assert (in[strlen(in)-1] == '\n');
          assert (sscanf (in, "%[^!]!%d", name, &age) == 2);
          sprintf (out, "%3d  %-s\n", age, name);
          fputs (out, printfile);
     }
     fclose (persons);
     fputs ("\nEnd of list\n", printfile);
     fclose (printfile);
     return  0;
}
```

As output by this program, *printfile.d* takes no account of page boundaries. The program must be a little more sophisticated if we want to split the output into pages, each with a page heading, a page number, and column headings. Chapter 8 begins by developing the program to meet this requirement.

7

Constants

7.1. Constants generally

A bad feature of the last two programs in chapter 6 is the appearance of the numbers 26 and 82 in the array declarations. Inclusion in a program of such so-called "magic numbers", even if used only once, is unsatisfactory. In these programs, 26 is the maximum number of characters in a record (line) in the *persons.d* file, plus one to allow for the null character which terminates the string. If the maximum record size were changed to 30, a programmer would have to find all the occurrences of 26 and change them to 31. In doing so, the programmer might easily miss an occurrence or might wrongly change a 26 which had nothing to do with line length - it might be the number of characters in the alphabet. Indeed, if we look at Program B at the end of chapter 6, we see that in the declaration of *in [26]*, the 26 is derived from the maximum size of a record in *persons.d*, while the 26 of *out [26]* is derived from the maximum size of the output line. By chance, these both happen to be 25. If we increased the number of spaces between the output columns, we would want to change the declaration of *out* but not that of *in*.

To make program maintenance easier, most languages (but not C or Cobol) provide a simple way of declaring *named constants*. Typically, the declaration of a named constant is like that of a variable with an initialization: it has a type, and its visibility is determined by the same scope rules (e.g. if declared at the start of a block, it cannot be referred to outside that block). As the terminology suggests, the program may modify the value of a variable but not that of a constant. In the last two programs of chapter 6, if *maxrec* were declared as an integer constant with value 25, then instead of using the number 26 we would refer to *maxrec + 1*. If at some later date we wanted to change the maximum record size, only the declaration of *maxrec* would need to be amended.

In standard Cobol, the best we can do is define a data item with a **value** clause and hope that the program will not inadvertently change its value. Standard C does provide facilities which enable us to specify something akin to named constants; but these facilities are error-prone and more complex than they need be. Before looking at them, let us briefly recapitulate what the word "constant" means in C terminology.

C uses the term *constant* to mean what Cobol calls a *literal*, or what is sometimes called an *unnamed constant*. As we have seen, in a C declaration like

>   **char** a[10] = {'x'};

10 is an integer constant and 'x' is a character constant (which, remember, is of type **int** - see section 2.10).

7.2. Integer constants - a special case

One statement in section 7.1 needs to be qualified. There is, in fact, a simple way of declaring true named constants in C. Saying

>   **enum** {
>   maxrec = 25,
>   maxinline = 81
>   };

enables us to use the names *maxrec* and *maxinline* in place of 25 and 81 respectively. The scope and visibility of these constants is governed by precisely the same rules as those for variable declarations. Surely this is just what is needed?

Well, it is, but there is a snag. This kind of declaration can be used only for constants whose values are integers. We could not, for instance, say

>   **enum** {
>   pi = 3.14159;   /* WRONG */
>   };

because 3.14159 is not an integer. Most C programmers feel that it is better to treat all named constants uniformly, rather than have one technique for integers and another for non-integers. Named integer constants are therefore usually specified as macros. Macros are introduced in section 7.4, and **enum** is described more fully in chapter 13.

7.3. *const* qualification

C provides two other unsatisfactory substitutes for named constants. One, which we have used already, is the declaration of a variable with the qualification **const**, as in chapter 6, where we declared

>   **const char** separator = '!';

Any explicit attempt by the program to modify the value of *separator* should give rise to at least a warning from your compiler; but, for instance, modification through the wrong use of a pointer is a possibility which, according to the C standard, results in "undefined behaviour" at run time. An identifier declared as **const** cannot be treated as being the name of a constant. It cannot be used in constant expressions (see section 2.8.2) and thus, in particular, cannot be used in a **case** constant of a **switch** statement or in an expression specifying the size of an array.

A const-qualified object therefore sits uneasily between being a variable and being a named constant. Such an object is intended to be placed in read-only storage if the underlying system provides such a facility. It is probably best thought of as a "read-only variable". However self-contradictory that description may seem, and however unsatisfactory the facility is, the security of your programs will be increased if you include the word **const** in the declaration of any object whose value is not to be modified by the block in which it is declared - provided of course that you can accept the limitations on its use.

The declaration

     const int * p;

means that, though the value of *p* itself can be modified, the integer it points to cannot (through the use of *p*). The declaration

     int * **const** p;

means that the value of *p* cannot be modified, but the integer it points to can. The declaration

     const int * **const** p;

means that neither *p* nor (using *p*) the integer it points to can be modified.

Each pointer in a chain can be modifiable or not. For example,

     char * **const** * c;

means that pointer *c* is modifiable, the pointer that *c* points to is not modifiable, and the character (array?) pointed to by that pointer is modifiable.

7.4. Macros

Traditionally, C programmers have used *macros* to overcome the language's failure to provide for named constants. Macros have a long history and are among the most powerful tools in programming. Their basis is systematic replacement of one sequence of characters by another. In the present context, we need look at only the simplest forms of C's macro-defining facility. By writing a program line

    #define MAXREC 25

(which is an example of a *macro definition*) we are saying: every time "MAXREC" appears in the program from this point on, replace it by "25", except when it appears within quotes. Regardless of the division of the program into functions and blocks, the effect continues through all subsequent program lines until either the end of the program text is reached or a line

> #undef MAXREC

cancels the definition. Conceptually at least, all *macro replacement* (in this case, substitution of "25" for "MAXREC") takes place during a *preprocessing* phase before compilation proper begins; the compiler therefore receives as its input the program with all the macro substitutions done and the *#define* and *#undef* lines removed.

There is another way in which macro definitions differ from variable declarations: each macro definition or cancellation must be on its own *on one line*. (If you want to spread a macro definition over several lines, put a backslash at the end of each of these lines except the last; the lines will then be treated as a single line.) In most C contexts, the new-line character is regarded just as a component of white space; in macro definitions and cancellations, it is syntactically distinct. The shape of a definition is:

white space including new-line

#define

white space not including new-line

the identifier to be replaced (the *macro name*)

white space not including new-line

the replacement text, which may include embedded white space, not including new-line

optional white space not including new-line

new-line

Do not put a semicolon at the end of the replacement text, unless you want it to be part of the replacement text. Most macro names in this book are in upper-case; this is not a language requirement, but it follows a long-standing convention of C programming.

In Program A at the end of chapter 6, 26 is one greater than the maximum record size, and 82 is one greater than the maximum length of an input line (including, in both cases, the new-line character). It would be better, therefore, to amend the array declarations to

```
#define MAXREC 25
#define MAXINLINE 81
char   in [MAXINLINE + 1] = {'\0'};
char  out [MAXREC + 1] = {'\0'};
char name [MAXINLINE + 1] = {'\0'};
#undef MAXREC
#undef MAXINLINE
```

The *#undef* lines are unnecessary, but it is a good habit to cancel a macro definition as soon as there will be no further use for it. This removes the danger of changing inappropriate things in other blocks and functions. However, for clarity, the *#undef* lines will be omitted in the examples that follow.

Similarly, the array declarations in Program B would be better as

```
#define MAXREC 25
#define MAXOUTLINE 25
char  in [MAXREC + 1] = {'\0'};
char  out [MAXOUTLINE + 1] = {'\0'};
char  name [MAXREC + 1] = {'\0'};
```

Confusion would then not arise between the two uses of the number 26.

Now let us think again about the maintenance of these two programs. We have made it easier to change the maximum input and output line lengths and the maximum record length in the file *persons.d*. But we have not considered the maximum lengths of the items that make up the lines and records. Also, since the maximum record length is derived from the lengths of these items, there is the danger of changing one of these and forgetting to make the resulting change to the maximum record length. Using MAXS to mean "maximum size of", a better approach is

```
#define MAXS_AGE 3
#define MAXS_NAME   20
#define MAXREC   (MAXS_NAME + MAXS_AGE + 2)
```

which results in every subsequent occurrence of MAXREC being replaced by

```
(20 + 3 + 2)
```

Alternatively, in Program A, where *separator* is declared as

```
const char  separator  = '!';
```

we could be pedantic about making the meaning clear by writing the last of the above three lines as

```
#define MAXREC   (MAXS_NAME + sizeof separator + MAXS_AGE + 1)
```

but we could not take this to its logical conclusion by substituting **sizeof** '\n' for the final term of the expression (i.e. 1), because '\n', being a character constant, is of type **int**. While the C standard says that the **sizeof** an object of type **char** is always 1, the **sizeof** an object of type **int** is implementation-dependent; on a 32-bit word machine, it is likely to be 4. The expression **sizeof** (**int**) will give you the size of an **int** in the implementation you use. Here the parentheses are significant - they indicate that the operand of **sizeof** is a type identifier. So we could amend the last line of the above to

```
#define MAXREC   (MAXS_NAME + sizeof separator + MAXS_AGE + \
     sizeof (char) )
```

which is perhaps less clear than we would ideally like it to be. (Notice, by the way, the use of a backslash at the end of a line, causing the next line to be treated as a continuation of the current line.) Every later occurrence of MAXREC would then be replaced by

(20 + **sizeof** separator + 3 + **sizeof** (**char**))

Having defined MAXS_NAME as 20, we would of course want to use MAXS_NAME instead of 20 in the statement in Program A:

if (**strlen** (name) > 20)
{**fputs** ("**Name exceeds 20 characters\n", **stdout**); **continue**;}

The first line of the statement can be written as

if (**strlen** (name) > MAXS_NAME)

but if we wrote the second line as

{**fputs** ("**Name exceeds MAXS_NAME characters\n", **stdout**); **continue**;}

MAXS_NAME would not be replaced by 20 because macro replacement does not take place within a string literal. One solution would be to use **printf** instead of **fputs**:

printf ("**Name exceeds %d characters\n", MAXS_NAME)

Another would be to include the definition

#define QMAXS_NAME "20"

and to say

{**fputs** ("**Name exceeds " QMAXS_NAME " characters\n", **stdout**);
continue;}

During preprocessing the first argument of **fputs** would become

"**Name exceeds " "20" " characters\n"

Since adjacent string literals are always concatenated to form a single literal, this in turn would become

"**Name exceeds 20 characters\n"

The snag is that this technique requires two definitions, one for use outside string literals and one for use within them:

#define MAXS_NAME 20
#define QMAXS_NAME "20"

Ideally, we would like to define MAXS_NAME as here and to derive the quoted version from it, so that the constant 20 appears only once. Deriving a method of doing so will give us an opportunity to look at macros with arguments and to learn a little more about how macro replacement is done.

7.5. Macros with arguments

Like functions, macros may have arguments. If we write

> #define MAX(x, y) (x>y ? x:y)

with no space between MAX and the first open parenthesis, then a later occurrence in the program text of

> MAX (bill, fred)

(whether or not white space follows MAX) will be replaced during preprocessing by

> (bill>fred ? bill:fred)

It is a good convention to put parentheses around the replacement text. For example, following the definition

> #define TWICE(i)   i + i

TWICE (4) would be replaced, as intended, by 4 + 4, and so 5 * TWICE(4) would be replaced by

> 5 * 4 + 4

giving 24 at run-time, rather than the probably intended result 40. The latter result would be obtained if the macro definition were

> #define TWICE(i) (i + i)

But this convention alone is not enough. If we defined another macro

> #define SQUARE(i) (i * i)

then the replacement of 2 * SQUARE (5 + 1) would be

> 2 * (5 + 1 * 5 + 1)

giving 22 instead of the probably intended 72. To avoid this kind of thing, it is best also to put parentheses round the arguments when they appear in the replacement text:

> #define SQUARE(i) ((i) * (i))

7.6. More about macros

(If you have had enough of macros for the time being, feel free to skip this section on your first read through.)

The following displays *Fred*:

> #define DISPLAY(a) **printf** ("%s", a)
> **char** xyz[] = "Fred";
> DISPLAY(xyz);

If, in a macro definition, an argument is immediately preceded in the replacement text by #, then the argument is placed unchanged in double quotes. The following displays *Fred+xyz*:

> #define DISPLAY(a) **printf** ("%s+%s", a, #a)
> **char** xyz[] = "Fred";
> DISPLAY(xyz);

because during the preprocessing phase the final line becomes

> **printf** ("%s+%s", xyz, "xyz");

If an argument (inserted without a preceding #) contains any macro names, these are replaced and what is generated is the argument with all internal replacements done. Finally, the generated text is scanned again to see if any further macro replacement can be done. The following displays *Alf*:

> #define DISPLAY(a) **printf** ("%s", a)
> #define xyz abc
> **char** abc[] = "Alf";
> DISPLAY(xyz);

In the call of DISPLAY in the last line, the argument *xyz* is recognized as a macro name, and becomes *abc*. The replacement text thus becomes

> **printf** ("%s", abc);

which, when the program is run, displays *Alf*.

The following, however, displays *Alf+xyz*:

> #define DISPLAY(a) **printf** ("%s+%s", a, #a)
> #define xyz abc
> **char** abc[] = "Alf";
> DISPLAY(xyz);

because the final line becomes

> **printf** ("%s+%s", abc, "xyz");

The first *xyz* is replaced by *abc*, but the second is not, because macro replacement is never applied within double quotes.

Now let us return to the problem we had at the end of section 7.4. Having defined MAXS_NAME as 20, we want to use MAXS_NAME to give us the string literal "20". The examples above demonstrate that we cannot just

> #define MAXS_NAME 20
> #define QUOTE(b) #b

and say QUOTE(MAXS_NAME), for that will give us

> "MAXS_NAME"

What we can do, though, is:

> #define MAXS_NAME 20
> #define Q(b) #b
> #define QUOTE(b) Q(b)

As a result of the third of these definitions, the replacement text for QUOTE(*anything*) is Q(*anything*). (It is not #*anything*, because macro calls in the replacement text are not recognized at definition time.) A later occurrence of QUOTE(*anything*) in the program text will be replaced by Q(*anything*), with any macro names within *anything* suitably replaced, and then the generated text is scanned again, Q(*anything*) being replaced by "*anything*". Thus QUOTE(MAXS_NAME) is replaced by Q(20), which in turn is replaced by "20".

With the above definitions, we can rewrite the statement of Program A (chapter 6)

> **if** (**strlen**(name) > 20)
> {**fputs** ("**Name exceeds 20 characters\n", **stdout**) ...

as

> **if** (**strlen**(name) > MAXS_NAME)
> {**fputs** ("**Name exceeds " QUOTE(MAXS_NAME) " characters\n",
>   **stdout**) ...

(remember that adjacent string literals are concatenated to form a single literal). Using the same definitions of Q and QUOTE, as well as

> #define SEPARATOR !

we could rewrite the statement in Program B

> **assert** (**sscanf** (in, "%[^!]!%d", name, &age) == 2);

as

> **assert** (**sscanf** (in, "%[^" QUOTE(SEPARATOR) "]" QUOTE(SEPARATOR)
>   "%d", name, &age) == 2);

This would be helpful if the separator were to be referred to in other statements in the program where it did not appear in a string literal. If at some later date we wanted to change the character separating *name* from *age*, only the definition of SEPARATOR would need to be changed.

This example has been given not for its trivial achievement, but to illustrate how macros may be used. It is no more than a simple illustration - there is much more that you can learn about macros if you are going to use them more ambitiously.

7.7. Derivation of constants from other constants

Generally, if the value of one constant is derived from that of another, that derivation should be reflected in the definitions of the constants; otherwise inconsistencies can arise during program maintenance. We noted in section 7.4 that the maximum record size in the file *persons.d* (MAXREC) was derived from the maximum size of a person's name and the maximum size of a person's age. You may have noticed that the maximum size of an age is itself derived from the maximum permissible value of age (assuming that ages are always non-negative). You may have noticed also that the minimum and maximum age values both appear in a statement in Program A of chapter 6:

> **if** (age < 0 ‖ age > 100)
> {**fputs** ("**Age not in range 0 to 100\n", **stdout**) ...

The 0 would be better expressed as MIN_AGE and the 100 as MAX_AGE. These are defined in the following definitions, which express the interdependencies of constants for Program A:

> #define MAXS_NAME   20
> #define MIN_AGE   0
> #define MAX_AGE   100
> #define MAXS_AGE   (**sprintf** (c, "%d", MAX_AGE))
> #define MAXREC   (MAXS_NAME + **sizeof** separator + MAXS_AGE + 1)
> **char** c[10];   /* used in computing max age size */

The condition in the above **if** statement would then be

> (age < MIN_AGE ‖ age > MAX_AGE)

and the first argument of **fputs** could be treated on the lines described in the last section, using the Q and QUOTE macros. More simply, **printf** could be used instead of **fputs**:

> **printf** ("**Age not in range %d to %d\n", MIN_AGE, MAX_AGE) ...

8
Functions

8.1. Introduction

Program B at the end of chapter 6 requires some modification in order to provide for the division of its output into pages. In Cobol, output pagination is a trivial matter, thanks to **linage** and **footing** and to the **end-of-page** clause of the **write** statement. In C, you have to keep track of how many lines have been output on the current page and to test this number before (or after) each line is written, e.g.

```
if (++linenumber > PAGESIZE)  {
        /* throw to new page, increment pagenumber,
            print headings, reset linenumber  */
    };
    fputs (  ...
```

In rewriting Program B, let us concentrate all the interaction with the output file, including line and page control, in a function whose *prototype* is

void writeline (**const char***);

A prototype declares a function, but does not define it. A prototype has no body, and it does not need to name its parameters - it merely gives the type of value returned (**void**, in this case) and the types of the parameters. In this case, there is a single parameter of type pointer to **const char**. (For the definition which we will construct later, the argument is intended to be a pointer to a character string which is to be sent by the function to the output file as one line. It will not include the new-line character. If the argument is a null pointer, that will be a signal to *writeline* that there are no further lines to be sent to the file.)

In chapter 3 it was recommended that every function be defined before being called, i.e. that the definition should appear earlier in the program text than the first call. That recommendation can now be modified. A C compiler, encountering a function call, will make what will usually be inappropriate assumptions about the type of value returned and the types of the arguments, unless the compiler has prior information about the function. We can ensure that it has the information it needs for a function *x* by defining *x* before it is called; alternatively, we may define function *x* elsewhere (perhaps after another function that calls it), but *ensure that a function prototype for x is available to the function that makes the call.* The above prototype for *writeline* contains the information necessary for the compiler to handle calls of *writeline* correctly, even when the compiler does not have a full definition of *writeline* available.

Here is a revised version of Program B which assumes that the output file is looked after by the function *writeline*:

```
           #include <stdio.h>
           #include <string.h>
           #include <assert.h>
/*1*/#define DETAIL_LINE "%3d  %-s", age, name
           #define COL_HEADINGS "AGE  SURNAME"

           main (void)
             {
/*2*/          void  writeline (const char*);
               FILE*  persons;
               #define RECSIZE 25
               #define OUTLINESIZE 25
               char  in[RECSIZE + 1] = {'\0'};
               char  name[RECSIZE + 1] = {'\0'};
               char  out[OUTLINESIZE + 1] = {'\0'};
               int  age;

/*3*/          persons = fopen ("persons.d", "r");
               while (fgets (in, sizeof in, persons) != NULL) {
                   assert (in[strlen(in) - 1] == '\n');
                   assert (sscanf (in, "%[^!]!%d", name, &age) == 2);
/*4*/              sprintf (out, DETAIL_LINE);
                   writeline (out);
               }
               fclose (persons);
               writeline (NULL);
               return 0;
             }
```

The commented numbers refer to these notes:

1. The macro COL_HEADINGS is not used in *main*; it will be used in *writeline*. The two macros DETAIL_LINE and COL_HEADINGS are defined together as a reminder to a maintenance programmer that a change to the format of DETAIL_LINE may involve a change also to the column headings.

2. Prototype declaration of the function *writeline*. Like the other declarations, this is local to the function *main*.
3. For clarity of exposition, the check for successful opening (see chapter 5) is omitted, as are those for the other file operations.
4. With macro replacement, this statement becomes

> **sprintf** (out, "%3d %-s", age, name);

We can follow the above by a definition of the function *writeline*:

```
        void  writeline (const char* text)
          {
/*1*/       #define PAGESIZE  60 /* must not be smaller than 4 */
/*2*/       static FILE*  printfile;
            static int  linenumber;
            static int  pagenumber = 0;

            if (pagenumber ==0)  {
/*3*/           printfile = fopen ("p.d", "w");
/*4*/           linenumber = PAGESIZE;
            }
/*5*/       if (linenumber >= PAGESIZE)  {
/*6*/           char  out[81];
                linenumber = 1;     /* about to print first line of page */
/*7*/           sprintf (out, "\fContent of persons file  -  page %d\n",
                        ++pagenumber);
                fputs (out, printfile);
                ++linenumber;
                fputc ('\n', printfile);     /* blank line */
                ++linenumber;
                fputs (COL_HEADINGS, printfile);
                fputc ('\n', printfile);
            }
            if (text == NULL)  {
/*8*/           fputs ("\nEnd of list\n", printfile); /* inadequate */
                fclose (printfile);
            }
            else  {
                ++linenumber;
/*9*/           fputs (text, printfile);
                fputc ('\n', printfile);
            }
            #undef PAGESIZE
          }
```

Notes:

1. PAGESIZE is the number of lines per page. (Every comment is replaced by one space character before the preprocessor phase.) If PAGESIZE is changed to a value less than 4, the function will behave as though it is 4.

2. *printfile, linenumber* and *pagenumber* are all declared as **static**, because their values must not be lost on exit from the function. If the word **static** were omitted, then, every time *writeline* was called, the values of *printfile* and *linenumber* would be undefined (we would lose both our contact with the file and the current line number) and the value of *pagenumber* would be zero. Since *pagenumber* is **static**, initialization to zero is redundant; it would happen by default. Explicit initialization, as here, is the programmer's way of telling the reader that the initial value of zero is used by the function.

3. Again, checks for successful execution of file-handling functions are omitted in the interest of clarity of exposition.

4. This statement ensures that a new headed page will be started on the first call of *writeline*. The same effect could be achieved by initializing *linenumber* when it was declared. Placing an assignment to *linenumber* at this point - just before testing it - makes the intention clearer. Alternatively, special code to start the first page could be written here.

5. Logically, a test for equality would be adequate. Use of >= makes the function more robust.

6. Declaration of *out* at the start of the block means that it can be referenced only within the block, and it makes reading easier by placing the declaration of *out* close to its use. This *out* is an entirely different object from the *out* declared in *main*, which can be referenced only within *main*. The two objects just happen to have the same name.

7. Remember that the character '\f' is the form feed, which causes a throw to the start of the next page.

8. The **fputs** statement here is inadequate because a check ought first to be made that there are at least two lines remaining on the current page. If there are not, then a new page ought to be started, with headings, before the "End of list" line is output. In other words, the statement beginning

    if (linenumber >= PAGESIZE) { ...

    should be repeated at this point. The situation could be handled by defining another function with some name like *newpage*, which would be called at both points. We will return to this matter later.

9. You might think that this and the following statement could be replaced by the single statement

    fputs (**strncat** (text, "\n", 1), printfile);

    but this would give trouble in the case of a call like

    writeline ("Top");

    because **strncat** modifies the string pointed to by its first argument. In the case of

    strncat ("Top", ...

it would be modifying a string literal. This is an error which results in undefined behaviour.

8.2. Recursion

Most calls of *writeline* will simply result in *linenumber* being incremented and the argument string, followed by a new-line, being output to *printfile*. But when it is appropriate to start a new page, or when the argument is null, other lines have to be output to *printfile*. Each of these lines - the heading lines and the lines indicating the end of the list - also consists of a string followed by a new-line, and requires *linenumber* to be incremented. In other words, *writeline* generates strings which are to be treated in the same way that *writeline* itself treats the strings of text passed to it. So why shouldn't *writeline* call itself to handle the lines it generates? For instance, in the above version of *writeline*, why don't we replace the lines

```
++linenumber;
fputs (COL_HEADINGS, printfile);
fputc ('\n', printfile);
```

by

```
writeline (COL_HEADINGS);
```

since this should do just what we want? The answer is that there is no reason why we shouldn't. In C, a function can "call itself". When you are defining a function, you can assume that the function already exists.

This is something you are forbidden to do in Cobol. You cannot use the statement **call** "x" within a program named *x*, nor can you use the statement **perform** *x* within a paragraph named *x*. You would be trying, during an *activation* of a program or a paragraph, to start another activation of the same program or paragraph. This would be a *recursive* call, and prohibition of such calls is Cobol's greatest single deficiency, a deficiency shared by only a few other languages.

When you **perform** a procedure or **call** a program in Cobol, you probably think in terms of concealed **go to** statements; control is transferred to the start of the procedure or program and, after its execution, control is returned to the statement logically following the **perform** or call. Do not think in this way in relation to function calls in C - it is not how you have been thinking of standard library function calls, and it is not how you should think of a call of a function that you have defined yourself. A function is best regarded as an operator (see section 3.3) that has been added to the basic language. When you call a function, you are concerned with only two things:

1. The value returned by the function, if any. For instance, the standard function **fgetc** returns an integer, and the function *writeline* defined above, being a **void** function, returns nothing.
2. Any action that the function takes which affects the state of something outside the function itself. For instance, the function *writeline* changes the state of the output

file. Indeed, that is the whole purpose of calling *writeline*, and it would be misleading in the C context to refer to such actions as *side-effects*, which is what they are called in other languages. (They are so called because in other languages functions are normally called solely for what they return; but, since C has no provision for procedures, functions have to be used in their place.)

When a function is called, you can assume that these two things will be taken care of, unless the program terminates abnormally (as when a run-time error occurs, an assertion fails, or the function calls **exit**, the equivalent of Cobol's **stop run**). There is not the possibility, as there would be in Cobol, of the function making a sneaky exit to somewhere else in the program.

And all this is true regardless of whether or not the function is called from within itself. When a function calls itself (i.e. makes a *nested* call of itself), it does not lose the values of its arguments or of its local automatic (i.e. non-**static**) variables; these values are unaffected by nested calls. To put it another way, every *activation* of a function has its own set of parameters and automatic variables, distinct from the corresponding objects in any other current activation. This set of objects comes into existence when the function is called, and ceases to exist when the function returns. By contrast, an object declared in a function as being **static** has an existence independent of any activation. When different activations of a function refer to a **static** object with a given name, they are all referring to the same object.

For an example, we look at a simplified version of *writeline*, which will be named *wline*. Its basic actions are the same as those of *writeline*, except that it does not concern itself with page numbers, it does not output special text at the end of the file, and it simply heads each page with a line saying "Listing". Notice the definitions of TRUE and FALSE. The function *writeline* used a zero value of *pagenumber* to indicate that the function was being called for the first time; in *wline* we are more explicit, using a static variable *first_call*. (Whether or not *first_call* should be reset to TRUE when the output file is closed is a matter of opinion.)

```
void  wline (const char* text)
{
      #define  TRUE   1
      #define  FALSE  0
      #define  PAGESIZE 60
      static FILE*  printfile;
      static int  linenumber;
      static int  first_call = TRUE;

      if (first_call == TRUE) {
           first_call = FALSE;
           printfile = fopen ("p.d", "w");
           linenumber = PAGESIZE;
      }
```

4

```
            if (text == NULL) {
                    fclose (printfile);
                    first_call = TRUE;
            }
            else {
                    if (linenumber >= PAGESIZE) {
                            linenumber = 0;
                            wline ("\fListing");
                    }
                    ++linenumber;
                    fputs (text, printfile);
                    fputc ('\n', printfile);
            }
    }
```

Suppose that the first call of this function is

> wline (" 25   James");

This causes an activation of *wline* in which the string addressed by *text* is
" 25   James". Since the function is being activated for the first time, the condition in
the first **if** statement is true, so values are assigned to the three static variables. As a
result of the assignment to *linenumber*, the condition in

> **if** (linenumber >= PAGESIZE) { ...

is true, so 0 is assigned to *linenumber*, and *wline* is called recursively. This has the
effect of suspending the current activation of *wline* and starting a new activation in
which the string addressed by *text* is "\fListing". Since *text* is a parameter, the object it
identifies in this new activation is different from that identified in the suspended
activation; but a name declared as **static** denotes the same object in both activations.
Thus the new activation makes use of the values which were assigned to *printfile*,
linenumber and *first_call* by the suspended activation. Within the new activation, the
statement

> **if** (linenumber >= PAGESIZE) { ...

is again reached. The condition value is false, *linenumber* is incremented to 1, the
string addressed by *text* (i.e. "\fListing") is output to *printfile* followed by a new-line,
and the activation terminates. The suspended activation is now resumed where it was
left off, so the first thing it does is to increment *linenumber* to 2. The string addressed
by *text* (i.e. " 25   James") is then output to *printfile* followed by a new-line, and this
activation terminates. Thereafter, repeated calls of *wline* from elsewhere will each
cause an activation of *wline*, in which there will be a nested activation only when the
end of an output page is reached.

Now consider what would happen if the definition of PAGESIZE were changed to

> #define PAGESIZE 0

and the function were called for the first time by

wline (" 25   James");

In every activation, the condition

(linenumber >= PAGESIZE)

would be true, so that every activation would execute the recursive call

wline ("\fListing");

thus starting a new activation, which, in turn, would start another activation, and so on for ever. No activation would ever be completed, because every one would be suspended on the start of another. (A run-time error would almost certainly occur when storage capacity was exceeded.) This is an example of *infinite recursion*, which is a common danger in recursive programming. You might expect the same situation to arise with

#define PAGESIZE 1

but it doesn't. Read the function definition again and see what would happen.

Traditionally, textbooks introduce recursion by showing a function whose prototype is

int factorial (**int**)

and which returns the factorial of its argument. Mathematicians use the notation *n!* to denote the factorial of an integer *n*. The factorial of *n* can be defined thus:

- If *n* is negative, the factorial of *n* is undefined;
- If *n* is zero, the factorial of *n* is 1 (i.e. 0! = 1);
- If *n* is positive, the factorial of *n* is the product of all integers from 1 to *n* inclusive (e.g. 4! = 1 × 2 × 3 × 4).

This is easily realized as a non-recursive C function (which returns zero if *n* is negative):

```
int  factorial (int n)          /* Version I1 */
{
       if (n < 0)  return 0;
       else  if (n == 0)  return 1;
       else  if (n > 0)  {
                      int  i;
                      int  product = 1;
                      for (i=1;  i <= n;  i++)
                             product *= i;
                      return  product;
              }
}
```

(Notice that the **else**s are unnecessary, since **return** terminates the activation. Inclusion or omission of **else** in such cases is a matter of programming style; the **else**s will be omitted in later examples in this chapter.)

A *recursive definition* is one in which the thing being defined appears in its own definition. There is a recursive definition of *n!*:

- If $n < 0$, *n!* is undefined;
- If $n = 0$, *n!* = 1;
- If $n > 0$, *n!* = $n \times (n - 1)$!

For example, 3! = 3×(2!) = 3×(2×(1!)) = 3×(2×(1×(0!))) = 3×2×1×1 = 6. This definition too translates easily into a C function, but this time - naturally - the function is recursive (again returning zero if *n* is negative):

```
int  factorial (int n)          /* Version R1 */
{
      if (n < 0)  return 0;
      if  (n == 0)  return 1;
      return  n * factorial (n−1);

}
```

Suppose that this function is called with a positive integer as its argument. Then each new activation of *factorial* has an argument value one less than that of the activation that called it. Eventually, therefore, *factorial* will be activated with argument value 0, an activation which will *not* start any further activation; on its completion, the activation that called it will continue (i.e. will complete the evaluation of its return expression) and then it too returns (i.e. is completed). The activation that called *it* then continues, and so on until the first activation completes by returning the required value. For example, if the call *factorial (3)* is made, there are four activations:

Activation	*Activation*	*Activation*	*Activation*

factorial (3)

....

multiply 3 by ——> factorial (2)

              ....

              multiply 2 by ——> factorial (1)

                              ....

                              multiply 1 by ——> factorial (0)

                                              ....

                                    1 <——— return 1

                        1 <——— return 1

          2 <——— return 2

return 6

Generally, for non-negative *n*, $(n + 1)$ activations are required to compute *factorial (n)*.

While version R1 of *factorial* provides a simple illustration of recursive programming, it would not in practice be a good function definition (nor, for the same reason, would the earlier non-recursive definition). The factorial of even quite a small integer is a very large integer (e.g. 10! = 3628800), so the function could easily cause arithmetic overflow by trying to calculate a value greater than the maximum permissible for an **int**. A Cobol program could detect this situation using **size error** and take appropriate action; you will be astonished to learn that, in a C program, there is no means of detecting integer overflow. Worse still, it is very unlikely even to give rise to a run-time error message; the result of the calculation will probably be stored as an apparently random integer value and program execution will continue. This is one of many examples of the insecurity of C programs.

There is in the standard library a header called *<limits.h>* which enables a program to find out certain things about the particular implementation of C being used. If we say

        #include <limits.h>

then the identifier INT_MAX stands for the maximum value that can be represented as an **int**. We can thus amend our non-recursive *factorial* function definition so that it returns zero when the argument is such that the factorial cannot be computed. We rewrite version I1 as:

```
int factorial (int n)          /* Version I2 */
{
    if (n < 0)  return 0;
    else  if (n == 0)  return 1;
    else  if (n > 0)  {
        int i;
        int product = 1;
        for (i=1; i<=n && INT_MAX/product >= i; i++)
            product *= i;
        if (i>n)  return product;
        else  return 0;
    }
}
```

A similar check may be introduced into the recursive version by writing the function as:

```
int factorial (int n)          /* Version R2 */
{
    if (n < 0)  return 0;
    if (n == 0)  return 1;
    if (factorial(n-1) == 0 || INT_MAX/factorial(n-1) < n)  return 0;
    return (n * factorial(n-1));
}
```

You may now find the recursive version (R2) more difficult to understand than the iterative one (I2). In version I2, computation starts at 1 and evaluates successively 1 × 2, 1 × 2 × 3, 1 × 2 × 3 × 4, and so on; the computation stops as soon as the next multiplication would cause overflow, so in that case it does not continue to *n*. But the recursive version (R2) starts at *n*, and calls itself recursively to obtain the factorials of successively lower values down to zero - multiplication occurs only after return from an activation. The recursive version must therefore make all calls from *factorial (n)* right down to *factorial (0)*. If at any stage it finds that the factorial value returned for the next lower integer is 0 (i.e. is uncomputable because of overflow), it must itself return 0. There will always be (*n*+1) activations. But, in order to make the necessary checks, two further sets of activations have been introduced. Where *n* is greater than zero, a call of *factorial (n)* will result in *three* calls of *factorial (n−1)*. Unless *n* = 1, these three calls will *each* result in three calls of *factorial (n−2)*, and so on. Let us denote the number of activations caused by a call of version R2 of *factorial (n)* by *a(n)*, assuming *factorial (n)* to be computable. In general,

$$a(n) = 3a(n-1) + 1$$

Check the following few examples against the programs and ensure that you understand how *a(n)* is derived from the program.

n	*a(n)*
0	1
1	4
2	13 (= 3×4 + 1)
3	40 (= 3×13 + 1)
4	121 (= 3×40 + 1)

As *n* increases, *a(n)* rises rapidly - to compute *factorial*(12) requires 797161 activations. Using most compilers, this will give very inefficient code, and it may cause a run-time error.

The number of activations can be dramatically reduced by introducing a variable *f*, to which we assign the value of *factorial (n−1)*, so that the function contains only one recursive call:

```
int factorial (int n)          /* Version R3 */
{
    int f;
    if (n < 0) return 0;
    if (n == 0) return 1;
    if ( (f = factorial (n−1)) == 0 || INT_MAX/f < n ) return 0;
    return (n * f);
}
```

The number of activations is now the same as for the non-checking recursive version (R1), i.e. *a(n) = n + 1*:

n	*a(n)*
0	1
1	2
2	3
3	4
4	5

but the program code in version R3 remains less intelligible than the iterative version (I2).

A better strategy would be for the function to check whether its argument value is greater than the maximum for which the factorial is computable. In some implementations, this number is 12 so, for these implementations, the function could begin

```
int factorial (int n)
{    if (n < 0 || n > 12) return 0;
     .....
```

but this would not be portable to an implementation with a different INT_MAX value. So perhaps when the function is first called in a run-unit, it can calculate (iteratively) the maximum value (*maxarg*) for which the factorial can be computed:

```
int factorial (int n)        /* Version R4 */
{
     #define TRUE 1
     #define FALSE 0
     static int first_call = TRUE;
     static int maxarg;

     if (first_call == TRUE) {
          int i;
          int product = 1;
          first_call = FALSE;
          for (i=1; INT_MAX/product >= i; i++)
               product *= i;
          maxarg = i-1;
     }
     if (n < 0 || n > maxarg) return 0;
     if (n ==0) return 1;
     return (n * factorial(n-1));
}
```

Two criticisms may be made of this version (R4). The first is not too serious - it is that three unnecessary tests are made every time the function is called recursively. When it is called from another function, *first_call* might be true, *n* might be less than zero, or *n* might be greater than *maxarg*. But the program logic ensures that, when the function is called by itself, all these conditions must always be false; time is therefore wasted in making the unnecessary tests during recursive activations. But the number of activations is small and this inefficiency can be disregarded. (The same situation, however, often arises with functions having a potentially large number of activations, and there is a way of avoiding the redundant tests in such cases. This need not concern us at present.)

The second criticism is more interesting. If you look at what version R4 does when it is first called in a run-unit (i.e. when *first_call* is true), you will see that, in the process of establishing the value of *maxarg*, it computes the value of every computable factorial. Since the number of computable factorials is small, why shouldn't the function, on its first call, store these values in an array, so that all the function ever has to do thereafter is return the appropriate value from the array? This, indeed, is the most sensible way to write a factorial function. (The only changes from version R4 are marked by null comments.)

```
     int factorial (int n)
     {
          #define TRUE  1
          #define FALSE 0
          static int  first_call = TRUE;
          static int  maxarg;
/**/     static int  fact[25] = {1};        /* 1 is value of 0! */

          if (first_call == TRUE) {
               int  i;
               int  product = 1;
               first_call = FALSE;
               for (i=1;  INT_MAX/product >= i;  i++)
/**/                fact [i] = (product *= i);
               maxarg = i - 1;
          }
          if (n < 0 || n > maxarg) return 0;
/**/     else return fact [n];
     }
```

The size of the array *fact* should really be (*maxarg* + *1*), but since we have so far learned about fixed-length arrays only, *fact* is declared large enough to accommodate the largest number of factorials likely to be computable using **int**s in any implementation (i.e. 25).

What emerges from our study of the *factorial* function is that the most intelligible and effective way of writing the function is non-recursive. This is not a criticism of recursion in general, for recursive solutions are often the most intelligible and effective. Nor does it mean that the factorial function is necessarily a bad introduction to recursion; the factorial function is useful for its simplicity, and the discussion arising from it should have helped you to consolidate your understanding of recursive programming.

For another example, suppose we want to define a function whose prototype declaration is

> int sumarray (**const int*** a, **int** minsub, **int** maxsub);

(Notice that parameters may optionally be named, as here, in a prototype. In a prototype these names have no significance to the program; it is the names in the function definition parameter list that are significant.) The first argument is intended to be a pointer to an array of integers (typically specified as the name of the array), and the second and third arguments are intended to be valid subscripts for that array. (Assume that any checking of the validity of the subscripts is done before the function is called - remember that the function knows nothing about the size of the array pointed to by its first argument.) The function returns the sum of elements in the array, from *a[minsub]* to *a[maxsub]* inclusive. If *minsub* is greater than *maxsub*, the function returns 0. A typical call to sum a complete array might be

> sumarray (sales, 0, (**sizeof** sales / **sizeof** sales[0]) – 1)

where *sales* is an array identifier. (Remember that **sizeof**, applied to an array identifier, gives the total number of bytes in the array. Thus

> **sizeof** sales / **sizeof** sales[0]

gives the number of elements in the array.)

Here is a straightforward iterative (i.e. non-recursive) version of *sumarray*:

```
int  sumarray (const int* a,  int minsub,  int maxsub)
{
      int  i, sum;

      for (sum=0, i=minsub;  i <= maxsub;  i++)
            sum += a[i];
      return  sum;
}
```

Recursive programming enthusiasts may define the sum differently. They say: "The *sum* of a sequence of elements is zero if there are no elements; otherwise it is the value of the first element plus the *sum* of the remaining elements". With this approach, the function can be defined as:

```
int  sumarray (const int* a,  int minsub,  int maxsub)
{
      if (minsub > maxsub)  return 0;
      else  return (a[minsub] + sumarray (a, minsub + 1, maxsub));
}
```

Suppose now that we have an array of **int** named *x*:

> **int** x[] = {10,5,7};

and we make the call

sumarray (x, 0, 2)

This call starts what turns out to be the outermost activation of four:

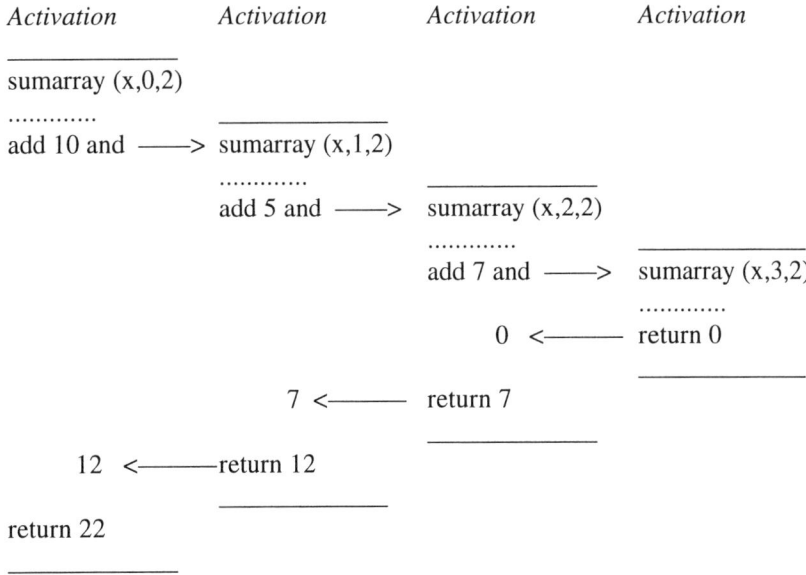

Activation   *Activation*   *Activation*   *Activation*

sumarray (x,0,2)

....

add 10 and ——> sumarray (x,1,2)

....

add 5 and ——> sumarray (x,2,2)

....

add 7 and ——> sumarray (x,3,2)

....

0 <——— return 0

7 <——— return 7

12 <———return 12

return 22

and returns 22. Notice that calling this function will never cause infinite recursion. The third argument is unchanged from one activation to the next, while the value of the second argument is increased by one; so there must eventually be an activation in which the second argument is greater than the third, thus preventing any further activations.

The above examples of recursive functions, chosen for their simplicity, are alternatives to iterative versions which are simpler or equally simple. But there are many situations in which recursive functions are simpler and more natural than iterative ones. We will return to recursion later. For the moment, look again at the *writeline* function with which this chapter started. Using recursive calls, *writeline* can be specified as follows; this version also deals with the point raised in note 8 about checking that there is enough space on a page for the "End of list" line and the blank line that precedes it. Recursive calls are marked by null comments (/**/).

```
void  writeline (const char* text)
{
        #define  PAGESIZE  60        /* must not be smaller than 4 */
        static FILE*  printfile;
        static int  linenumber;
        static int  pagenumber = 0;
```

```
              if (pagenumber ==0)  {
                   printfile = fopen ("p.d", "w");
                   linenumber = PAGESIZE;
              }
              if (linenumber >= PAGESIZE)  {
                   char  out[81];
                   linenumber = 0;        /* about to print first line of page */
                   sprintf (out, "\fContent of persons file  -  page %d\n",
                        ++pagenumber);
/**/               writeline (out);
/**/               writeline ("");                        /* blank line */
/**/               writeline (COL_HEADINGS);
              }
              if (text == NULL)  {
/**/               writeline ("");
/**/               writeline ("End of list");
                   fclose (printfile);
              }
              else  {
                   ++linenumber;
                   fputs (text, printfile);
                   fputc ('\n', printfile);
              }
              #undef  PAGESIZE
         }
```

(Remember that the argument of

      writeline ("")

is a pointer to a null string, but the argument of

      writeline (**NULL**)

would be a null pointer.)

To be recursive, a call of a function *f* need not be within the definition of *f* itself. If *f* calls another function, *g*, which then calls *f*, the latter call is recursive: the initial activation of *f* is suspended during activation of *g*, and the activation of *g* is suspended when it initiates another activation of *f*. Two activations of *f* then exist, as they would if *f* were called directly from *f*. Of course, there need not be just one intermediate function: rather than calling *f*, *g* might call *h*, which in turn might call *f*; the call of *f* would still be recursive.

The fact that two functions, *f* and *g*, call each other usually results in recursion. But not always - no recursion would be implied if *f* and *g* contained no direct or indirect calls of each other apart from those shown here:

```
int  f (const int fp)
{      .....
       .....
       if (fp == 0)  { printf ("%d", g(1)) .....
       .....
       .....
}

int  g (const int gp)
{      .....
       .....
       if (gp == 0)  { printf ("%d", f(1)) .....
       .....
       .....
}
```

As an illustration of indirect recursive calls, we now change our *writeline* function so that, instead of outputting page headings itself, it calls another function, *writeheadings*, to do so. The changed program is shown on the next page. In order to illustrate also the C equivalent of passing an argument by reference in Cobol, we define *pagenumber* in *writeline*, but increment it in *writeheading*. Notice that the parameter of *writeheading* is a pointer to an **int**, and that *writeline* passes to it the address of (i.e. a pointer to) *pagenumber*.

In the program overleaf, *writeline* calls *writeheading*, and *writeheading* calls *writeline* - the two functions are mutually recursive. Since the definition of *writeline* precedes that of *writeheading*, *writeline* includes a prototype declaration for *writeheading*. As long as PAGESIZE is greater than 2, infinite recursion cannot occur, because *writeheading* will never call *writeline* at a time when *linenumber* is greater than or equal to PAGESIZE; thus there will never at any time be more than one activation of *writeheading*. You may care to work out what would happen if PAGESIZE were 3, and then try running the program to confirm your findings. Would precisely the same happen with the immediately preceding version of *writeline*? It might be wise to include an assertion that PAGESIZE is not less than 4, in case an error is made when the program is later amended.

```
void writeline (const char* text)
{
     void  writeheading (int*);
     #define  PAGESIZE  60
     static FILE* printfile;
     static int  linenumber = 0;
     static int  pagenumber = 0;

     if (pagenumber == 0) {
          printfile = fopen ("p.d", "w");
          writeheading (&pagenumber);
     }
     if (linenumber >= PAGESIZE) {
          linenumber = 0;
          writeheading (&pagenumber);
     }
     if (text == NULL) {
          writeline ("");
          writeline ("End of list");
          fclose (printfile);
     }
     else {
          ++linenumber;
          fputs (text, printfile);
          fputc ('\n', printfile);
     }
}

void  writeheading (int* page)
{
     char  out[81];

     sprintf (out, "\fContent of persons file  -  Page %d", ++(*page));
     writeline (out);
     writeline ("");
     writeline (COL_HEADINGS);
}
```

8.3. Scopes of identifiers

We have seen that a non-static object (i.e. one that is - perhaps implicitly - **auto**), defined at the start of a function definition, comes into existence at the start of an activation of the function and ceases to exist when the activation is completed. A static object, however, exists for the whole duration of program execution.

A static object has a *lifetime* which is the whole execution of the program, but if it is defined in a function it is available for use only during activations of the function. Therefore there are likely to be times during the lifetime of a static object when it cannot be referenced - times, in other words, when it is invisible. An identifier is *visible* (i.e. can be used) only within a region of program text called its *scope*.

8.3.1. Scope within a block

The scope of any identifier is from its declaration to the end of the current block. Thus, in a block which begins

```
{     int  a = 5;
      int  b = a + 1;
      static char  c;
      void d (char*);  .....
```

the identifiers *a, b, c* and *d* are visible until the '}' which closes the block. They are therefore visible also within any other blocks nested within the block (unless hidden by a local declaration - see section 8.3.2), but they are not visible outside the block.

The declarations of *a* and *b* could not be interchanged, because, if the first two declarations were

```
      int  b = a + 1;
      int  a = 5;
```

the reference to *a* in *b*'s declaration would be outside *a*'s scope, which starts immediately after *a*'s declaration. Within a block or a function, the storage class (**static** or **auto**) of the associated object does not affect visibility. If the declaration of *d* (a function prototype) included a parameter name, that name would *not* be visible in the block (or anywhere else - it would act only as documentation), though the function identifier *d* is visible in the block.

8.3.2. Scope within a function

Only the function name is visible outside the function. (It is also visible inside it.) The identifiers of the parameters have a scope which extends from the beginning of the block which forms the function body to its end. This block may contain other blocks. It is generally unwise to use the same identifier for different objects within one function; if you do so, the simple rule is that if a block, *b*, contains a declaration of identifier *i*, any other currently visible declaration of *i* is hidden until the end of block *b*. (This rule resembles that for nested programs in Cobol, if we think of a C block as a Cobol program, and think of all identifiers as being those of Cobol records declared as **global**.) The following outline example should clarify the situation - but it is certainly not intended to show how identifiers should be chosen when you write a program!

```
              int  a (char* b)
/*block 1*/    {      char  c;
                      int  d[5];
                                    /*Also visible in block 1:
                                       a  (function name)
                                       b  (parameter)           */

                    .....
/*block 1.1*/         {      char  c (int);
                             int  a;
                                          /*Also visible in block 1.1:
                                             b  from block 1
                                             d  from block 1         */
/*block 1.1.1*/                {     int  a=5;
                                     int  b=a+1;
                                     static char  c;
                                     void  d (char*);
                                             /*Nothing else is visible in block 1.1.1,
                                               because all earlier declarations are
                                               hidden (but see section 8.3.3)          */

                                     .....
                               }
                             .....
/*block 1.1.2*/                {     char  e;
                                             /*Also visible in block 1.1.2:
                                               a  from block 1.1
                                               c  from block 1.1
                                               b  from block 1
                                               d  from block 1        */

                                     .....
                               }
                             .....
                      }
                    .....
/*block 1.2*/         {      int  f;
                                          /*Also visible in block 1.2:
                                             a  from block 1
                                             b  from block 1
                                             c  from block 1
                                             d  from block 1        */

                             .....
                      }
                    .....
              }
```

8.3.3. Scope within a source file

In Cobol, a *run-unit* may be formed by linking several separately-compiled *programs*. Similarly, in C, a *program* may be formed by linking several *source files*; what we have so far called a C program is really a C source file. C uses the word *file* with two distinct meanings. As we saw in chapter 5, "file" normally means the same kind of thing as it does in Cobol - a data file. A *source file*, like a file containing a Cobol program, is a file containing program text that can be compiled on its own. Linking several C source files together is a topic for a later chapter. The remainder of this chapter deals with the structure and interpretation of a single source file.

Our source files so far have contained only function definitions. But a source file may contain declarations (or definitions - see later in this section) of things other than functions, i.e. objects. The scope of an identifier declared outside any function (i.e. at *source file level*) is from its declaration to the end of the source file. This, of course, is why a function should be declared (by prototype) if it is to be called by another function whose definition precedes its own. The prototype of a function *f* may be either within functions which call *f* (as in section 8.2, where a prototype for *writeheading* was contained in the definition of *writeline*), or at source file level, as in:

```
void  writeheading (int*);

void  writeline (const char* text)
{
      #define  PAGESIZE  60
      .....
      writeheading (&pagenumber);
      .....
}

void  writeheading (int* page)
{
      char  out[81];
      .....
      writeline (out);
      .....
}
```

It should be clear from this example that declarations made at source file level are visible within all function definitions within their scope, except where hidden within a block by a parameter name or a local declaration. Assuming that there is no local *i* or *j* within the function definitions, the source file outlined below is such that *i* may be referenced in functions *p* and *q*, and that *j* may be referenced only in *q*.

int i;

char p (....
{   .....
       .....
}

int j;

void q (....
{   .....
       .....
}

Since function *p* is not in the scope of *j*, *j* is not visible within *p*. If we want to refer to *j* within *p*, we can move the declaration of *j* to precede the definition of *p*. Alternatively, we can leave the declaration of *j* where it is, and include in *p* an **extern** declaration of *j*. Let us see what an **extern** declaration is.

So far, we have glossed over the difference between a *declaration* and a *definition*. A declaration describes the characteristics of an object or function; a definition is a declaration which also allocates storage for it. With one exception, all the declarations in this book so far have been definitions. Our declarations of **int** and **char** variables, variables of various pointer types, and arrays were all definitions, resulting in allocation of storage for objects of the appropriate types. The single exception was a function prototype; a prototype is a declaration which allocates no storage for the function, but provides enough information to allow the function to be called. Before the program can run, there must be somewhere a definition of the function. In our earlier program extract, the definition of *writeline* contained a *declaration* of *writeheading*; the *definition* of *writeheading* followed the definition of *writeline*.

In the same way, we can declare objects at one point in a program and define them at another. This is done by declaring the objects as **extern**. If, anywhere within a function, we declare

     extern int k;

we are saying that the *definition* of *k* occurs outside the function - the definition will be at source file level in the current source file or another source file. Furthermore, we are saying that if other functions in the same source file also declare

     extern int k;

they are referring to the same object. (The same rule applies in Cobol to objects declared as **external**.)

The scope rules for visibility of identifiers declared as **extern** are the same as those for other identifiers. For instance, changing a declaration from

> **extern int** k;

to

> **int** k;

does not change *k*'s scope.

Since **extern** declarations do not allocate storage, objects cannot be assigned initial values in such declarations - it is incorrect to say

> **extern int** k = 5;   /*incorrect*/

For the same reason, an **extern** declaration cannot specify that the object is **static** or **auto**.

Returning to the last example, we see that the scope rules ensure that no declaration of *i* is needed within function *p*, nor are declarations of *i* and *j* within function *q*. But there is nothing to stop us making such redundant declarations - indeed, from the point of view of program maintenance, there is much to be said for declaring all source file level variables as **extern** in the functions that use them. It may then make more sense to declare all source file level variables before declaring the functions:

```
int  i;
int  j;

char  p ( .....
{     extern int  i, j;
      .....
      .....
}

void  q ( .....
{     extern int  i, j;
      .....
      .....
}
```

The **extern** declarations are redundant, but they have the effect that each function declares fully its interfaces with its environment - not only its parameters, but also its references to external variables.

You will remember that the lifetime of a **static** object is the whole duration of program execution, and that the lifetime of an **auto** object is one activation of the function in which it is declared. Since source files are never activated (i.e. are never called - only functions can be called), all objects declared at source file level have static duration, i.e. their lifetime is the whole duration of program execution. This will be true whether or not they are explicitly declared as being **static**. When we learn about linking source files together, we will see that explicit declaration of source file level objects as **static** has an important (and surprising) implication.

Finally, look back at the functions *writeline* and *writeheading*. The somewhat contrived use of *pagenumber*'s address as an argument in the calls of *writeheading* can now be dropped. Since both functions make use of *pagenumber*, it can be defined at source file level, so that the outline of the complete source file looks like this:

```
                #include  <stdio.h>
                #include  <string.h>
                #include  <assert.h>
                #define  DETAIL_LINE  "%3d  %-s", age, name
                #define  COL_HEADINGS "AGE  SURNAME"

                main (void)
                {
                      void  writeline (const char*);
                      .....
                      .....
                      return  0;
                }

/*1*/ static int  pagenumber = 0;

                void  writeline (const char*  text)
                {
                      void writeheading (void);
                      #define PAGESIZE  60
                      .....
/*2*/         extern int  pagenumber;    /* replaces original declaration */
                      .....
                      .....            /* calls of writeheading are now in the form
                      .....                 writeheading ()       */
                }


                void  writeheading  (void)
                {
/*2*/         extern int  pagenumber;
                      char  out [81];

                      sprintf (out, "\fContent of persons file  - Page %d",
                              ++pagenumber);
                      .....
                      .....
                }
```

Notes:

1. Source file level declaration (definition) of *pagenumber*. It is helpful to the reader to have the declaration immediately preceding the functions that use it, rather than before the definition of *main*. Variables declared at source file level are by default initialized to zero; but explicit initialization draws the reader's attention to the fact that the program depends on *pagenumber*'s value being initially zero.

2. Since the scope rules ensure that *pagenumber* is visible within *writeline* and *writeheading*, these **extern** declarations are redundant (but it is, arguably, good practice to have them).

Source file level declarations can be misused. The most extreme misuse is to declare all objects at source file level. You then have the kind of situation that exists in Cobol, where **perform**ed procedures have access to data with which they have no concern, thus decreasing program security and making understanding and debugging difficult. Another misuse, undesirable for the same reasons, is for communication between a calling and a called function to take place through source file level objects instead of by argument-passing. You cannot go far wrong if you adopt the principle of making the scope of an identifier as small as possible. Try to declare each thing in such a way that it is visible only to those blocks or functions that have a reason to see it. We will return to this point in a later chapter.

8.3.4. Exceptions

There are certain identifiers whose scopes differ from the norm:

1. A parameter name, (optionally) included *in a function prototype*, has effectively no scope, for its scope ends at the end of the prototype.

2. An identifier which acts as a macro name (i.e. which immediately follows #define) has a scope which is unaffected by the function and block structure of the program. Its scope ends at the end of the source file, or before that if it is the subject of an #undef:

```
     .....
     char  f (void)
     {
             char  c;
             #define  M  25
             .....

             .....
     }                       /* scope of c terminates here */


     int  g (int gx)
     {     .....
             #undef  M       /* scope of M terminates here */
             .....
```

3. A label (an identifier which is the object of a **goto**) has a scope extending from the start of the function body in which it appears to the end of that function body. See section 2.8.5 for examples of labels.

9

Typedef and
Dynamic Storage Allocation

Chapter 8 was very long. To redress the balance, here is a nice short chapter introducing some concepts which will be used in chapter 10.

9.1. Giving names to types

If what appears to be a declaration is preceded by the word **typedef**, the thing being described is a *type*, instead of being a variable. For instance

> **int*** intpointer;

declares a variable named *intpointer*, whose type is **int***; but

> **typedef int*** intpointer;

defines a type whose name, *intpointer*, becomes a synonym for **int***. We can then declare variables as being of type *intpointer*, rather than type **int***:

> intpointer x, y;

This is just the same as declaring

> **int*** x;
> **int*** y;

but, given my approach to declaring pointer variables, it allows a more sensible way of declaring several pointer variables on the same line than

> **int*** x, *y;

A commoner use of **typedef** is exemplified by

> **typedef char** Surname [21];

which says that *Surname* means "an array of 21 **char**s". *Surname* identifies a type, not a variable. The initial upper-case letter is a useful convention (but no more than that) to indicate to a reader that *Surname* identifies a type. The subsequent declaration

>   Surname owner, user;

is treated as being equivalent to

>   **char** owner [21];
>   **char** user [21];

The existence of **typedef** therefore adds nothing to the functionality of the language. But, by declaring *owner* and *user* to be of type *Surname*, we impart information to a reader of our program. We also ensure that, if we later want to change the way a surname is to be represented in the program, we need change only the **typedef** for *Surname*, rather than changing the declarations of all variables intended to be assigned surname values.

As with other types, these variables may be initialized on declaration, as in

>   Surname owner = "Inglis";

Of course, in addition to the above, we might use *#define* to specify the size of a surname, as we did in earlier chapters. The commonest uses of **typedef**s are in making certain aspects of programs more portable and, as we will see, in defining structure types.

9.2. Void pointers

Sometimes programs, particularly systems programs, want to refer to storage addresses without having to specify the type of object stored. They want, in other words, to have a generic, or *untyped,* pointer facility. This is provided in C by a type of pointer - a **void** pointer - which "points to an object of void type". Such a pointer variable, *vp*, would be declared as

>   **void*** vp;

The value of a void pointer may at any time be **NULL** or be a pointer to an object of any type. Do not confuse a void pointer with a null pointer - the latter term is simply a loose way of saying that a pointer has the **NULL** value.

You will remember that assignment between pointers of different types is forbidden. However, *any* pointer value may be assigned to a void pointer variable, and a value of type **void*** may be assigned to a variable of any other pointer type. You can use these characteristics to assign indirectly between pointers of different types via a void pointer, but you will usually be asking for trouble if you do. However, one respectable use of the type **void*** arises when we want to allocate or deallocate storage at run time. This is the subject of the next section.

9.3. Dynamic storage allocation

Every object we have used in our programs so far has been declared before its use. Within the scopes of their declarations, these objects can be referred to either by their declared names (identifiers) or by using pointers. But many programming languages, including C, give us the additional facility of creating objects which are *unnamed*. Such objects have no identifiers and they can be referred to *only* by the use of pointers. They may be created at any time during program execution. Like named objects, unnamed objects must be of a specified type; which is another way of saying that the pointers by which we access them must be of specified types.

What a program has to do in order to create an unnamed object is:

* get the right amount of storage for the object; and
* set a pointer pointing to that storage.

Since the object has no name, we must then be careful not to lose the pointer value (e.g. by allowing a variable containing that value to go out of scope, or by assigning a new value to the variable without first preserving its current value). The pointer value is our only means of identifying the object.

Here is how we might create a new unnamed **int** and set p pointing to it:

> **int*** p;
> ....
> ....
> p = **malloc** (**sizeof** (**int**));

The standard C function **malloc** finds an area of previously free storage, of the size indicated by its argument. The value it returns, of type **void***, is a pointer to that area. The start of the area is suitably aligned for any type of object. The effect of the statement above is to give us a new unnamed integer object, which is pointed to by p and whose initial value is undefined. We can then, if we choose, assign a value to the new object in an expression such as

> *p = 0

or

> **sscanf** (a, "%d", p)

where a is of type **char***; and we can use the new object in the same ways as we use named objects.

But of course it isn't quite that simple. Firstly, in order to use **malloc** (or **free** or **calloc** or **realloc**, each of which we'll look at presently), we should have a line

> #include <stdlib.h>

Secondly, it is possible that **malloc** cannot find an area of storage of the size required, in which case it returns the **NULL** pointer value. The above assignment to *p* should therefore be on the lines:

> **if** ((p = **malloc**(**sizeof** (**int**))) == **NULL**)
>> {/* probably write a diagnostic message, and abandon */}

(*<stdlib.h>* is one of the headers containing the definition of **NULL**.) Thirdly, the most likely reason for **malloc** running out of store is that the program keeps acquiring storage for objects and never releases it back to the pool of available storage (i.e. never *deallocates* it). To release storage no longer needed, we use the function **free**, which takes as its single argument a pointer value *which at some earlier stage has been acquired using* **malloc** (or **calloc** or **realloc**), or which is **NULL** (in which latter case nothing happens) - if it is given any other argument value, **free**'s behaviour is undefined. The function **free** returns no value. To deallocate the storage acquired (*allocated*) by the above call of **malloc**, we would say

> **free** (p);

assuming that the value of *p* has not been changed in the meantime.

It is always best to specify the argument of **malloc** using the **sizeof** operator, rather than using an explicit constant value, for the sizes of types may differ between implementations. An **int**, for instance, may be of different sizes in different implementations. Always bear in mind, too, that because of storage boundary alignment the size of a composite object may not be the same as the total of the sizes of its members. For any type, T, however,

> **sizeof** T[3]

is always the same as

> (**sizeof** (T)) * 3

(By the way, the outer parentheses are unnecessary because of operator precedence.)

Like **malloc**, the function **calloc** returns a pointer, of type **void***, to an area of previously free storage or returns the **NULL** value if it fails to find an area of the required size. It differs from **malloc** in two respects:

- **calloc** sets the area of storage so that all the bits are zero. (But beware - according to the Standard, this is not necessarily the same as the null pointer value or a floating-point zero.)
- **calloc** takes two arguments. The intention is that **calloc** is used to allocate storage for an array. The first argument gives the number of members and the second the size of one member. To obtain a pointer to storage acquired for an array of 20 integers, the call would be

> **calloc** (20, **sizeof** (**int**))

The calls

>   **calloc** (6, **sizeof** (**int**))

and

>   **malloc** (**sizeof** (**int**[6]))

are equivalent, except that in the former case the allocated space is initialized to zero values.

The function **realloc** is used to change the size of an object, usually an array, perhaps by copying it to another location in storage where extra space is available. It can be useful when the number of elements required is unpredictable. The function gives defined results only when the space for the object was previously obtained by a call of **malloc**, **calloc** or **realloc** itself and has not subsequently been **free**d. If the space cannot be allocated, **realloc** returns **NULL**, but does not affect the existing pointer value or the thing it points to. Otherwise, it returns a pointer, of type **void***, to the start of the space where the expanded or contracted object is now stored. If the new size is greater than the old, the value of the added storage is undefined.

Here is a toy example which, for clarity, disregards the possibility of **malloc** or **realloc** returning **NULL**. Given the declaration

>   **char*** a;

the statement

>   a = **malloc** (**sizeof** (**char**[10]));

sets *a* pointing to the start of an area in which a 10-character array can be stored. (The Standard defines **sizeof** (**char**) as 1, so the argument could be written as 10. But the sizes of other types are implementation-defined, so it is a good habit to use the **sizeof** operator.) The values of *a*[0] through *a*[9] are undefined, but we can now of course assign values to them. Later, to increase the size of the array to 15 characters, we use:

>   a = **realloc** (a, **sizeof**(**char**[15]));

a now points to the first element of an array of 15 characters. The values of *a*[0] through *a*[9] are unchanged, and the values of *a*[10] through *a*[14] are undefined. If we subsequently say

>   a = **realloc** (a, **sizeof**(**char**[6]));

the values of *a*[0] through *a*[5] remain unchanged, and the values of *a*[6] through *a*[14] are lost.

10

Aggregate Types and Unions

Apart from arrays, the types of C objects we have looked at so far resemble elementary data items (i.e. data items with pictures) in Cobol. An aggregate type in C resembles a Cobol group item: it consists of a number of members, each of which is of a particular type - perhaps itself an aggregate type. There are two kinds of aggregate object in C: *arrays* and *structures*. This chapter also introduces *unions*; though not aggregate objects, unions have much in common syntactically with structures. Unions are like Cobol redefinitions.

10.1. Arrays

Though simple C arrays are easily understood and used, understanding the principles of C arrays is not straightforward. The tricky part is in sections 10.1.3 and 10.1.4; if you find it difficult, you can skip the last part of section 10.1.3 and come back to it later.

10.1.1. Declaration and reference

In the Cobol description

```
01.
    02 a pic x, occurs 5.
```

the array as a whole is not given a name. (Pre-1985 compilers may require the word **filler** after the 01.) Thus, only individual elements may be accessed, as *a(1)*, *a(2)*, ... or *a(5)*. There is no way of referencing the array as a whole. This is the same as the C declaration

> **char** a [5];

which makes access possible by reference to *a[0]*, *a[1]*, ... or *a[4]*, the subscript being specified generally as an expression.

The Cobol description of a matrix of two rows and three columns:

```
01.
    02  occurs 2.
        03  a  pic x  occurs 3.
```

is similar to the C declaration

char a[2][3];

References to the array elements in C are in the form

a[r][c]

(where, of course, *r* and *c* are expressions) which is the equivalent of Cobol's form, *a (r, c)*. The same pattern is extended to arrays of more than two dimensions. In C, each subscript expression is bracketed separately, the order of the dimensions being (as in Cobol) the same as in the declaration. Be very careful not to write the above as *a [r, c]* - remember what the comma means in C (see section 3.2).

Like Cobol, C regards an array of two dimensions as being an array of one dimension, each member of which is an array of elements. (And so on - an array of three dimensions, for instance, is an array of arrays of arrays of elements.) An array declared as

char a[2][3];

is stored as a sequence of six characters in the order

a[0][0], a[0][1], a[0][2], a[1][0], a[1][1], a[1][2]

which is the same storage arrangement as that used by Cobol.

10.1.2. Initialization

One way to initialize this array is to reflect the array dimensions in the initializer structure:

char a[2][3] = { {'a', 'b', 'c'}, {'d', 'e', 'f'} };

which, conventionally regarding the first dimension as row and the second as column, initializes the array to

a b c
d e f

This is how the array would be displayed by the code

```
int  i, j;
for  (i=0;  i<2;  i++)  {
        for  (j=0;  j<3;  j++)
                printf ("%c ", a[i][j]);
        printf ("\n");
}
```

Because the array is stored as illustrated at the end of section 10.1.1, precisely the same initialization would be achieved by the declaration

char a[2][3] = {'a', 'b', 'c', 'd', 'e', 'f'};

The declaration

char a[2][3] = { {'a'}, {'b', 'c'} };

initializes the array contents to

    a \0 \0
    b c \0

An array of character strings is, of course, an array of arrays of **char** and can be initialized as in the following example, where the declaration is split over several lines only for readability.

char suit [4][9] = {   {"clubs"},
                          {"diamonds"},
                          {"hearts"},
                          {"spades"}
                };

(The second dimension, 9, allows for the longest of these strings, including the terminating null - see chapter 4.)

Arrays whose elements are of types other than **char** can be initialized in the same way. For instance, either

int i [2][4] = { {2, 2}, {1, 2, 3, 4} };

or

int i [2][4] = {2, 2, 0, 0, 1, 2, 3, 4};

initializes array *i* to

    2 2 0 0
    1 2 3 4

10.1.3. Array types

You will recall that the name of an array is usually regarded as that of a pointer to the first element of the array. Following the declaration

int x [5];

x has usually been treated as being of type *pointer to* **int**, just as *y* would be following the declaration

int* y;

But *x* does not have the same properties as *y*. In particular:

- We cannot assign a value to *x*; we can assign only to the individual elements of *x*. We *can* assign a pointer value to *y*.
- **sizeof** *x*, as we have seen, is the size in bytes of the complete array (i.e. 5 * **sizeof** (**int**)), but **sizeof** *y* is the size in bytes of a pointer. Both **sizeof** **x* and **sizeof** **y* give the size in bytes of an integer.
- *&x* is of type "pointer to an array of five **int**s"; *&y* is of type "pointer to pointer to **int**".

The type of *x* is, in fact, an array of five integers (written as **int** [5]). In many contexts, as we have seen, this type is treated in the same way as *pointer to* **int**. For instance, element *x*[1] may be accessed by

* (x + 1)

(remember that the pointer increment is the size of an integer, since **int** is the type pointed to by *x*); or, if we have the prototype

void f (**int***);

we can call function *f* with *x* as the argument:

f (x)

An object of type **int** [5] may be a member of an array: an object of type

int [3][5]

consists of three occurrences of objects of the type

int [5]

A declaration

int n [3][5];

says that *n* is an object of type **int** [3][5]. This object consists of three objects, each of type **int** [5]. (Each of these three objects consists of five objects of type **int**.) A reference to

n [1]

is a reference to the second of the three objects. Since that object is an array, the context of the reference will determine its interpretation. If we refer to $*n[1]$, or pass $n[1]$ to a function as an argument, $n[1]$ is treated like type **int***, i.e. it is a pointer to the second row of the array. If we apply the **sizeof** operator to $n[1]$, the value is $(5 * \textbf{sizeof (int)})$.

We now look briefly at an example of a three-dimensional array of characters. It may be initialized on declaration in one of two equivalent ways:

> **char** c[2] [3] [3] =   {   { {"abc"}, {"def"}, {"ghi"} },
> { {"jkl"}, {"mno"}, {"pqr"} }
> };

or

> **char** c[2] [3] [3] =   {'a', 'b', 'c', 'd', 'e', 'f', 'g', 'h', 'i',
> 'j', 'k', 'l', 'm', 'n', 'o', 'p', 'q', 'r'};

A reference to c[1][0][1], for instance, will be a reference to the array element initialized to 'k'. As long as the array elements are referred to in this way, using three subscript expressions, multi-dimensional arrays in C present no problems and resemble arrays in other languages. A Cobol programmer may be tempted also to reference "chunks" of the array by using fewer than three subscripts. Resist this temptation unless you are quite sure what you are doing. Arrays of more than two dimensions are relatively uncommon in C programs, and a full treatment here would be of interest to only a small minority of readers; but the following table will give you some idea of the ways in which the above array *c* could be referenced. If you understand how the values of the following expressions are derived, multi-dimensional arrays will hold no terrors for you. If you don't, don't worry too much.

expression	value	
c[1][2][1]	'q'	
*c[1][2]	'p'	(*i.e.* c[1][2][0])
**c[1]	'j'	(*i.e.* c[1][0][0])
***c	'a'	(*i.e.* c[0][0][0])
sizeof c	18	(number of bytes)
sizeof c[1]	9	(number of bytes)
sizeof c[1][1]	3	(number of bytes)
sizeof *c	9	(*i.e.* **sizeof** c[0])
sizeof *c[1]	3	(*i.e.* **sizeof** c[1][0])
sizeof *c[1][1]	1	(*i.e.* **sizeof** c[1][1][0])

Because each dimension of an array is itself an array, each string in an array of strings may be referenced individually. Given the declaration

> **char** strikers[10][20];

we could, for example, assign to the third string:

      strncpy (strikers [2], "Shearer", **sizeof** strikers[2] – 1)

or test the value of the first string:

      if (**strcmp** (strikers [0], "Wright") == 0) ....

or obtain the length of the last string:

      strlen (strikers [9])

10.1.4. Arrays of pointers

Compare the earlier definition of *suit,* (**A**), with a similar definition, (**B**):

            A   **B**

```
char  suit [4][9] = { {"clubs"},          char*  suit [4]   = {  {"clubs"},
                      {"diamonds"},                            {"diamonds"},
                      {"hearts"},                              {"hearts"},
                      {"spades"}                               {"spades"}
          };                                       };
```

Definition A reserves storage for 36 characters and initializes the four adjacently-stored 9-character arrays; definition B reserves storage for 4 pointers only, initializing them to point to four constant character strings. The differences are:

- With A, the four 9-character arrays are in fixed positions in storage; with B, each of the four pointers may point to a character array of any length anywhere in storage. For instance, with B, **malloc** might be used to obtain storage for a character string, and the value returned by **malloc** could be assigned to one of the four pointers.
- With B, a new pointer value may be assigned to *suit*[1], since *suit*[1]'s type is **char***. With A, *suit*[1]'s type is **char**[9]; the character string may be changed (e.g. using **strncpy** *(suit*[1], ...)) but assigning a value to the array identifier *suit*[1] would make no sense.
- With A, the character strings can be changed, as in

      strncpy (suit[3], "shovels", **sizeof** suit[3] – 1)

  With B, a similar attempt to change the string pointed to by *suit*[3] would, given the above initialization, be an attempt to modify a string literal's value; this is not something you should ever want to do, and the effect is undefined. But, as we have seen, a new value could be assigned to the pointer *suit*[3] so that it no longer pointed to a string literal. The string pointed to could then be modified.
- With A, the value of **sizeof** *suit*[1] is 9, since *suit*[1] is an array of 9 characters; with B, it is the same as **sizeof** (**char***).
- With A, the value of **sizeof** *suit* is 36; with B it is four times **sizeof** (**char***).

5

10.1.5. Arrays as function arguments

So far, when we have "passed an array to a function", we have declared the function as taking a parameter of the appropriate pointer type; then, when we called the function, we passed an array name (or a pointer to an array element) as the corresponding argument. For instance, given the declarations

>   **char** xlist [10];
>   **int** search (**const char*** x);

we can make the call

>   search (xlist)

There is an alternative, and equivalent, way of declaring the function:

>   **int** search (**const char** x[ ])

which arguably makes the intention clearer to a reader. It is not clear from the first form (**const char*** x) whether the argument is to be a pointer to a character or a pointer to an array of characters; the second form shows that it is the latter. Perhaps it might be even clearer to say

>   **int** search (**const char** x[10])

if the function body actually operates on a ten-character array. This will not, however, prevent us from using as an argument an array of a different size, since *only a pointer is passed as the actual argument*. In all these cases, we would still call the *search* function by

>   search (xlist)

When an argument is to be a pointer to an array of two or more dimensions, the simplest way to handle it is to specify the parameter as an array name with all dimensions specified, except the first. (If the first dimension is specified, it is ignored by the compiler, as above.) Regardless of the value of *n*, a function *f* which operates on an *n* by 4 array of integers would be declared as

>   **void** f (**int** ia[ ][4])

and, within the body of *f*'s definition, the elements of the array would be referenced using normal subscript notation, e.g.

>   ia [i][j]

It should be obvious that, if the function is to use subscript notation to reference the elements, the compiler must be given (as part of the parameter declaration) the second and later dimensions so that it can generate code to convert subscript values into the addresses of array elements.

If the function *f* is intended to operate on arrays with different numbers of rows, it will be necessary to pass the first dimension as a separate argument. The declaration might be

> **void** *f* (**int** ia [ ][4], **int** rows)

and a call passing a pointer to an 8 by 4 array named *ib* to the function would be

> f (ib, 8)

If a function is intended to operate on arrays in which dimensions other than the first are to be variable, there is clearly no way in which the calculation of element addresses can be taken care of by the compiler. In this case, you will have to declare one parameter as a pointer to the array and other parameters for the dimensions, and the addresses of elements will have to be calculated explicitly in the function body.

10.1.6. Arrays as structures

We now return briefly to the Cobol example at the start of section 10.1.1. The array as a whole can be given the name *aa*:

> **struct** xx {
>   **char** a [5];
> } aa;

This declares a type of **struct** (C's way of saying "structure") named **struct** *xx*, which consists of array *a*, and also an instance of type **struct** *xx* named *aa*. The declaration resembles Cobol's

> ```
> 01  aa.
>       02  a pic x,  occurs 5.
> ```

in allowing the program to refer to the whole array (structure) as *aa*. But the C contexts in which the name *aa* may be used are much more limited than in Cobol. Assignments to and from *aa* are possible only when the other item involved is also a type *xx* structure, and the value of *aa* can never be compared with that of any other structure. Structures are treated in detail in the next section.

10.2. Structures

Like an array, a "structure" , or **struct**, is an aggregate type. A **struct** in C is very like a group data item in Cobol. For instance, compare the Cobol description

> ```
> 02    today.
>       03 day      pic 99  comp.
>       03 month  pic 99  comp.
>       03 year     pic 9(4) comp.
> ```

and the C declaration

```
struct {
      int day;
      int month;
      int year;
} today;
```

which declares *today* as a variable, whose type is a structure consisting of three *members* (*day, month, year*). The points of similarity and difference are:

1. As with a Cobol group item, the members of a **struct** are stored together in order, and the precise storage mapping depends on the implementation. The size of a structure is not necessarily the same as the sum of the sizes of its members. For instance, both Cobol's

    | 02   event. |
    | 03 event-type **pic** x. |
    | 03 year **pic** 9(4) **comp**. |

    and C's

    ```
    struct {
          char event_type;
          int  year;
    } event;
    ```

    may result in the presence of one or more bytes of garbage between *event_type* and *year*, due to storage boundary alignment.

2. In Cobol an item subordinate to a group item may be an elementary item (i.e. an item with a picture) or another group item. Similarly in C, a member of a **struct** may be a simple type or a composite type - perhaps another **struct** or an array.

3. Just as we may refer in Cobol to

    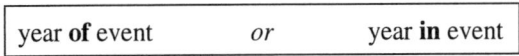

    year **of** event   *or*   year **in** event

    so we refer in C to

        event.year

    the dot being known as the *selection operator*. This operator is in a group with ( ), [ ], and -> (the last of which we will meet soon), which all have higher precedence than any other operator.

4. As in Cobol, the same identifier may be used for members of different structures. In Cobol, qualification of the identifier *year* by writing *year of event* is necessary only if there is another description of *year* (e.g. another variable) with which it could be confused. But in C the identifier *year* declared above *must* be referred to as *event.year*, even if there is no other object named *year*.

5. In Cobol, if several group items have the same structure, each of them has to be described in full. C has a much better arrangement: several variables may be declared as being structures of the same type. The declaration

```
struct {
      int day;
      int month;
      int year;
} today, end_of_term;
```

declares two variables, *today* and *end_of_term*, both of which have the structure indicated.   Members may then be referenced by such expressions as *end_of_term.month* and *today.day*.

6.   In Cobol, we can assign from one group item to another. In C, this is possible only between structures *of the same type*. Thus the assignment

```
end_of_term = today
```

is permissible, but

```
event = today
```

is not.

7.   In Cobol, the values of group items may be compared. In C, comparison of the values of structure objects is never allowed;   even testing for equality between structure objects of the same type, as in

```
if (today == end_of_term)  ....
```

is prohibited.

The fifth of these observations highlights an essential difference between Cobol and C. When we declare a structure object in C, we are also defining a *type* of variable. The type itself may be given a name (called a *tag*), as in the declaration

```
struct date {
      int day;
      int month;
      int year;
} today, end_of_term;
```

which gives the name "**struct** date" to the structure type, and makes it possible to declare further variables as having the same structure, as in

```
struct date speech_day;
```

Commonly, no variables at all are declared when we define the structure itself:

```
struct date {
      int day;
      int month;
      int year;
};
```

could be followed, somewhere else in the program where it is visible, by the declaration

        struct date today, end_of_term, speech_day;

Alternatively, and possibly most satisfactorily, **typedef** can be used to give the structure type a name, so that the word **struct** becomes unnecessary in declarations of variables:

```
typedef struct {
        int day;
        int month;
        int year;
} Date;
```

Because this is a **typedef**, the name following the '}' is not the name of a variable but the name that the programmer is giving to the structure itself - it becomes the identifier of a *type*, and may be used in the same ways as the identifiers of other types, like **char*** or **int**. The tag could be retained after the word **struct**. For most practical purposes it would be redundant, but we will shortly see a use for it. The above **typedef** enables us to declare variables as in

        Date today, end_of_term, speech_day;

A member of a structure may be used in the same ways as any other variable of its type. For instance, here is a program fragment which sets a variable, *between*, to indicate whether *speech_day* is after *today* and before *end_of_term*. It illustrates the use of structures as function arguments.

```
int comparedate (Date d1, Date d2)
/* returns neg, 0, pos if d1<d2, d1=d2, d1>d2 respectively */
{
        if (d1.year < d2.year)  return -1;
        if (d1.year > d2.year)  return 1;
        if (d1.month < d2.month)  return -1;
        if (d1.month > d2.month)  return 1;
        if (d1.day < d2.day)  return -1;
        if (d1.day > d2.day)  return 1;
        return 0;
}
....
....
        between = (comparedate (today, speech_day) < 0)
                && (comparedate (speech_day, end_of_term) < 0);
....
```

Of course, the definition of the type *Date* must be visible in both *comparedate* and the function from which it is called.

A word about the programming style of this last example. The point is one that has been mentioned briefly in connection with earlier examples, but here it thrusts itself on your attention. It is this. For safe program maintenance, each **if** except the first should really be preceded by **else**, as should the final **return**. It is quite common practice in C not to use an **else** where the action controlled by the matching **if** always causes a **return** (or **break** or **continue**) to be executed. Though I have misgivings, I have adopted this style in this book as being a style which is usually characteristic of C programs.

10.2.1. Initialization of structures

Structure variables are initialized in the same way as array variables - by listing the values of the members, all of which values must be constant expressions. For instance, assuming our earlier definition of *Date*, the declaration

> Date expiry_date = { 10, 4, 1996};

initializes *expiry_date.day* to 10, *expiry_date.month* to 4, and *expiry_date.year* to 1996. As with arrays, if fewer initial values appear in the braces than there are members, the remaining members have the value zero (or the value corresponding to zero for the type concerned). The declaration

> Date toms_birthday = {24,12};

initializes *toms_birthday.year* to zero.

If a member of a structure is itself a structure or an array, its initialization is usually placed in a nested pair of braces (or may, in the case of a **char** array, be a quoted string). For example, given the further definitions

> **typedef char** Surname [21];

> **typedef struct** {
>   Surname s;
>   Date birthday;
>   } Birthrec;

then a possible declaration is

> Birthrec sam = { {'S', 'm', 'i', 't', 'h'}, {9, 3, 1978} };

or

> Birthrec sam = { "Smith", {9, 3, 1978} };

But, if you initialize structures on declaration, it is all too easy to amend the definition of a structure type (perhaps by adding a new member between two existing members) and to forget to change the initializations of all objects of that type. It is safer to initialize structures by explicit assignment to the individual members.

10.2.2. Arrays and structures

Since an array or a structure may be a member of a structure or an element of an array, it is important to keep a clear head when referencing individual members and elements. Given the above declaration, the expression

>   sam.s

refers to a 21-character array containing the string value "Smith". The value of

>   sam.s[2]

is the character 'i', and the value of

>   sam.birthday.month

is the integer 3. The value of

>   sam.birthday

is a structure of type *Date*.

We may declare an array of structures of type *Birthrec*, representing forty persons:

>   Birthrec b[40];

Assignment of *sam* to the twentieth element of *b* is simple:

>   b[19] = sam

To refer to the year of birth of the twentieth person, we say

>   b[19].birthday.year

(Given the foregoing assignment, the value is 1978.) To refer to the first letter of the second person's surname, we say

>   b[1].s[0]

Like other objects, structures may be pointed to. We could, for instance, declare pointers to structures of type *Birthrec*:

>   Birthrec* bp1;
>   Birthrec* bp2;

We might then make *bp1* point to *sam* and *bp2* point to *b[19]*:

>   bp1 = &sam
>   bp2 = b + 19   *or, better:*   bp2 = &b[19]

after which the assignment

>   *bp2 = *bp1

would be equivalent to

>   b[19] = sam

10.2.3. Inter-structure pointers

Let us now declare two structure types, in the order

```
typedef struct {
        char  address[60];
        int  occupants;
} House;
```

```
typedef struct {
        char  name[16];
        int  age;
        House* residence;
} Person;
```

One type, *House*, consists of a postal address (*address*) and the number of occupants (*occupants*). The other type, *Person*, consists of a person's *name* and *age* and where the person lives (in the form of a pointer to a structure of type *House*). We now declare one variable (*home*) of type *House*, and two (*jack, jill*) of type *Person*:

```
House  home;
Person  jack, jill;
```

If the person represented by *jack* lives in the same house as the person represented by *jill*, we could construct this data structure:

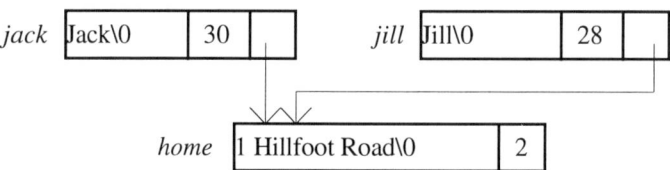

by the following statements:

```
strncpy (home.address, "1 Hillfoot Road", sizeof home.address - 1);
home.occupants = 2;
strncpy (jack.name, "Jack", sizeof jack.name - 1);
jack.age = 30;
strncpy (jill.name, "Jill", sizeof jill.name - 1);
jill.age = 28;
jack.residence = jill.residence = &home;
```

The program may contain statements which exploit the "linkage" between the two structure types, as in

```
printf ("Jill lives at %s", (*jill.residence).address);
```

which will display "Jill lives at 1 Hillfoot Road". The inner parentheses are necessary because the selection operator (.) has higher precedence than *. (Remember that there is a complete precedence table in Appendix 1.) Without the parentheses, the expression

> *jill.residence.address

would be interpreted as

> *(jill.residence.address)

which is clearly wrong, since *address* is not declared as a pointer. An easier way to write the above statement correctly is:

> **printf** ("Jill lives at %s", jill.residence ->address);

This statement introduces the -> operator. On its left is an expression (*jill.residence*) yielding a pointer to a structure, and on the right is the name of the member whose value becomes the value of the whole expression (*jill.residence->address*).

In selecting a member of a structure,

- the dot (.) operator is preceded by an expression identifying a structure, e.g.

  home.address

- the arrow (->) operator is preceded by an expression yielding a *pointer* to a structure, e.g.

  jill.residence->address

  Dot and arrow have the same precedence and they associate left to right, so the implied bracketing is

  (jill.residence)->address

  The parenthesized sub-expression selects the value of the *residence* member in the structure identified by the name *jill*. This value is then used as a pointer to a structure from which the value of the *address* member is selected.

A structure may contain one or more members whose values are pointers to structures of the same type as itself. For instance, here is a different definition of the Person structure, in which an additional member, *spouse*, points to another Person structure representing the first person's husband or wife:

```
/**/    typedef struct Person {
                char  name[16];
                int  age;
                House* residence;
/**/            struct Person* spouse;
            } Person;
```

Notice the two lines marked by the null comments. The reason why we can't just specify a member as

Person* spouse;

is that at the point where this declaration occurs, *Person* is as yet undefined - it is still in the process of being defined. (*House*, in contrast, was defined earlier in the program.) To overcome this problem, we introduce a tag for the structure by inserting "Person" between the **struct** and the '{' in the first line of the definition. (The tag could be a different name from that of the type we are defining, but there is no point in needlessly inventing new names.) When a tag is referred to, the tag has to be preceded by the word **struct**, as in

struct Person* spouse;

above.

We can now construct this structure:

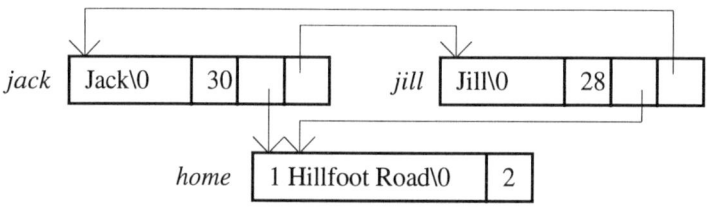

by adding to our earlier code the statements

jack.spouse = &jill;
jill.spouse = &jack;

and we can then exploit this linkage by such statements as

printf ("Jack's wife is %s, aged %d",
       jack.spouse->name,
       jack.spouse->age);

which displays "Jack's wife is Jill, aged 28", or:

printf ("Jack's wife lives at %s",
       jack.spouse->residence->address);

which displays "Jack's wife lives at 1 Hillfoot Road".

Please ensure that you understand these examples before moving on to the next section.

10.2.4. Dynamic data structures

In the examples we have just looked at, all the **struct**s concerned were *named* variables (*jack, jill, home*). Where data structures are represented using **struct**s linked by pointers, it is much more common to use unnamed variables, obtaining storage space by calling **malloc** and releasing it by calling **free**. The advantages of working in this way will become clear shortly; for now, let us just look at how the data structure of the preceding section may be treated. We define the structure types as before:

```
typedef struct {
    char address[60];
    int occupants;
} House;

typedef struct Person {
    char name[16];
    int age;
    House* residence;
    struct Person* spouse;
} Person;
```

Instead of declaring *jack* and *jill* as being of type *Person*, we declare them as being of type *Person**; similarly, we declare *home* as being of type *House**:

```
Person* jack;
Person* jill;
House* home;
```

To avoid cluttering our program with tests for unsuccessful calls of **malloc**, we define a function which reports an error and abandons the program if **malloc** fails:

```
void* getstorage (int size)
{
    void* p;
    assert ( (p = malloc (size)) != NULL);
    return p;
}
```

We can now obtain the storage for the structures we require and set up their values. Look carefully at the differences between these statements and what we wrote before:

```
home = getstorage (sizeof (House) );
strncpy (home->address, "1 Hillfoot Road", sizeof home->address - 1);
home->occupants = 2;
jack = getstorage (sizeof (Person) );
strncpy (jack->name, "Jack", sizeof jack->name - 1);
jack->age = 30;
jack->residence = home;
jill = getstorage (sizeof (Person) );
strncpy (jill->name, "Jill", sizeof jill->name - 1);
jill->age = 28;
jill->residence = home;
jack->spouse = jill;
jill->spouse = jack;
```

This may not seem much of an advance on what we did before. We have in effect replaced the three **struct** variables (*jack, jill, home*) by three pointer variables with the same names. We still have one variable corresponding to each **struct** we have created. But the advantage of using pointers is that this need not be the case. We can, for instance, arrange a number of **structs** as a single higher-level "structure" with only one pointer to the complete structure. The word "structure" is used here in a more general sense, not as meaning a C **struct**. C **structs** are commonly components (or *nodes*) of these more general structures. One such general data structure is a *singly-linked list*, exemplified by:

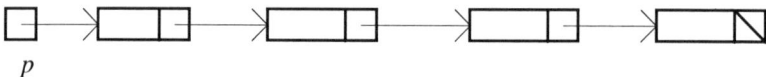

p

where *p* is a pointer variable pointing to the first node in the list. In C terms, each node is a **struct**, one of whose members is a pointer to the next node. In the last node, that member has the **NULL** pointer value (represented above by a diagonal line), indicating that there are no further nodes. If the value of *p* itself is **NULL**, the list is empty.

Each node in the list could be a complex **struct**, and could perhaps include pointers to other things as well as to the next node in the list. We might, for instance, introduce another member into our *Person* definition which, like *spouse*, would be of type **struct** *Person**, and whose function would be to link together all the Person **structs** we created. But, for simplicity, let us look at an example where a node consists only of an **int** and the pointer to the next node. We could declare the node structure, the pointer variable *p* (initialized to **NULL**), and a working variable *w*:

```
typedef struct Node {
        int i;
        struct Node* link;
} Node;

Node* p = NULL;
Node* w;
```

To add a new node to the list, we make it point to the node that *p* currently points to (or **NULL** if *p* is **NULL**), and set *p* pointing to it:

```
w = getstorage (sizeof (Node) );
w->i = /*whatever value we want to store at the node*/;
w->link = p;
p = w;
```

In terms of the above diagram, the new node will be inserted "between" *p* and the previous first node, if any.

To remove the first node from the list and assign its information to some variable *x*, we must first check that the list is not empty:

```
if (p != NULL) {
        w = p;
        x = w->i;
        p = w->link;
        free (w);
}
else /* report attempt to remove from empty list */;
```

If you know about stacks, you will see that these code fragments use the list like a stack.

10.2.5. Singly-linked lists - a queue

A queue is a data structure from which values are normally removed in the same order as that in which they were inserted. It models everyday queues, like people waiting for medical treatment, or, to take a computing example, processes waiting to use a common resource. In the following example, a singly-linked list is used to implement a queue; to keep the example simple, we assume that each item in the queue is just one character. We use two pointer variables, one pointing to the *front* of the queue (the next item to be removed) and one pointing to the *rear* (the last item added to the queue). A queue in which three characters, 'x', '+' and 'y', have been placed in that order would look like this:

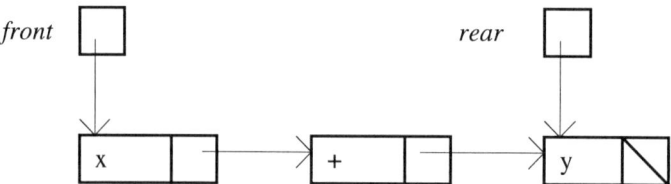

When the queue is empty, *front* has the **NULL** value.

Assuming that the function *getstorage* is defined as in the preceding section, the declarations and definitions required to implement the queue are:

```
typedef struct Node {
        char value;
        struct Node*  link;
} Node;
Node* front;
Node* rear;
```

```
void* getstorage (int size)
{ /* as defined previously */ }
```

```
int qempty (void)   /* returns 1 if queue empty;  0 otherwise */
{     return (front == NULL);  }
```

```
void qput (char c)  /* inserts its argument value on the queue */
{
      Node*  temp;

      temp = getstorage (sizeof (Node) );
      temp->value = c;
      temp->link = NULL;
      if (front == NULL)
            front = temp;
      else rear->link = temp;
      rear = temp;
}
```

```
      int qget (void) /* returns, as int, the char at the front of the
                              queue, or -1 if the queue is empty */
   {
         Node* temp;
         char tempchar;

         if (front == NULL) return -1;
         tempchar = front->value;
         temp = front;
         front = front->link;
         free (temp);
         return tempchar;

   }
```

Notice that *qget* calls **free** to release back to the pool of available storage the space occupied by the node removed from the queue.

As an exercise, you may care to add a further, slightly more complex, function

   int qescape (**char** c)

which looks for the first occurrence in the queue of a node containing its argument value and removes that node. It returns 1 if successful or 0 if the argument value is not found in the queue. The function should deallocate the node and adjust the linkage so that the form of the queue still conforms to its specification.

10.3. Unions

The C declaration

```
      union {
            int a;
            char b;
      } ab;
```

whose *members* are then referred to as *ab.a* and *ab.b*, is like the Cobol description

```
02 ab.
      03 a pic s9(4) comp.
      03 b redefines a pic x.
```

in that *a* and *b* identify alternative mappings of the same storage area. The size of the area is determined by the largest of the alternatives, allowing for any storage boundary alignment. In the above example, the programmer's intention is that the actual data stored may at any time be either an integer or a character - but, of course, never both at the same time. In C, *a* and *b* are referred to as *members* of the union. A union may have more than two members, just as a Cobol area may have more than one redefinition.

In Cobol, a redefined item may be initialized, but its redefinitions must not.   The description of *a* in the above could include a **value** clause:

```
02  ab.
        03  a  pic s9(4) comp, value 1.
        03  b  redefines a  pic x.
```

but a **value** clause could not be specified for *b*. In C likewise, only the first-named member of a union may be initialized; this is done by writing the initialization after the complete declaration, so that the above declaration could be

```
union  {
        int  a;
        char  b;
} ab = 1;
```

The initial value for a union must be specified as a constant expression.

In C, as in Cobol, it is the programmer's responsibility to ensure that the appropriate identifiers are used. In the above example, if the program tries to retrieve the value of *b* when in fact an integer was last stored in the area, the result is undefined. In C, as in Cobol, the alternatives may be structures of arbitrary complexity and members of unions may themselves include other unions.

One major nuisance in C is that the members of a union can be accessed only if a name is given to the union as a whole (*ab* in the above example) and that name is used as part of the identifier of every member (e.g. *ab.a* in the above example).   In Cobol, the declaration of *ab* is unnecessary;   even if it is present, *a* and *b* are perfectly good references to the two members, as long as they are unique identifiers. When unions and structures are nested within other unions and structures, it can take a whole line of C code just to reference a member.

As an example of the use of unions, and as an extension to what we have learned about structures, we now consider how an arithmetic expression might be represented. To keep things simple, assume that:

- all operands are integer constants;
- all operators are binary (i.e. every operator has two operands); a unary plus or minus is regarded here (but not in C) as part of a number rather than as an operator.

Some examples are shown here, in both infix and prefix notation (see section 3.3):

```
5                    5
6 * -8               * 6 -8
(7+3) * 4            * + 7 3 4
6 + 2 * 5            + 6 * 2 5
21 + (2*3) - 8       + 21 - * 2 3 8
```

Here is one way in which these expressions may be represented as *trees*:

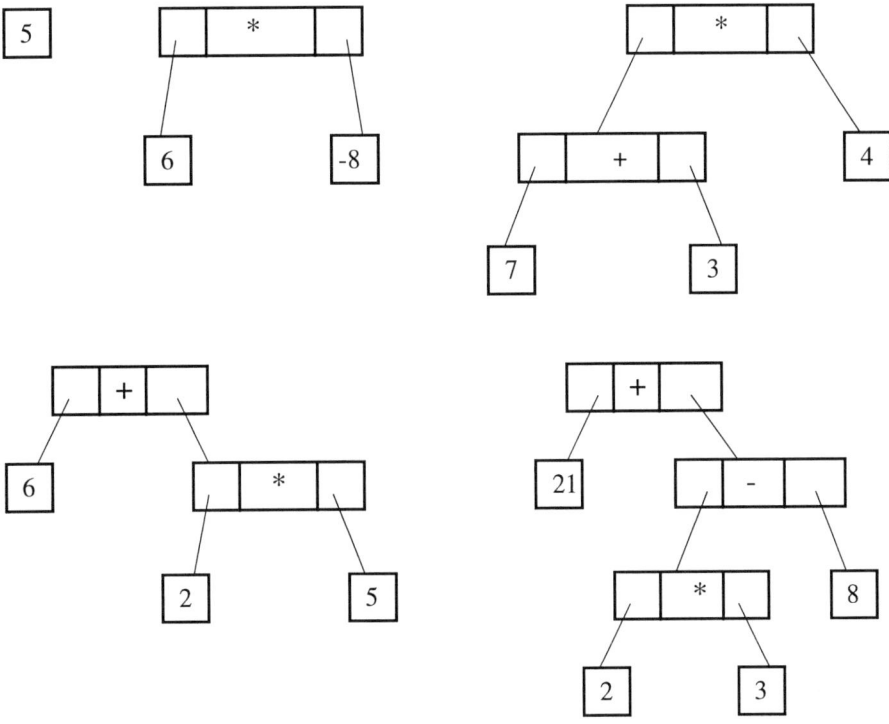

You will see that every node in a tree (i.e. every box in these diagrams) represents an expression, and that there are two kinds of node:

- a node containing only a number - the simplest form of expression;
- a node containing an operator and pointers to the two nodes representing the expressions to which the operator is to be applied. The nodes pointed to may be of either kind.

In C, a node of the first kind could be declared as

      int number;

and a node of the second kind as (assuming we can decide what to substitute for X):

```
struct {
    X* operand1;
    char operator;
    X* operand2;
} enode;
```

The pointers *operand1* and *operand2* have to point to some type X.   The node representing the sub-expression may be of either kind, so we want to define a type which encompasses both kinds of node. To do so, we could declare a union type:

```
typedef union Exprn {
    struct {
        union Exprn* operand1;
        char operator;
        union Exprn* operand2;
    } enode;
    int value;
} Exprn;
```

so that each node is of type *Exprn*. (Remember that *operand1* and *operand2* are really of type *Exprn**, but we have to precede their declarations with the word **union** because the type is not fully defined at their point of declaration.)   But this would cause a problem - when we accessed a node, there would be no way of determining whether it was *enode* or *value*. In order to distinguish between the two kinds of node, we therefore introduce another item, *exprntype*. The union is now enclosed in a **struct**:

```
typedef struct Exprn {
    char exprntype;  /* 'o'=operator; 'v'=value */
    union {
        struct {
            struct Exprn* operand1;
            char operator;
            struct Exprn* operand2;
        } enode;
        int value;
    } data;
} Exprn;
```

Now suppose that a variable *p*, of type *Exprn**, is pointing to such a node. We can determine whether or not the node is the kind with an operator and two pointers (i.e. an *enode*):

```
if (p->exprntype == 'o') ...
```

and, having established that it is, we can reference the pointer to its second operand by

```
p->data.enode.operand2
```

Using such notation, we can define a recursive function to return the value of the expression tree pointed to by the (non-null) value of *root*:

```
int evaluate (Exprn* root)
{
    int op1, op2;

    switch (root->exprntype) {
        case 'v': return root->data.value;
        case 'o':
            op1 = evaluate (root->data.enode.operand1);
            op2 = evaluate (root->data.enode.operand2);
            switch (root->data.enode.operator) {
                case '+': return op1 + op2;
                case '-': return op1 - op2;
                case '*': return op1 * op2;
                case '/': return op1 / op2;
            }
    }
}
```

11
Translation Units

11.1. Introduction

Having used standard library functions, you will be aware that component parts of a C program need not be stored in the same source file, nor compiled together - in the terminology of the C standard, a program consists of one or more "translation units". To illustrate the facilities available, we consider a simple program for date conversion. It is unlikely that you would want to write such a program yourself, since most systems already provide more generally useful tools of this kind.

Our limited program provides a unique daynumber for each calendar date between 1 January 1980 and 31 December 2099 inclusive. The daynumber is the ordinal number of the day, starting at 1 January 1980. The function *dayno* returns the daynumber corresponding to a given calendar date, and the function *cal_date* returns the calendar date corresponding to a given daynumber. The function *main* is just a simple test harness to enable the programmer to check that the other functions work correctly. To keep the example small, daynumbers and calendar dates are assumed to be valid, though it would be easy to add functions to perform validation checks.

11.2. The program in one file

Here is how the program may be written as one translation unit (apart from the library functions it uses):

```
/*          VERSION 1          */
#include <stdio.h>
#include <string.h>
```

```
#define  BASEYEAR  1980
#define  LIMITYEAR  2099
#define  LEAPYEAR(y)  ( (((y)%4==0 && (y)%100!=0) || (y)%400==0 )
          /* 1=leap year,  0=not leap year */
#define  YEARSIZE(y)  (LEAPYEAR(y) ? 366 : 365)
#define  MONTHSIZE(M,Y)  ( days_in_month[M] + (M==2 && \
LEAPYEAR(Y)) )
          /* adds 1 (true) or 0 (false) */

typedef  int  Dayid;
typedef  struct {
          int  day;
          int  month;
          int  year;
       } Date;

Dayid  dayno (Date);
Date  cal_date (Dayid);

const int  days_in_month[13] = {0,31,28,31,30,31,30,31,31,30,31,30,31};

main (void)
{
    #define  MAXLINE  80
    char  in[MAXLINE+2] = {'\0'};
    Date indate;
    Dayid inday;

    fgets (in, MAXLINE+2, stdin);
    while (strcmp (in, "end\n") != 0)  {
        if (sscanf (in, " day-no = %d", &inday) == 1)  {
            indate = cal_date (inday);
            printf ("date is %d/%d/%d\n",
                        indate.day, indate.month, indate.year);
        }
        else  if (sscanf (in, " date = %d/%d/%d",
                        &indate.day, &indate.month, &indate.year) == 3)
                printf ("day number is %d\n", dayno (indate) );
            else  printf ("??\n");
        fgets (in, MAXLINE+2, stdin);
    }
    return  0;
    #undef MAXLINE
}
```

```
int  dayno_in_year (Date d)
{
     int  i, dn;

     for (i=1, dn=0; i < d.month; i++)
          dn += MONTHSIZE(i, d.year);
     return dn + d.day;
}


Date  date_in_year (int dn, int y)
{
     Date  d;
     int  i, j;

     for (i=1; dn > (j = MONTHSIZE(i,y)); i++)
          dn -= j;
     d.day = dn; d.month = i; d.year = y;
     return  d;
}

Dayid  dayno (Date d)
{
     int  y;
     Dayid  dn;

     for (dn=0, y = BASEYEAR;  y < d.year;  y++)
          dn += YEARSIZE(y);
     return  dn + dayno_in_year (d);
}

Date  cal_date (Dayid dn)
{
     int  y;

     for (y = BASEYEAR;  dn > YEARSIZE(y);  y++)
          dn -= YEARSIZE(y);
     return  date_in_year (dn, y);
}
```

Notes:

• The functions *dayno* and *cal_date* are called in *main*, but defined after *main*; so the declaration by prototype of these two functions is necessary. The prototypes could be inside the definition of *main*, rather than, as here, preceding it at source file level.

- The values corresponding to BASEYEAR and LIMITYEAR may be changed, but problems will arise with dates up to the mid eighteenth century. There is also the fact that a large range of dates may result in daynumber values exceeding the capacity of an **int**. Indeed, even the maximum daynumber value for the range 1980 to 2099 (which is 43830) may exceed the value of INT_MAX in some implementations, in which case the **typedef** of *Dayid* may specify **long int** (to be explained later) instead of **int**. This is one kind of situation in which a **typedef** can aid program portability.
- The macros LEAPYEAR, YEARSIZE and MONTHSIZE are alternatives to functions. We could decide later to replace one or more of them by functions with the same names, taking the same parameters, and returning **int** values. There would be no consequent need to change anything else in the program. But notice that the function to replace the MONTHSIZE macro would either have to be defined after the declaration of the array *days_in_month* or would have to include an **extern** declaration for the array.

11.3. The program in two files, compiled together

Alternatively, the program could be stored in two or more source files. We could, for example, store the program text up to the end of *main* in one file, *days1.c*, and the rest of the text in another, *days2.c* (though this would not be a very suitable way to split the program). Part of the program text is stored in file *days1.c*:

```
/*          VERSION 2:  in file days1.c        */
/* Content of this file is unchanged text from version 1, down to end of
        function main, with one #include line appended */

#include <stdio.h>
#include <string.h>

#define BASEYEAR 1980
    ....
    ....
    ....
    ....
main (void)
{
    ....
    ....
    ....
}
#include "days2.c"
```

The rest of the program is stored in file *days2.c*:

```
/*          VERSION 2:  in file days2.c          */
/* The function definitions in this file are unchanged from version 1 */
```

int dayno_in_year (Date d)
{
    .... unchanged ....
}

Date date_in_year (**int** dn, **int** y)
{
    .... unchanged ....
}

Dayid dayno (Date d)
{
    .... unchanged ....
}

Date cal_date (Dayid dn)
{
    .... unchanged ....
}

The program still consists of one translation unit (apart from the library functions it uses). For compilation purposes, it is equivalent to the previous version; before compilation proper begins, each *#include* line is replaced by the text from the file which is named in that line. Thus the effect of the last line of *days1.c* (*#include "days2.c"*) is that compilation of *days1.c* is the same as compilation of Version 1 of the program.

The system of course has to find the files named in the *#include* lines. Notice the difference between the line at the start of the *days1.c*

    #include <stdio.h>

and the line at the end

    #include "days2.c"

The difference between the effects of *<filename>* and *"filename"* is that the system will search in different places for the specified file. There is one set of files which is searched if *<filename>* is used, and another which is searched if *"filename"* is used. In the latter case, if *filename* is not found in the appropriate set of files, a further search is made in the set of files appropriate to *<filename>*. The C standard leaves it to the implementor to define precisely how these two sets of files are identified by a particular computer system. (Indeed, the Standard says that a library header is not necessarily a source file, and that the character sequence delimited by '<' and '>' need not be a valid source file name.) Commonly, *<filename>* refers to a file in the C library, and *"filename"* refers to a file in a user's directory.

So the *#include* lines that we have been putting at the start of our programs normally copy files *<stdio.h>* etc., from the standard library on to the beginning of the program. If your system lets you look at these files, or if your compiler has a "preprocess only" option, you will be able to see that they contain function prototypes, macro definitions, and other things necessary to enable you to use the facilities provided by particular library units.

11.4. The program in two files, compiled separately

A program is normally designed as a collection of modules which may be compiled and tested independently of each other. The advantages of this approach are well known - it makes the individual modules intellectually manageable, makes testing and debugging easier and more methodical, aids fault diagnosis and correction, and enables a module to be used in different programs. An experienced programmer would therefore not write even this small date conversion program in the form shown so far. The programmer would instead write two modules, one containing the date conversion functions and the other containing the *main* function. The first of these modules could then be incorporated into any program which wanted to make use of its functions.

Naturally, any such program would be using daynumbers and structures of type *Date*, and there may be other programs which use daynumbers and *Date* structures but do not require the conversion functions. It is important to ensure that all programs (and of course the date conversion functions themselves) use the same definitions for *Dayid* and *Date*. So it makes sense to store the appropriate type definitions in a file which can be included in any file requiring them. We can place these type definitions in a file named *dtypes.h*:

```
typedef int Dayid;
typedef struct {
        int day;
        int month;
        int year;
    } Date;
```

Naming this file *dtypes.h* rather than *dtypes.c* is here merely a matter of convention, to indicate that this is a "header" file, intended for inclusion at the beginning of another source file.

Those programs that need to use conversion between the two types will need also prototypes for the functions *dayno* and *cal_date*. (They will not need prototypes for *dayno_in_year* and *date_in_year*, since these are used only as sub-functions of the other two conversion functions.) So that such programs may use just a single *#include*, we can place the type definitions and the function prototypes together in another header file named *dconv.h*:

```
#include "dtypes.h"
Dayid  dayno (Date);
Date cal_date (Dayid);
```

Notice how duplication of the type definitions is avoided by using *#include* to include the other header file in this one.

Look again at Version 1 of the program. We intend to rewrite it as it should have been written in the first place - as two independently-compilable modules (translation units):

- the function *main*, together with any external definitions and declarations needed to make it compilable;
- the other functions (i.e. the date conversion functions), together with any external definitions and declarations needed to make them compilable.

Consider the second of these modules. You will notice that the five *#define* lines (i.e. the macro definitions) at the start of Version 1 are for use in the conversion functions only; they are not used in *main*. The same is true of the array *days_in_month*. Given the header file *dtypes.h* defined above, the second of our modules can be written as below and placed in file *dconv.c*. (Notice the convention of giving this file the same name as that of the header (*dconv.h*) which enables other separately-compiled modules to use it, but with a different extension letter - *c* instead of *h*.)

The four function definitions are unchanged from Version 1, except that two of them are now declared to be **static**, as is the array *days_in_month*; this will be explained later. The only other point to note is that there is a *#include* for the header file *dtypes.h*, whose contents are shown above.

```
/*       VERSION 3:  in file dconv.c           */
/*    package of date conversion functions     */

#define  BASEYEAR  1980
#define  LIMITYEAR  2099
#define  LEAPYEAR(y)  ( ((y)%4==0 && (y)%100!=0) || (y)%400==0 )
          /* 1=leap year,  0=not leap year */
#define  YEARSIZE(y) (LEAPYEAR(y) ? 366 : 365)
#define  MONTHSIZE(M,Y) ( days_in_month[M] + (M==2 && \
LEAPYEAR(Y)) )
          /* adds 1 (true) or 0 (false) */

#include  "dtypes.h"

static const int days_in_month[13] =
                  {0,31,28,31,30,31,30,31,31,30,31,30,31};
```

```
static int dayno_in_year (Date d)
{
    int i, dn;

    for (i=1, dn=0; i < d.month; i++)
        dn += MONTHSIZE(i, d.year);
    return dn + d.day;
}

static Date date_in_year (int dn, int y)
{
    Date d;
    int i, j;

    for (i=1; dn > (j = MONTHSIZE(i,y)); i++)
        dn -= j;
    d.day = dn; d.month = i; d.year = y;
    return d;
}



Dayid dayno (Date d)
{
    int y;
    Dayid dn;

    for (dn=0, y = BASEYEAR; y < d.year; y++)
        dn += YEARSIZE(y);
    return dn + dayno_in_year (d);
}

Date cal_date (Dayid dn)
{
    int y;

    for (y = BASEYEAR; dn > YEARSIZE(y); y++)
        dn -= YEARSIZE(y);
    return date_in_year (dn, y);
}
```

The other module consists of the function definition for *main*, together with a *#include* line for *dconv.h* which, as we have seen, contains the type definitions for *Dayid* and *Date* as well as the prototype declarations for the functions *dayno* and *cal_date*:

```
/*      VERSION 3:  in file dtest.c          */

#include <stdio.h>
#include <string.h>
#include "dconv.h"

main (void)
{
    #define MAXLINE 80
    char in[MAXLINE+2] = {'\0'};
    Date indate;
    Dayid inday;

    fgets (in, MAXLINE+2, stdin);
    while (strcmp (in, "end\n") != 0) {
        if (sscanf (in, " day-no = %d", &inday) == 1) {
            indate = cal_date (inday);
            printf ("date is %d/%d/%d\n",
                        indate.day, indate.month, indate.year);
        }
        else  if (sscanf (in, " date = %d/%d/%d",
                        &indate.day, &indate.month, &indate.year) == 3)
                printf ("day number is %d\n", dayno (indate) );
            else  printf ("??\n");
        fgets (in, MAXLINE+2, stdin);
    }
    return  0;
    #undef MAXLINE
}
```

Each of the source files *dconv.c* and *dtest.c* may be compiled independently of the other to produce an *object file*. Before the modules can be executed together, the two object files must be *linked* to produce executable code. The facilities for performing these operations are not part of the C language, and the precise commands required will depend on your operating system and on the particular C compiler you are using.

Linkage of two or more object files involves resolving all inter-file references. In Version 3 above, the object file produced by the compiler from *dconv.c* would contain no references to anything outside itself. Every function and object that the program uses is fully defined in *dconv.c* itself. (Remember that the preprocessing phase replaced the *#include* line by the contents of file *dtypes.h*.)

In the file *dtest.c*, however, there are three *#include* lines. The first two result in the inclusion of prototype declarations for library input and output functions used in *main*, and for the string-handling function *strcmp* used in *main*. The *definitions* of these functions will have to be found in the library. The line

```
#include  "dconv.h"
```

results in the inclusion of prototype declarations for the functions *dayno* and *cal_date*. The object file produced by the compiler from *dtest.c* therefore contains the information that, in order to produce an executable program, the *definitions* of all these functions must be found during linkage. When the object files produced from *dtest.c* and *dconv.c* are linked, the definitions of *dayno* and *cal_date* are found in the *dconv.c* object file, and the library function definitions are found automatically.

11.5. Inter-file references

All objects and functions referenced in a source file should be declared in that source file or in a file which is *#included* in it. Remember that a declaration is usually also a definition. The declaration

char x;

acts also as a definition of *x*, reserving storage for the object. Within a function, the declaration

extern char x;

is *not* a definition. No storage is reserved by the declaration. If several functions each contain that declaration, they are all referring to the same object, whose definition will appear at source file level (i.e. not within a function) in the same file or in another file with which the code produced from that source file will be linked.

A definition within a function is always local - it cannot be seen from outside the function. *In section 11.5.1, the term* "definition" *will be used to mean* "definition at source file level", *i.e.* "definition outside functions".

11.5.1. Objects

Within a set of files which are to be linked together:

1. There should not be two or more (non-static - see **3** below) object definitions with the same identifier.
   Example: there should not be a definition of an object named *x* in one source file and a definition of another object named *x* in another source file.
2. An object defined in one source file may be referenced in another source file if it is declared as **extern** in the latter.
   Example: an object defined in source file A by

   char x;

   may be referenced by a source file B if B contains the declaration

   extern char x;

3. It follows from **1** and **2** that any source file may reference an object defined in another source file. From the point of view of program modularity, this is undesirable. To make a definition invisible to other files, the word **static** is inserted at the start of the definition.

Example: Suppose that source files A, B and C are to be linked. If source file A contains the definition

> **static char** x;

then the definition is private to file A and cannot be seen by other files during linkage. Thus if source file B contained

> **char** x;

this would define a different object from that defined in A. Further, if source file C contained the declaration

> **extern char** x;

this would be a reference to the object x defined in B. Neither B nor C would have any knowledge of the object x defined in A.

Notice, in Version 3 of the earlier date conversion program, that the array *days_in_month* is **static**, since it is purely for use by the conversion functions. The consequences are that we can remove or change its definition, or change its initialization, knowing that no other source files will be affected and that no problem will arise if another source file also defines an object named *days_in_month*.

This use of the word **static**, which has its roots in the history of the language, is unfortunate in two ways:

- The word **static** in a C program can mean two different things, depending on the context of its use:
  (a) applied to an object declared *within a function*, **static** means that the object continues to exist when control passes out of the function; on the next call of the function, its value is unchanged. (See section 3.6.)
  (b) applied to an object defined at *source file level* (i.e. not within a function), **static** means that the object is private to the source file. (All objects defined at source file level are static in the sense of (a) .)
- If an object defined at source file level is *not* specified as **static**, it can be referenced by code in other files. In other words, the default situation is that code in other files can access all objects defined at source file level. It would be safer if the default situation were that these objects were private.

It is therefore arguably good practice to specify all objects defined at source file level as being **static**, except when it is intended that code in other files may access them. There should be few exceptions, since most interaction between translation units should take place by parameter passing and by the use of header files.

11.5.2. Functions

Since function definitions cannot be nested in C, all function definitions are at source file level. Function *declarations*, in the form of prototypes, always have the **extern** property. (It is a matter of taste whether or not you precede a function prototype with the word **extern**.) As with objects, all declarations of functions with the same name are taken as referring to the same function definition. Within a set of files which are to be linked together:

1. There should not be two or more (non-**static** - see **3** below) function definitions with the same identifier.
2. A function defined in one source file may be called within another source file if a prototype declaration of that function appears in the latter.
3. It follows from **2** and **3** that any source file may call a function defined in another source file. To make a function definition invisible to other files, the word **static** is inserted at the start of the function's definition.

Notice, in Version 3 of the date conversion program, that the definitions of the functions *dayno_in_year* and *date_in_year* are specified as **static**, leaving us free to remove them later (e.g. if we change the algorithms in the other two functions), knowing that this will have no impact outside the source file *dconv.c*.

11.6. Conditional compilation

Since *#include* can be used several times in the same source file, and since an included file may contain other *#includes*, there is a danger of including the same declarations more than once in a source file. As an example, consider the two header files used in section 11.4:

<table>
<tr><td>

dtypes.h

typedef int Dayid;
typedef struct {
    int day;
    int month;
    int year;
  } Date;

</td><td>

dconv.h

#include "dtypes.h"
Dayid dayno (Date);
Date cal_date (Dayid);

</td></tr>
</table>

Suppose that another header file, *dprint.h*, contains

```
#include "dtypes.h"
void printdate (Date);
```

Now suppose that a source file *sf*, which converts dates and prints them, contains the lines

```
#include "dconv.h"
#include "dprint.h"
```

After preprocessing, source file *sf* will contain two identical pairs of type definitions for *Dayid* and *Date*, a state of affairs which will distress the compiler. (This situation cannot arise with standard library header files because the Standard says that multiple inclusions of a library header file in a given scope have precisely the same effect as a single inclusion. Nor can it arise with identical *#define* lines, whether they are in library headers or not.) One advantage of defining header files is that they can be included in many different source files; much of that advantage would be lost if we had to keep arranging things to avoid multiple inclusions. One way to deal with the situation is to define *dtypes.h* like this:

```
#ifndef DTYPES
    #define DTYPES
    typedef int Dayid;
    typedef struct {
        int day;
        int month;
        int year;
    } Date;
#endif
```

These lines are processed by the preprocessor. In the second line, we see for the first time a macro definition with no replacement text; DTYPES in this case is defined as being replaced by nothing at all. The reason for this definition is that the line

```
#ifdef DTYPES
```

tests if DTYPES is currently defined, and the line

```
#ifndef DTYPES
```

tests if DTYPES is *not* currently defined. The preprocessor lines suggested above for *dtypes.h* ensure that, if *dtypes.h* has already been included, the lines between *#ifndef* and the matching *#endif* disappear from the source file. If *dtypes.h* has *not* already been included, then DTYPES becomes defined, and the two **typedef**s remain in the source file. As long as DTYPES is not defined elsewhere, the overall effect is that a source file may ultimately have several lines saying

```
#include "dtypes.h"
```

but only the first of them will be replaced by the two **typedef**s.

There are equivalent ways of writing the directives *#ifdef* and *#ifndef*. For a name X:

#ifdef X	*is equivalent to*	#if defined X
#ifndef X	*is equivalent to*	#if ! defined X

(The unary operator *defined* evaluates to 1 (true) if the name X is defined, and to 0 (false) if it is not.) In general, *#if* tests a constant expression. *#if*s may be nested, and each may take one of two forms. One form is

```
#if    ....        /* constant expression */
       ....        /* lines to be compiled if true */
       ....
#else
       ....        /* lines to be compiled if false */
       ....
#endif
```

The *#else* part is optional. The constant expression following *#if* is subject to certain restrictions and peculiarities which need not be detailed here; in practice, very simple expressions are usually used. The other form, with as many *#elif*s as required, provides an alternative to nesting when one of several options is to be chosen for compilation:

```
#if    ....        /* constant expression 1 */
       ....        /* lines to be compiled if expression 1 is true */
       ....
#elif ....         /* constant expression 2 */
       ....        /* lines to be compiled if expression 2 is true */
       ....
#elif ....         /* constant expression 3 */
       ....        /* lines to be compiled if expression 3 is true */
       ....
#else
       ....        /* lines to be compiled in all other cases */
       ....
#endif
```

Again, the *#else* part is optional.

One customary use of *#if* is to select particular code for an implementation-dependent operation. A single macro might be defined, whose name is the name of the target machine:

```
#define  SUN
....
....
#if defined  SUN
       ....        /* lines to be compiled for SUN */
       ....
#elif defined  VAX
       ....        /* lines to be compiled for VAX */
       ....
(etc.)
```

By changing the *#define* line above, we can ensure that the appropriate code for the target machine is compiled in those parts of the program that are machine-dependent.

As was mentioned in an earlier chapter, a library header file *<limits.h>* contains a definition of INT_MAX - the implementation's maximum value for an **int**. Suppose that part of a program has to use a variable whose maximum possible value is 50000. If INT_MAX is smaller than 50000, extra code has to be compiled, or perhaps **long int** used instead of **int**. Again, *#if* might be used:

```
#include  <limits.h>
    ....
    ....
#if  INT_MAX < 50000
        ....   /*  code to declare or use long int  */
        ....
#else
        ....   /*  code to declare or use int  */
        ....
#endif
```

Another use of *#if* is to include debugging code in a program. During testing, the program is compiled with the line

```
#define DEBUG
```

at the beginning. For production use, it is compiled without that line. At each point in the program where debugging code is to be inserted, the debugging statements are placed in a *#if* or *#ifdef* directive; for instance:

```
#ifdef  DEBUG
        printf ("Reached start of function x\n");
        printf("Argument values are %d, %d\n", i, j);
#endif
```

This is like using **with debugging mode** together with D in the indicator area of selected lines in a Cobol program. Alternatively, some C compilers provide options to do the same kind of thing without the need to modify the source code.

Conditional compilation is a useful feature, but it should not be overused. Very often, rather than using preprocessing directives, you can obtain the same effect by using tests in the language itself. In these cases, it is usually better to have a larger program rather than one which is shorter but less intelligible.

12

Types and Type Conversion

12.1. Introduction

A C program manipulates the contents of regions of computer storage known, in the terminology of the Standard, as *objects*. The choice of name is unfortunate, since these objects are very different from the "objects" in object-oriented programming.

The interpretation of a value stored in a C object is determined by the object's *type* (**int, char***, etc.), which is specified in the declaration of the object's identifier or is otherwise implied in the expression which causes access to the object (e.g. the constant 15 implies an unnamed constant object of type **int**). Like an object, a function has a type, based on the type of its return value. A function is characterized by the type of its return value and the number and types of its parameters. There are also *incomplete types*, where a declaration does not supply information about the size of the type; probably the commonest example is the declaration of a parameter as an array of unspecified size. The Standard regards the special type **void** as "an incomplete type that cannot be completed". Incomplete types will be omitted from the discussion in this chapter. *Enumeration types* too will be omitted, but will be introduced briefly in a later chapter.

This chapter is mainly concerned with object types. It introduces object types that have not been used in earlier chapters, and it explains how the Standard categorizes types and how data are converted from one type to another.

12.2. Basic types

In this section we look briefly at each of the basic types. In C, these are represented in pure binary and not, as in Cobol, by sequences of binary-coded characters.

12.2.1. Integer types

So far, we have used just one type, **int**, for all our integer variables. In fact, there are six different integer types, disregarding for the moment the character types, which, together with the enumeration types and the integer types described here, are classed as *integral* types. The six integer types are:

> **short int**   **unsigned short int**
> **int**   **unsigned int**
> **long int**   **unsigned long int**

These types correspond to **computational** types in Cobol. Generally, the Cobol default is unsigned (i.e. you write S in the picture to get a signed variable), but the C default is signed (i.e. you write **unsigned** if you don't want it to be signed). In declarations of objects of all these types except plain **int**, the word **int** may be omitted.

"A plain **int** object has the natural size suggested by the architecture of the execution environment." For most architectures, this is likely to mean that an **int** object will be one word of storage. Objects of **unsigned** types occupy the same amount of storage as those of the corresponding signed types, but can represent only non-negative values, with a potentially greater range of positive values than the corresponding signed types. The implication is that the most significant bit is treated as a magnitude bit in an **unsigned** type, and as a sign bit in a signed type, using two's or one's complement representation. For a particular implementation, INT_MIN, INT_MAX and UINT_MAX (all defined in the standard header *<limits.h>*) give respectively the lower and upper bounds of the range of values representable in an **int** object, and the upper bound of the range representable in an **unsigned int**. The lower bound for an **unsigned int** is of course zero. All the **unsigned** types have the characteristic that overflow "can never occur", by which the Standard means that there will be no run-time indication if a computation yields a value which is outside the appropriate range. For instance, an **int** object may be 16 bits long in a particular implementation, giving UINT_MAX the value 65535; the arithmetic is then such that $65535 + 1 = 0$ and $0 - 1 = 65535$; in general, overflow is just lost.

The intended use of **short int** and **unsigned short int** objects is to provide, where the underlying architecture is suitable, more economical storage of integers whose known range of values is considerably smaller than the **int** and **unsigned int** ranges. With an appropriate machine architecture, objects of these **short** types may be half-words. The header *<limits.h>* defines the implementation's ranges by SHRT_MIN, SHRT_MAX and USHRT_MAX.

The **long int** and **unsigned long int** types are intended to cater for integer variables whose ranges of values exceed those of **int** and **unsigned int**. These **long** types may be double words. The header *<limits.h>* defines the implementation's ranges by LONG_MIN, LONG_MAX and ULONG_MAX.

The Standard says that every implementor must provide for *at least* the following magnitudes; in effect, it says that the minimum size of a **short int** or an **int** is 16 bits and the minimum size of a **long int** is 32 bits:

SHRT_MIN −32767	INT_MIN −32767	LONG_MIN −2147483647
SHRT_MAX 32767	INT_MAX 32767	LONG_MAX 2147483647
USHRT_MAX 65535	UINT_MAX 65535	ULONG_MAX 4294967295

In any implementation, the range of **short int** (or **unsigned short int**) values is a subset of the range of **int** (or **unsigned int**) values, and the range of the latter is a subset of the range of **long int** (or **unsigned long int**) values. This of course means that an implementor may choose to make **short int** the same size as **int**, or to make **int** the same size as **long int**, or to make all three the same size, using, in the last case, a storage unit of at least 32 bits.

As we will see, it can occasionally be important to know, or to control, the storage representation of an integer constant written in a program. (For instance, what is the type of the constant 30000?) Here are the rules. An integer constant is of type **int** if it is in the appropriate range (i.e. INT_MIN <= constant value <= INT_MAX); if not, it is of type **long int** if it is in the appropriate range; failing that, and given that it is positive, it is of type **unsigned long int**. The programmer can control the type of an integer constant by appending the letter U or L or both. For example, 24 is of type **int**, 24U is of type **unsigned int**, 24L is of type **long int**, and 24UL is of type **unsigned long int**; the value represented (24) is the same in all four cases.

You will remember that some <*stdio.h*> library functions - **sscanf**, **sprintf**, **printf** and others not covered in this book - take a format string as an argument. In the format string, %d is used for integers, %c for characters and %s for strings. For the various types discussed here, the appropriate format string specifications are shown below. In the case of **sscanf**, the corresponding arguments will, of course, be *pointers* to objects of the stated types.

 %u for an **unsigned int** argument,

 %hd for a **short int** argument,

 %hu for an **unsigned short int** argument,

 %ld for a **long int** argument,

 %lu for an **unsigned long int** argument.

12.2.2. Floating types

Like integer objects, *floating* objects are used to store numeric values, and may participate in expressions. Floating-point representation of numbers is too big a subject to be covered here. From the programmer's point of view, the important features of floating-point representation are:

- It can be used for fractional numbers, or numbers with fractional parts.
- It can be used for integers which lie outside (as well as inside) the ranges of the integer types.

• The representation may be very slightly inaccurate.

So, if the value of a variable is to include any fractional part, or if it may exceed the capacity of a **long int** (or **unsigned long int**, as appropriate), the variable must be declared to be one of the floating types. The possible inaccuracy of the stored value need not usually be a matter for concern; the main consequences are that it is dangerous to involve a floating-point number in a test for strict equality, and that it would be unwise to use floating-point numbers to represent sums of money in business applications.

There are no unsigned floating types. The different floating types are characterized not just by ranges of values but also by the precision with which these values are represented. The three floating types are **float, double** and **long double**, and they have the same kind of relationship with each other as do **short int, int** and **long int.** Typically, **long double** gives the best range and precision and occupies more storage. Like those of the integer types, the characteristics of the floating types for a particular implementation are available in a standard header, in this case *<float.h>*. Most of the details are of interest to numerical analysts rather than to programmers.

Floating constants in a program are distinguished from integer constants by including either a decimal point or the letter E (or, equivalently, e) or both. If present, E is followed by an exponent value giving the decimal scaling of the number. Here are some examples:

constant	value represented
16.0	16
1.57	1.57
1.57E−2	0.0157
2E3	2000
−0.024E2	−2.4

The type of a floating constant may be specified by appending the letter F (for **float**) or L (for **long double**). If neither letter is appended, as in the examples above, a floating constant has the type **double**.

For output of floating-point numbers, the format strings used by **sprintf** and **printf** may include %f or %e (or %g, which we will ignore). These have much in common with %d, which is described in section 6.1: a minus sign indicates left justification, a plus sign indicates that the converted value will start with a plus sign if it is positive, and a minimum field width and/or a precision may be specified. For instance, %9.3f (or %9.3Lf if the corresponding argument is of type **long double**) in a format string means that the converted value will have a minimum field width of 9, with 3 digits after the decimal point. If no precision is specified (as in %9f) the number of digits following the decimal point is 6. If necessary, the converted value is rounded, not truncated.

The difference between %f and %e is that %f converts an argument to "normal" notation (e.g. "−15.7") and %e converts it to "scientific" notation (e.g."−1.57e01") with one significant digit before the decimal point. If %E is used instead of %e, the exponent is preceded by an upper-case E (e.g. "−1.57E01").

For input, **sscanf** format strings, also, may contain %f or %e (or %g). In this context, they are equivalent, and only %f will be referred to in this paragraph. Remember that **sscanf** matches character sequences and converts the matched sequences into internal representation (see section 6.2). As with %d, a maximum field width may be specified. %f is used where the object pointed to by the corresponding argument of **sscanf** is of type **float**, %lf where it is of type **double**, and %Lf where it is of type **long double**. These specifications will match a sequence of digits optionally preceded by a plus or minus sign, optionally containing a decimal point character, and optionally followed by the letter E or e followed by an exponent value. A simple integer in the input character string can therefore be matched by %d or %f.

12.2.3. Character types

Most programming languages include the notion of a *character*. Traditionally, since the nineteen-sixties, the smallest unit of storage addressable at the hardware level has been such that each unit (*byte*) is of a convenient size to store a binary representation of one character; typically the size of a byte is 8 bits. (It remains to be seen how the increasing use of characters from larger alphabets will affect this tradition - C provides multi-byte characters for this purpose.) A byte thus usually provides for storage of 256 distinct values. The precise representation of a given character depends on the character encoding scheme in use. For instance, ASCII encoding represents the letter A by the number 65 (01000001 in binary), but EBCDIC encoding represents the same letter by the number 193 (11000001 in binary). Most C implementations use ASCII encoding.

After a character is input from a keyboard or other device, it is represented internally in its binary encoding; on output to a monitor or a printer or other graphic device, the binary encoding becomes a signal to the device; if the signal represents a printable character, that character is displayed or printed. In a program, therefore, character constants and string literals could be regarded as just a convenient way of specifying binary patterns.

In most languages, none of this really concerns the programmer. A Cobol programmer simply works with sequences of characters and need not be aware of the binary patterns by which the characters are represented in storage. The things a Cobol program can do with characters or character sequences - moving them around, comparing them, sorting them - are just the things we would want to do with them if they were not in a computer system.

C, by contrast, has a very curious view of what we might want to do with characters or character sequences. Though we can move individual characters around, we have to use standard library functions (or write our own) in order to move sequences of characters. Again, though two individual characters may be compared with each other, convenient comparison of character sequences requires the use of functions. Even comparison of individual characters is not a true character comparison based on a program-definable collating sequence; it is nothing more than a comparison of the numbers represented by the binary patterns which represent the characters - and, to make it more interesting, these numbers may (sometimes!) be negative. Character *arithmetic*, however, is included in the basic language! It is much easier in C to multiply two characters together or to square the difference between one character and another than it is to move a sequence of characters from one place in storage to another. What grotesque world, you may ask, do these C people live in?

The first thing to learn about the character types is that they are really integer types, or, more strictly, what the Standard calls "integral types". The type **char** might have been better named "very **short int**". The Standard does allow an implementor to define character objects as being the same size as **short int** objects, but it is usual for a character object to be one byte and for a **short int** object to be somewhat larger.

If C's attitude to characters cannot be justified, it can at least be explained. C started life as a kind of "structured assembler" - a language with the very laudable aim of combining the program structuring and abstraction capabilities of third-generation languages with the low-level control provided by assembly languages. In relation to certain machine architectures and a large range of system programming tasks, it proved eminently successful. Its shortcomings as an application programming language come, to some extent, from its origins in the PDP/Unix world. Its deficiency in the area of character manipulation could have been avoided if its designers had considered not just the architecture and instructions of conventional binary word machines but also those of, say, the IBM mainframes of the time. A look at Cobol might have helped too. But enough tilting at windmills.

There are three character types. In keeping with the other integral types, but in opposition to common sense, two of these are **signed char** and **unsigned char**. In the former case, you would expect the eight-bit pattern 11111110 to be interpreted as −2 (assuming two's complement); in the latter case it would be interpreted as 254. This corresponds to the interpretations of the other integral types - but there is a difference. Plain **int** means **signed int**, but plain **char** does not mean **signed char**. The third character type therefore is just plain **char** - whether this is the same as **signed char** or the same as **unsigned char** depends on the implementation. Thus, though two implementations use the same encodings, you may get different results when you compare two **char** variables whose values are, say, 00001001 and 10001110; the second of these may be positive in one implementation and negative in the other. There are also problems in the area of type conversion.

Fortunately, the problems do not arise in many applications. If you work with a conventional C implementation with 8-bit bytes and 7-bit ASCII encoding, no character will ever be negative. Further, if the only characters you use are those in the *basic source character set*, all these characters are guaranteed by the Standard to be positive. (So an implementation using EBCDIC would surely be one in which **char** is the same as **unsigned char**.) The Standard defines the basic source character set as consisting of the 26 upper-case letters of the English alphabet, the 26 lower-case letters, the 10 decimal digits, the space character, horizontal and vertical tabs, form feed, new-line, and the following 29 characters:

```
!   "   #   %   &   '   (   )   *   +   ,   -   .   /   :
;   <   =   >   ?   [   \   ]   ^   _   {   |   }   ~
```

If you work with a larger character set and you want your programs to be portable, you are going to have to think hard about the implications of choosing **signed** or **unsigned char**. You may end up defining your own type and writing your own library functions for comparisons and other operations. The character types are a mess which, in the end, you may have to sort out for yourself.

12.3. Derived types

We have already met every kind of derived type:

1. *A function type* "is said to be derived from its return type". Thus "function returning **int**" and "function returning **double**" are different types.
2. *A pointer type* may be derived from a function type or from an object type. Thus "pointer to **int**" is a different type from "pointer to function returning **int**" and from "pointer to **char**".
3. *An array type* "is said to be derived from its element type". Thus "array of **int**" is a different type from "array of pointer to **int**". An array is characterized by its element type and the number of elements in the array.
4. *A structure type* "describes a sequentially allocated nonempty set of member objects, each of which has an optionally specified name and possibly distinct type".
5. *A union type* "describes an overlapping nonempty set of objects, each of which has an optionally specified name and possibly distinct type".

12.4. Type conversion

As in Cobol, expressions may include numbers which are of different types, and a value of one type may be assigned to a variable of another type. In Cobol, the rules about how a value of one type is converted to another type are simple and unsurprising. C's rules are more complex, largely because there are more types.

We will be considering only the basic types, i.e. the types described in section 12.2. The only derived types to which conversion is applicable are the pointer types. There is no implicit conversion between different pointer types; explicit conversion can be done by casts (section 12.5.1); it is also possible to convert between different pointer types by converting to and from the type **void*** (see section 9.2), but these facilities should rarely be needed in routine application programming. All that you need to learn about interaction between pointer types and integer types is already covered in section 3.8.

This section describes only the basic conversion rules. Section 12.5 explains how these rules are applied in particular contexts.

12.4.1. Conversion between integral types

Remember that integral types include **char**, **signed char** and **unsigned char**. Depending on your implementation, or perhaps on your own choice if the implementation allows you to choose, the plain **char** type will be the same as either **signed char** or **unsigned char**.

We consider now the rules for conversion from one integral type (which we'll call the *old* type) to another (the *new* type). As in Cobol, *if the original value can be represented in an object of the new type, then the value is unchanged.* The C conversion rules are therefore of interest only when there is conversion between a signed and an unsigned type and in cases of the kind that would raise a **size error** condition in Cobol. Table 12.1 summarizes the conversions. The table rows represent the *old* types and the columns the *new* types, and each table entry indicates what happens when a value represented as the *old* type is converted to the *new* type. *The numbers in the table refer to the conversion rules listed below.* Bear in mind when reading the rules that objects of different types may be the same size in an implementation. For the examples in the numbered rules, *assume an implementation in which **char** is 8 bits, **short int** and **int** are both 16 bits, and **long int** is 32 bits.*

As stated here, the rules assume that two's complement representation is used. An implementor who uses one's complement will have the not inconsiderable task of achieving numerically identical effects.

TO \ FROM	signed char	short int	int	long int	unsd. char	unsd. short	unsd. int	unsd. long
signed char	-	1	1	1	4	5	5	5
short int	2	-	1	1	6	4	5	5
int	2	2	-	1	6	6	4	5
long int	2	2	2	-	6	6	6	4
unsigned char	3	3	3	3	-	1	1	1
unsigned short	3	3	3	3	6	-	1	1
unsigned int	3	3	3	3	6	6	-	1
unsigned long	3	3	3	3	6	6	6	-

Table 12.1: Integral conversions.

The numbers in Table 12.1 refer to the following conversions:

1.   The value is unchanged.

2.   (*a signed type to a potentially smaller signed type*)
- If *new* and *old* are the same size, the value is unchanged.
- Otherwise, *new* is smaller than *old*:
  - If the value is within the range for *new*, the value is unchanged.
  - Otherwise, the result is implementation-defined. It is likely that bits at the more significant end will be truncated, but the Standard does not say that this is what happens; presumably the intention is that the implementation may provide a run-time error message.

  Example: Conversion of the value 65537, of type **long int**, to **int**. The implementation may give a run-time error, or it may, by truncating, give the value 1 of type **int**, or it may do anything it chooses. Consult your implementor's manual.

3.   (*unsigned to signed*)
- If *new* is larger than *old*, the value is unchanged.
- Otherwise:
  - If the value is within the range for *new*, the value is unchanged.
  - Otherwise, the result is implementation-defined, as in **2** above.

  Example: Conversion of the value 32769, of type **unsigned short int**, to **int**. Since we are assuming that **short int** and **int** are both 16 bits, with two's complement representation, the range of **unsigned short int** is 0 to 65535, and that of **int** is –32768 to 32767. The implementation may give a run-time error, or it may give the value –32767 of type **int**, or it may do anything else. Consult your implementor's manual.

4.   (*a signed type to the corresponding unsigned type*)
- If the value is non-negative, the value is unchanged.
- If the value is negative, the result is the original bit-pattern reinterpreted as an unsigned value.

  Example: Conversion of the value –2, of type **int**, to **unsigned int** gives 65534, since the bit-pattern is 11111111 11111110.

5.   (*a signed type to a potentially larger unsigned type*)
- If the value is non-negative, the value is unchanged.
- If the value is negative, the original value is "promoted" to the signed type which corresponds to the unsigned type *new* (i.e. if *new* is larger than *old*, additional 1 bits are generated at the more significant end), and then the result is the bit-pattern interpreted as an unsigned value, as in **4** above.

  Example: Conversion of the value –2, of type **signed char**, to **unsigned int**. The original representation, 11111110, is first promoted to type **int**, giving 11111111 11111110, which is then reinterpreted, as in **4** above, as 65534.

6. (*any integral type to a potentially smaller unsigned type*)
- If *new* and *old* are the same size, rule **4** above applies.
- Otherwise, *new* is smaller than *old*, and the result is the non-negative interpretation of the original bit-pattern, reduced to the size of *new* by truncation at the more significant end.

   Example: Conversion of the value –513, of type **int**, to **unsigned char** gives 255, since the representation of –513 is originally 11111101 11111111, which is truncated to 11111111 and interpreted as being unsigned.

Like most other languages, then, C ensures that wherever possible a value is unchanged when it is converted from one type to another. But how does a C program detect that the new value is different from the original? In other words, how does it detect that a conversion has "failed"? The answer is simple and astonishing - it can't. C has no equivalent of Cobol's **size error** clause. The conversion simply produces some other value, and the program continues to execute as though nothing untoward has happened. The Standard is unequivocal on this point in relation to conversion to unsigned types, but leaves it to the implementor to decide what to do when conversion to a signed type fails. Most implementors seem content to ignore the overflow and let the program proceed with the new value, giving no run-time indication.

Another aspect of these rules that may dismay a Cobol programmer is that the effect of a conversion often depends not just on the types involved, but also on their relative sizes, or equivalently their ranges. This means that a particular conversion may change the value in one implementation but leave it unchanged in another. Though you can still write a program in an implementation-independent way by testing against the values in <*limits.h*>, you will find it hard work after the simplicity of Cobol's **size error**.

But things aren't as bad as they seem. A clear message emerges from these conversion rules: *never use unsigned types*, unless it is absolutely necessary (and it rarely is necessary in application programming). The one exception is **unsigned char**, which would be troublesome only with an implementation in which **char** and **short int** were the same size. As long as you are able to work with integers in the range LONG_MIN through LONG_MAX, never even *consider* using unsigned types; unsigned data items are harmless in Cobol, but in C they can be lethal. If you use only the signed types, the integral conversions are straightforward, for only the top left-hand quarter of Table 12.1 is ever needed. (It is helpful in this connection that, unless the letter u is appended, an integer constant is always regarded as being signed, except when it exceeds LONG_MAX - see section 12.2.1.) The rule is then very simple and intuitive - the value is always unchanged *unless the new type is smaller than the old and the new type cannot represent the value*, in which case the result is implementation-defined.

12.4.2. Conversion between integral and floating types

When a value of a floating type is converted to an integral type, the fractional part is discarded. If the integral type cannot represent the integral part, the behaviour is undefined; this is true regardless of whether the integral type is signed or unsigned.

When a value of an integral type is converted to a floating type, there is no problem apart from a possible loss of precision of very large values.

12.4.3. Conversion between floating types

When a **float** is converted to **double** or to **long double**, or when a **double** is converted to **long double**, its value is unchanged.

When a **double** is converted to **float,** or when a **long double** is converted to **double** or to **float**, the value is unchanged except when:

- the value is outside the range representable by the new type. This situation results in undefined behaviour.
- the value is within the range, but cannot be represented exactly. This situation results in a less precise representation of the value.

12.5. Conversion contexts

12.5.1. Explicit conversion

A conversion may be explicitly invoked by a program. If an expression is preceded by a type name in parentheses, the value of the expression is converted to the named type, using the rules we have been looking at. For instance, in

> **(float)** 8

the type of the expression 8 is integer; because it is preceded by **(float)** - referred to as a *cast* - the type of the whole expression becomes **float**. Similarly, given the declaration

> **int** i = 8;

the value of the expression

> **(float)** (i+2)

is 10 and of type **float**.

12.5.2. Conversion in expressions

Most type conversion in C is implicit, and you need to be aware of how it is applied. Ex-Cobol programmers need to be particularly careful. Suppose that, in an implementation of Cobol, **comp-1** usage is equivalent to C's **float** type. Suppose also that we have these data descriptions:

> 01 i **pic** 9, **value** 3.
> 01 j **pic** 9v99, **value** 3.
> 01 k **comp-1**, **value** 3.

then every one of the ten expressions

> | | | |
> |---|---|---|
> | 3 / 2 | i / 2 | k / 2 |
> | 3 / 2.0 | i / 2.0 | k / 2.0 |
> | 3.0 / 2 | j / 2 | |
> | 3.0 / 2.0 | j / 2.0 | |

yields the "typeless" value 1.5. It is only when that value is *used*, for instance by assigning it to a variable, that the Cobol programmer needs to consider "type conversion". For example, if it were assigned to *i*, only the integral part would be retained.

Things are more complicated in C. Type conversion may occur at every step in the evaluation of an expression. Whenever an operator is applied to two operands, type conversion may occur. We will look at the detailed rules in a moment, but the general idea is that, if the operands are of different types, one of them is converted to the type of the other before the operator is applied to them. The common type of the operands is also the type of the result. Given the declarations

> **int** i = 3;
> **float** k = 3.0F;

Table 12.2 shows the types and values of the results of some of the expressions used in the Cobol example above. (Remember from section 12.2.2 that the constants 3.0 and 2.0 are of type **double**. Had the F been omitted from 3.0F in the declaration of *k*, it would have made no difference, since conversion to type **float** would be implied.) You will see that, when the operands are of types **int** and **double**, the **int** operand is converted to **double**; when they are of types **float** and **int**, the **int** operand is converted to **float**; and when they are of types **float** and **double**, the **float** operand is converted to **double**. Notice particularly that, if both operands are of type **int**, the result is of type **int**, giving the integer 1 (the dividend) as the value of the expressions 3/2 and *i*/2.

Expression	Operand types	Converted to	Result type	Value
3 / 2	int / int	-	int	1
i / 2	int / int	-	int	1
3.0 / 2.0	double/double	-	double	1.5
3.0 / 2	double/ int	double/double	double	1.5
3 / 2.0	int / double	double/double	double	1.5
i / 2.0	int / double	double/double	double	1.5
k / 2	float / int	float / float	float	1.5
k / 2.0	float / double	double/double	double	1.5

Table 12.2: Evaluation of some simple expressions.

Assuming again that Cobol's **comp-1** is equivalent to C's **float**, the Cobol code

```
01 i pic 9, value 3.
01 j pic 9, value 2.
01 e comp-1.
....
....
        compute  e = i / j * 2.6
```

assigns to *e* the value 3.9. Cobol's precedence and associativity rules make the **compute** statement equivalent to

```
compute  e = (i / j) * 2.6
```

and the expression on the right of the = will give the true arithmetic value. The programmer's only concern is whether that value can be assigned to the variable *e* without rounding or truncation. (In this case, it can.) In other words, "type conversion" is not an issue in the evaluation of an arithmetic expression; it becomes important only when the computed value of the expression is used.

Now let us look at how the C assignment expression below is evaluated:

```
int  i = 3;
int  j = 2;
float e;
....
....
e = i/j*2.6
```

Precedence and associativity are the same as in Cobol, so the sub-expression *i/j* is evaluated and multiplied by 2.6. Since *i* and *j* are both of type **int**, evaluation of *i/j* gives the value 1 of type **int**. The two operands of the * operator are thus of types **int** and **double**. So the **int** operand (1) is converted to **double** and multiplied by 2.6, giving the value 2.6 of type **double**. In simple assignments, the type of the expression on the right is converted to the type of the expression on the left, so the 2.6 is now converted to **float**, becoming the value of *e* and of the complete assignment expression - a result which a Cobol programmer would regard as bizarre.

To get the result (3.9) which the Cobol programmer would expect, *i* and *j* (or one of them) could be cast to type **double** (which would correspond to the type of the constant 2.6):

> e = (**double**) i / (**double**) j * 2.6

Notice that it would not be any good saying

> e = (**double**) (i/j) * 2.6

because the cast to **double** would be applied to an expression whose value is 1.

We now take a more detailed look at the rules for conversions within expressions, confining the discussion to the basic types and to these operators: unary + and -, and the binary (i.e. dyadic) arithmetic, relational and equality operators. Two concepts are involved.

1. *The integral promotions.* "Promotion" just means "upward conversion". These promotions are applied to the operands of the unary + and - operators, and may be applied also as part of the "usual arithmetic conversions" (see below). Assuming that **char** is smaller than **int**, the meaning of *integral promotion* is:

- If the operand is of type **char, signed char, unsigned char** or **short int**, it is converted to type **int**.
- If the operand is of type **unsigned short int**, then:
  - If **short int** is smaller than **int** in the implementation, the operand is converted to **int**.
  - Otherwise, the operand is converted to **unsigned int**.

(**unsigned char** would be treated in the same way as **unsigned short int** if **char** were the same size as **int** in the implementation.) For instance, if *c* is of type **signed char**, the expression

> - c

is evaluated like this: the value of *c* is first converted to **int**, and then negated, giving a result of type **int**. Remember that a character *constant*, like 'A', requires no conversion; it is already of type **int**. The integral promotions always preserve the original value.

2. *The usual arithmetic conversions.* These are applied in the case of binary operators. The object is to make both operands the same type before applying the operator, which then produces a result of that type if the operator is an arithmetic operator. Relational and equality operators give a result of type **int** (0 for false, 1 for true). Given this approach, the conversions are what you would intuitively expect. The Standard describes the *usual arithmetic conversions* with admirable lucidity:

- "First, if either operand has type **long double**, the other operand is converted to **long double**.
- Otherwise, if either operand has type **double**, the other operand is converted to **double**.
- Otherwise, if either operand has type **float**, the other operand is converted to **float.**
- Otherwise, *the integral promotions are performed on both operands.* Then the following rules are applied:

  - If either operand has type **unsigned long int**, the other operand is converted to **unsigned long int**.
  - Otherwise, if one operand has type **long int** and the other has type **unsigned int**, if a **long int** can represent all values of an **unsigned int**, the operand of type **unsigned int** is converted to **long int**; if a **long int** cannot represent all the values of an **unsigned int**, both operands are converted to **unsigned long int**.
  - Otherwise, if either operand has type **long int**, the other operand is converted to **long int**.
  - Otherwise, if either operand has type **unsigned int**, the other operand is converted to **unsigned int**.
  - Otherwise, both operands have type **int**".

Take, for example:

> **char** c;
> **double** d;
> **float** f;
> ....
> .... c * 2 > d + f ....

In the evaluation of c * 2, integral promotion is applied to c's value, making it of type **int**; both operands then have type **int**, as has the result of the multiplication. In evaluation of d + f, the value of the **float** operand (f) is converted to **double**, and the addition produces a result having type **double**. The two operands of the > operator thus have types **int** and **double**, so the **int** value is converted to **double**; the result of the comparison is of type **int**.

The conversion rules appear more complex than they are because of the rules about unsigned types. Otherwise they are straightforward. If you avoid unsigned types, you will rarely have any trouble.

The "integral promotions" and the "usual arithmetic conversions" do *not* apply to the simple assignment operator (=). Here the rule is the same as in Cobol - the value of the expression on the right is converted to the type of the assignment expression. Thus, in the unlikely event of the value of the above expression being assigned to f:

> f = c * 2 > d + f

the **int** value produced by the expression on the right would be converted to **float** and become the new value of f. As far as type conversion is concerned, an assignment expression like

> f *= 5

is treated in the same way as

> f = f * 5

12.5.3. Conversion of function arguments

For historical reasons, there is a strange anomaly in C. If you try to use a variable identifier in a program context where no declaration of the identifier is visible, your compiler will give you an appropriate error message. But if you try to call a function in a context where no declaration of the function is visible, the compiler will (and the Standard says it *should*) treat it as a function returning **int** and will perform certain default conversions on the arguments. If you do such a thing by mistake, you can only hope that the error will become obvious at run time (or, if you have a kind compiler, at compile time); if you do it deliberately, you deserve everything that happens to you. This book assumes that you are acting sensibly.

The function declarations we have used so far specify the type of each parameter. When a function with such a declaration is called, *the value of each argument is converted to the type of the corresponding parameter as though by assignment.* Given the declaration

> **void** f (**int** i);

the call

> f (1.5)

is equivalent to the call f *(1)*, since the argument 1.5, of type **double**, is converted to type **int**.

You may have wondered how a function like **printf** could be declared; the number of arguments is variable, and different calls of the function may have arguments of different types. We will see later how such functions are defined, but one thing is clear - the declaration cannot specify a parameter with a fixed type for every argument. With such functions - functions with a variable number of arguments - some of the arguments will have no corresponding parameters and thus no type information will be available for the conversion. These arguments have the *default argument promotions* applied to them. This means that "the integral promotions are performed on each argument and arguments that have type **float** are promoted to **double**". We will return to this topic in chapter 13.

12.6. Summary

This chapter has been the least pleasant to write and no doubt the least pleasant to read. But type conversion is important; you have to know about it. In practice, it gives remarkably little trouble if you remember that:

- unsigned types are best avoided whenever possible;
- unless it is implied by an assignment operation, *implicit* type conversion between signed integral types or between floating types never changes the value;
- character constants are of type **int**;
- floating constants are by default of type **double**.

13
Other Features

This chapter describes some features of C which have not been explored in earlier chapters. In some cases, the feature has already been introduced but is now described in more detail.

13.1. Functions with variable numbers of arguments

Every function definition we have looked at so far is such that the function is called with a fixed number of arguments, and each argument corresponds to a parameter with a specified type. But, as was observed in chapter 12, we have been using library functions like **printf** for which each call may have a different number of arguments; and, even if the number is the same, we can have two calls like these:

> **printf** ("%d", i)
> **printf** ("%s", s)

where the second argument is expected to be an integral expression in the first call and an expression of type **char*** in the second. On any call, the **printf** function can use the value of its first argument to determine how many other arguments there should be and what their types are. This section describes how such functions are defined.

As an illustration, let us define a function *mean* whose return value, of type **double**, will be the average of the values of its arguments (also of type **double**), excluding the first. The first argument, of type **int**, is a count of how many other arguments follow it. For example, the call

> mean (3, 1.5, 3.8, 4.6)

will return 3.3. Another possible call is

> mean (0)

which we will define as returning zero. A prototype declaration of the function is

> **double** mean (**int** arg_count, **...**);

The ellipsis (the three dots) at the end of the parameter list indicates that a variable number of arguments, of unknown types, may follow the first argument. There must be at least one parameter before the ellipsis.

In order to use the facilities described here, we must specify:

> #include <stdarg.h>

The standard header *<stdarg.h>* defines three macros - **va_start**, **va_arg** and **va_end** - and declares a special type, **va_list**, which is used by these macros. What the function *mean* must do in order to access its arguments is:

1. Declare a variable of type **va_list**, as in

    va_list arg;

2. Call the macro **va_start**, using that variable as its first argument, and, as its second argument, the name of the parameter of *mean* immediately preceding the ellipsis:

    va_start (arg, arg_count)

3. Access each argument of *mean* in turn by repeatedly calling **va_arg** like this:

    va_arg (arg, **double**)

    The second argument of **va_arg** specifies the type of value which **va_arg** itself will return, and may be different on each call of **va_arg**. (You can see how useful this is in defining a function like **printf**; you can also see why **va_arg** is defined as a macro, not a function.) The first time we call **va_arg** after **va_start**, it returns the value of the argument of *mean* which immediately follows *arg_count*. Each subsequent call of **va_arg** (with an appropriate type name as its second argument) returns the value of the next argument of *mean* in sequence, in much the same way as successive **read** statements in Cobol sequential access read successive records from a file.

    Because of the way the macro works, the type specified as the second argument of **va_arg** is limited. It must be a type name to which a * can be applied to make it into a pointer to an object of that type. For example, **char** [ ] could not be specified, since **char** [ ] * would not be a pointer to a character array. But **int** would be acceptable, since **int*** is a pointer to an **int** object; so would **char***, since **char**** is a pointer to an object of type **char***.

4. Finally, to avoid later undefined behaviour, call **va_end**:

    va_end (arg)

Assuming inclusion of *<stdarg.h>*, the definition of *mean* could therefore be:

```
double  mean (int arg_count, ... )
{
    va_list  arg;
    double  total;
    int  i;
```

```
                 if (arg_count <= 0)  return 0;
                 else  {
                       va_start (arg, arg_count);
                       for (i=0, total=0;  i < arg_count;  i++)
                             total += va_arg (arg, double);
                       va_end (arg);
                       return  total / arg_count;
                 }
           }
```

There is one nasty trap associated with variable numbers of arguments. The call

　　　mean (2.0, 5.6, 4.0)

will correctly return the value 4.8 because, you will remember, an argument value is converted to the type of the corresponding parameter "as if by assignment". The first argument, being a floating constant, is of type **double**, and the first parameter is of type **int**. The argument 2.0 therefore becomes integer 2 (as would also, for instance, the argument 2.95). But when the call is

　　　mean (2, 5.6, 4)

things are very different. Though the call of **va_arg** in *mean* specifies type **double**, the value of the last argument (4), which is of type **int**, is *not* converted to **double**. Any argument which corresponds to the ellipsis in the parameter list has only the *default argument promotions* applied (see section 12.5.3). There is therefore no conversion from **int** to **double**, so the type of the argument is incompatible with the type specified in the call of **va_arg**; the Standard says that this situation causes undefined behaviour.

I tried this using an implementation which I called from Microsoft Windows on a PC. The resulting message was dramatic:

> *"This application has violated system integrity due to an invalid general protection fault and will be terminated.*
>
> *Quit all applications, quit Windows, and then restart your computer"*

And it wasn't kidding. The C environment couldn't be reentered until the whole system was restarted. This may seem a rather extreme reaction to a simple type-matching failure, but you've probably run enough C programs by now not to be surprised by it. Just imagine the fun you'd have trying to locate the fault in a large program! For further fun, try accessing an argument that is not present.

In a function declaration, the ellipsis, if present, must be the last thing in the parameter list, but more than one parameter may precede the ellipsis. Suppose that our *mean* function additionally prints a string, which is supplied as an additional (first) parameter. The function definition now begins

> **double** mean (**char*** ptext, **int** arg_count, **...**)

and is unchanged except that a line

> **printf** ("%s\n", ptext);

is added before the **if** statement.

Finally, recall the *max_of_3* function in section 3.5. A more useful function would be one that returned the maximum value from a variable number of integer expressions. Assume for simplicity that there will be at least one such expression. The first argument is an integer expression whose value is the number of arguments following it; for example, the call

> max (3, –5, –20, 2)

would return 2. (The first argument, 3, says how many arguments follow it.) The function may be defined as below. Remember that, as well as *<stdarg.h>*, the headers *<limits.h>* and *<assert.h>* must be included, because INT_MIN and **assert** are used.

```
int  max (int argc, ... )
{
      va_list  argp;
      int  highest, i, val;

      assert (argc > 0);
      va_start (argp, argc);
      for (i=0, highest = INT_MIN;  i < argc;  i++)
            if ( (val = va_arg (argp, int)) > highest)
                  highest = val;
      va_end (argp);
      return highest;
}
```

13.2. The function *main*

So far, we have treated the function *main* as a special case. The time has come to explain what is "special" about it. One thing you may have thought was special is that we have never declared a return type for *main*. In fact, we can omit the return type in the declaration of *any* function, and the default return type **int** will be assumed. The prototype

> widget (**double**);

is equivalent to

> **int** widget (**double**);

but this temptation to sloppiness is not to be dwelt upon. So *main* returns an **int**. This is why you were advised in section 2.6 to insert the statement

> **return** 0;

at the end of *main* in every program. Remember that *main* is called from the outside environment (usually the operating system) and that it is to that environment that it returns. A return value of zero indicates successful program completion. Any other return value indicates unsuccessful completion of some implementation-defined kind.

So far, we have always declared *main* as having no parameters, by saying

> main (**void**)

Alternatively, *main* may be declared as having parameters. Quite often, we want to execute a program, giving it a number of arguments.

Most programmers will be familiar with operating system command lines in which the name of a program to be run is accompanied by arguments to the program. Suppose that the action of a program named *profile* is to provide details of named persons. The program may be called by a command line like

> profile Mannock Westerdale

In a C development environment, the arguments (the names *Mannock* and *Westerdale*) may be supplied to the program through a "Run Arguments" dialogue box. Alternatively, the operating system may provide a mechanism by which other application programs may call a C program, passing values to it. Regardless of the origin of its call and of how its arguments are provided, the C program will be identified by a file name and its execution will mean execution of its *main* function. (In Cobol, the equivalent is entry to the first paragraph of the procedure division.) The function *main* must be able to access a variable number of program arguments, each of which is a character string. How does it do so?

The method is more flexible and more complex than that provided by the **using** clause in a Cobol procedure division heading. In a C program which may be supplied with arguments at run time, *main* is declared as having two parameters. The parameters, being of course local to *main*, may be given any names you choose, but most programmers follow tradition (and the Standard) by naming them *argc* and *argv*. The declaration of *main* in this case is

> main (**int** argc, **char*** argv [ ])

and it is the responsibility of the system software and the compiler to ensure that the arguments are supplied in the appropriate form. *argv* is an array of pointers to strings, and *argc* is the number of pointers in the array. The string pointed to by *argv [0]* is the program name, and (if the value of *argc* is greater than 1) the strings pointed to by *argv [1]* through *argv [argc − 1]* are the program arguments. Thus, when *main* starts executing in our *profile* example, the value of *argc* is 3, and the elements of *argv* point to strings:

> *argv* [0] points to the string "profile"
> *argv* [1] points to the string "Mannock"
> *argv* [2] points to the string "Westerdale"

Here is a simple program which prints its arguments in reverse order:

```
#include <stdio.h>
main (int argc,  char* argv [])
{     int  i;
      for (i = argc - 1;  i > 0;  i--)
            printf ("%s\n", argv [i]);
      return 0;
}
```

A common use of program arguments is to specify the files to be used by a program. Look again at the *copyfile* functions defined variously in section 5.8.1. The controlling program shown at the start of that section obtained the names of the source and destination files by conducting a dialogue with the user. Now let us assume instead that the program is named *copyf* and that its execution is initiated by the command line

>   copyf f1 f2

where *f1* and *f2* are the names of the source file and the destination file respectively. In *copyf*, *main* could be defined thus:

```
main (int argc,  char* argv [ ])
{
      int  copyfile (const char* to,  const char* from);

      if (argc != 3)
            fputs ("Two file names needed\n", stdout);
      else {
            switch (copyfile (argv[2], argv[1])) {
            case 0:    fputs ("Copied successfully\n", stdout);  break;
            case 1:    fputs ("Source file cannot be opened\n", stdout);  break;
            case 2:    fputs ("Destination file cannot be opened\n", stdout);
                       break;
            }
      }
      return 0;
}
```

13.3. Disablement of assertions

You will remember from section 3.7 that the call

>   assert (a < b)

would, in the event of $a < b$ being false, cause execution to be aborted and an error message to be sent to **stderr**. It was suggested that **assert** might be used in debugging and also to trap those extreme types of errors that would be unlikely to arise in normal circumstances.

The effect of placing the line

> #define NDEBUG

(note that there is no 'O' after the 'N') anywhere before the

> #include <assert.h>

line is that any **assert** calls following are disabled;   the expression acting as the argument of **assert** is not evaluated. (The NDEBUG definition actually results in every assertion being replaced by ((**void**) 0).) Note carefully that this effect is obtained only if NDEBUG is defined at the point where *<assert.h>* is *include*d.   Later definitions of NDEBUG or occurrences of

> #undef NDEBUG

make no difference at all.   NDEBUG cannot therefore be used to enable or disable selected assertions; it's all or nothing.

The intention is, of course, that assertions used for debugging can be disabled when the program is used in production by adding a simple definition at the start of the program; the definition can be removed if the program is later amended and is to be tested again. This is much easier than removing all the individual assertions and putting them all back later for further testing. However, if you use assertions for purposes other than debugging (and it is arguably good practice to do so), the NDEBUG facility is of little value.

If you are misguided enough to put an expression with side-effects in an assertion, remember that the side-effects will not take place when the assertion is disabled, because then the expression will not be evaluated. The expression

> **assert** (++i < 6)

makes sense only if the variable i is used solely for debugging purposes.

13.4. Enumerated types

We have seen a use of enumeration in section 7.2, where

> **enum** {
>   maxline = 25, maxinline = 81
> };

was used as a means of defining integer constants. Indeed, you are unlikely to find many other uses. In general, the = may be followed by an integral constant expression which has a value representable as an **int**. The effect is that each identifier inside the brackets (i.e. each *member* of the enumeration) is declared as a constant of type **int** and may be used wherever such a constant is permitted. The = and the constant expression may be omitted; in the case of the first identifier listed, the implied value is zero; in the case of any other identifier, the implied value is one greater than that of the immediately preceding identifier. For example

```
enum {
        a, b, c=5, d=9, e, f=5, g
};
```

is equivalent to

```
enum {
        a=0, b=1, c=5, d=9, e=10, f=5, g=6
};
```

You may have noticed the syntactic similarity between an **enum** and a **struct**. Like a **struct**, an **enum** may have a tag:

```
enum team {
        Aberdeen, Celtic, Dundee, Rangers
};
```

in which case a type, **enum** *team*, is declared; or an **enum** may be the subject of a **typedef**:

```
typedef enum {
        Aberdeen, Celtic, Dundee, Rangers
} Team;
```

In either case, Aberdeen is 0, Celtic is 1, Dundee is 2, and Rangers is 3. The declaration

```
typedef enum {
        red, yellow, blue
} Colour;
```

defines another type. With these declarations, we are not really concerned with the integer values; we simply want each listed identifier in a given enumeration to have a distinct value. Variables of these types may be declared, with or without initialization, and may be used in the ways you would expect:

```
Colour shirt_colour;
Team cup_winner = Rangers;
Team* leader;
....
....
....
```

```
        cup_winner = Aberdeen;
        if (shirt_colour == red) ....
        ....
        leader = &cup_winner;
```

Team and *Colour* are different enumerated types. Enumerated types are integral, like **char** and the integer types. The choice of the integer type corresponding to an enumerated type is left to the implementor.

C's enumerated types resemble those of Pascal, but lack the strong typing and the accessory functions of the latter. Since a member of an enumeration may be used anywhere as an integer constant, it is valid to say

```
        cup_winner = yellow;
        shirt_colour = Dundee;
```

The variables *cup_winner* and *shirt_colour* are of different types. Since both are integral, and thus arithmetic, types, the Standard appears to permit inter-type arithmetic and assignment; but your compiler may give you a warning. Do you really need to do such things anyway?

13.5. Pointers to functions

Before reading the rest of this section, ensure that you understand the following declarations. The first four introduce nothing new, but the last two may puzzle you. Don't worry about why the syntax of these two is so unnatural; just memorize it so that you can use it.

Declaration	*Type*
int i;	*i* is **int**
int* p;	*p* is pointer to **int**
int fi (**int**);	*fi* is function returning **int** and taking one **int** argument
int* fp (**int**);	*fp* is function returning pointer to **int** and taking one **int** argument
int (* pf) (**int**);	*pf* is pointer to function returning **int** and taking one **int** argument
char* (* cpf) (**int**);	*cpf* is pointer to function returning pointer to **char** and taking one **int** argument

In most contexts, the name of a function, like the name of an array, is treated as a fixed pointer to the function. (Naturally, a new value cannot be assigned to it.) The resulting mess is even worse than in the case of arrays, and the appalling syntax doesn't help. The explanation you are about to read is as lucid as I can make it.

The name of a function is the most obvious example of a *function designator*, which the Standard defines as "an expression that has function type". The Standard goes on:

"Except when it is the operand of the **sizeof** operator or the unary **&** operator, a function designator with type 'function returning *type*' is converted to an expression that has the type 'pointer to function returning *type*'." It also states that the **sizeof** operator cannot be applied to a function designator.

Applied to a function designator, the **&** operator yields a pointer to the function. Applied to a pointer to a function, the * operator yields a function designator.

These rules have interesting consequences. Given the declarations

> **int** (*fun) (**void**);   /* *fun* is pointer to function returning **int** */
> **int** getno (**void**);   /* *getno* is designator of function returning **int** */

fun can be made to point to *getno* by any one of the following assignments (listed in increasing order of eccentricity):

fun = &getno	normal application of **&** (*getno* is *not* converted to pointer before **&** is applied)
fun = getno	function designator *getno* is converted to pointer
fun = *getno	*getno* is converted to pointer; * converts pointer into function designator; function designator is converted to pointer
fun = **getno	as previous example, followed by further conversion to function designator and back to pointer

The result will be the same no matter how many *s precede the identifier *getno*.

In a function call, the expression preceding the parentheses is of a "pointer to function" type. When we call a function, *f*, the name *f* is, as usual, converted to a pointer; so any expression yielding a pointer to *f* may be used in place of the name *f*. Following on from the above example, after the pointer value has been assigned to *fun*, the function *getno* may be called by any one of the following expressions:

> getno ( )
> (*fun) ( )
> fun ( )
> (&getno) ( )
> (*getno) ( )
> (**getno) ( )
> (**fun) ( )

and so on. The parenthesization is necessary because the argument parentheses (at the end of each expression) have higher precedence than the * and **&** operators. For instance, if the second example were written as

> * fun ( )

the expression would mean "the thing pointed to by the integer returned by *fun*".

Up to now, you may have found this section amusing, annoying, or just uninteresting, but it all makes good practical sense. The really important message is that the only differences between a function name and a pointer to a function relate to the **sizeof** and **&** operators. Otherwise they can be used interchangeably.

Now let us look at the use of function pointers as function arguments. Suppose that a structure type, *Symptoms*, contains a patient's medical symptoms, and the symptoms of particular patients may be stored in *Symptoms* variables *s1* and *s2*:

```
typedef struct {
        ....  ....
        ....  ....
} Symptoms;
Symptoms  s1, s2;
```

Dr. Dobbs, Dr. Kildare and Dr. Finlay all have their own methods of diagnosing from a set of symptoms. Their methods are embodied in three functions, each returning a character string representing a diagnosis. The prototypes of these functions are

```
char*  dobbs (Symptoms);
char*  kildare (Symptoms);
char*  finlay (Symptoms);
```

Part of a program may print the details from *s1*, and then print a diagnosis using the second doctor's method by the statement

```
printf ("Diagnosis:  %s\n", kildare (s1) );
```

This is just a normal use of **printf**: the second argument is evaluated in the usual way. But a pointer to a function *f* can be passed as an argument to function *g*, so that *g* itself can call *f*. This gives us a means of telling a function at call time how it is to do part of its computation. We may define a function which prints details of a patient's symptoms together with a diagnosis:

```
void patient_print (Symptoms s;  char* doctor (Symptoms));
{
        ....  ....      /* print details from s  */
        printf ("Diagnosis:  %s\n", doctor (s) );
        ....  ....
}
```

The declaration line specifies two parameters: *s* is an object of type *Symptoms*, and *doctor* is of type "pointer to a function returning a pointer to **char** and taking an object of type *Symptoms* as its single argument". Thus the type of the parameter *doctor* matches those of the functions *dobbs, kildare* and *finlay*. To print the details of the patient represented in *s1*, along with the patient's diagnosis using Dr. Finlay's method, the above function would be called by the statement

```
patient_print (s1, finlay);
```

Subject to the limitations noted earlier, pointers to functions of various types may be used in the same way as other pointers. We might, for instance, say

> **char*** (* pd) (Symptoms);

which declares *pd* to be a variable of type "pointer to a function which returns pointer to **char** and takes one argument of type *Symptoms*". We could then assign to that variable a pointer to the function *dobbs*:

> pd = dobbs

Another thing we might do is declare and initialize an array of such pointers:

> **char*** (* method [3]) (Symptoms) = {dobbs, kildare, finlay};

after which we might call our *patient_print* function by

> patient_print (s2, method[1]);

which would be equivalent to

> patient_print (s2, kildare);

We will see further uses of function pointers as arguments in the next two sections.

13.6. Sorting

In Cobol, the **sort** statement sorts a collection of records, usually the contents of one or more files; conceptually, it is an *external* sort, suitable for sorting large numbers of records into a specified sequence. The **qsort** function in C is quite different; all it can sort is the elements of an array, though these elements can of course be arbitrarily complex records (**struct**s); the sort is carried out in main store. To use **qsort**, you need

> #include <stdlib.h>

In Cobol, the records may be sorted on several ordered keys, and **ascending** or **descending** may be specified for each key. In C, sorting is always in ascending order (but, as we'll see soon, we can easily obtain descending order), and the whole business of key precedence has to be taken care of by a user-written function.

In order to use **qsort** on an array of objects of type *t*, we must supply a function which compares the values of two objects of type *t*. The function must take two arguments, both of type **const void***, which point to the objects to be compared. It must return an integer which is negative, zero or positive, to indicate whether the value of the first object is less than, equal to or greater than that of the second. A function to compare two integers might be written as:

```
int icomp (const void* v1, const void* v2)
{
        const int* i1 = v1;
        const int* i2 = v2;
        return *i1 < *i2 ? -1 : (*i1 == *i2 ? 0 : 1);
}
```

(A less secure version would just return the value of *i1* - *i2*.) A function to compare two strings is a little more interesting - remember that the value of a string variable is a pointer to the string, and that an array of strings is an array of pointers to strings. Conveniently, the **strcmp** function returns just the values we want, so the function could be:

```
int scomp (const void* v1, const void* v2)
{
        const char** c1 = v1;
        const char** c2 = v2;
        return strcmp (*c1, *c2);
}
```

Given a pointer to a function such as these, **qsort** sorts the array into ascending order. Now suppose we want to have an array of integers sorted instead into descending order - all we have to do is ensure that the function returns a positive value instead of a negative, and a negative value instead of a positive. With the above definition of *icomp*, we can provide this function for a descending sort (note the minus sign preceding *icomp*):

```
int descicomp (const void* v1, const void* v2)
{       return - icomp (v1, v2); }
```

The function **qsort** returns **void** and takes as its arguments:

1. A pointer to the initial element of the array, or part of the array, to be sorted (commonly just the array name).
2. The number of elements.
3. The size of each element.
4. A pointer to a function such as one of the three functions defined above.

We might use **qsort** to sort the members of an array of integers (*ia*) into ascending order:

```
int ia [IA_SIZE];
....

....
qsort (ia, IA_SIZE, sizeof (int), icomp);
```

or to sort an array of string pointers into ascending order (the ordering being based on the values of the strings, not of the pointers):

char* sa [SA_SIZE];
....

....

qsort (sa, SA_SIZE, **sizeof** (**char***), scomp);

Now consider a structure containing details of the performance of a football team:

typedef struct {
    char* name;
    int points;
    int goals_for;
    int goals_against;
} Team_record;

One team is above another in the league table if:

- it has a greater number of points.
- the teams have the same number of points, and it has more *goals_for*.
- the teams are equal on points and *goals_for*, and it has fewer *goals_against*.
- the teams are equal on points, *goals_for* and *goals_against*, and its name comes before the other's in alphabetical sequence. (No two teams have the same name.)

In Cobol terms, the ordering of a league table would involve just a **sort** statement using **descending** points, **descending** *goals_for*, **ascending** *goals_against*, and **ascending** *name*, in that order. In C, we have to provide a function which determines, for any two teams, which comes before the other. Given such a function, *tcomp*, we can sort an array of team records into league table order by:

Team_record ta [LEAGUE_SIZE];
....

....

qsort (ta, LEAGUE_SIZE, **sizeof** (Team_record), tcomp);

and the function *tcomp* could be defined in terms of our earlier function *icomp*:

int tcomp (**const void*** v1, **const void*** v2)
{
    int b;
    const Team_record* t1 = v1;
    const Team_record* t2 = v2;

    if ((b = icomp (&(t1->points), &(t2->points))) != 0)
        return –b;
    if ((b = icomp (&(t1->goals_for), &(t2->goals_for))) != 0)
        return –b;

```
        if ( (b = icomp ( &(t1->goals_against), &(t2->goals_against) ) ) != 0)
            return b;
        return strcmp (t1->name, t2->name);
    }
```

13.7. Searching

Cobol's **search all** statement searches an array for an element containing a specified key value. If it is to work correctly, the members must be stored in ascending order of key value; a binary search is probably used (the Cobol Standard says coyly that "a non-serial type of search operation may take place"). In the same way, C's **bsearch** function will probably use a binary search; it too expects the array to be ordered. To use **bsearch**, you need

        #include <stdlib.h>

Like **qsort**, **bsearch** must be given a comparison function. A comparison function for use with **bsearch** takes the same type of arguments and returns the same kind of value as one for use with **qsort** - indeed, for a given array, the same function is often used for both purposes.

Here is an example of the use of **bsearch** to set *p* pointing to an element whose value is 5 in an array of integers ordered on ascending value. **bsearch** returns a pointer to the element found; if no appropriate element is found, the **NULL** pointer value is returned. If several elements have the same value, a pointer to one of them is returned; precisely which one is indeterminate.

        int ia [IA_SIZE];
        int k = 5;
        int* p;
        ....
        ....
        p = bsearch (&k, ia, IA_SIZE, sizeof (int), icomp);

The arguments of **bsearch** are: a pointer to the value to be found (*&k*), a pointer to the first element of the array (*ia*), the number of elements (IA_SIZE), the size of one element (**sizeof** (**int**)), and a pointer to the comparison function (*icomp* - as defined in section 13.6).

For another example, suppose that the array *lt* contains a football league table, ordered as described in section 13.6. The only component of the *Team_record* structure on which the complete table is ordered is, of course, *points*; we can therefore use **bsearch** to find a team with a given number of points, but not, for instance, a team with a given number of *goals_for*. The following prints the name of a team which has 44 points. (The function *descicomp* is defined in section 13.6.)

```
Team_record  lt[LT_SIZE];
int  pcomp (const void* v1, const void* v2)
{
        const Team_record*  t2 = v2;
        return descicomp (v1, &(t2->points) );
}
/* USE: */
int  p = 44;
Team_record* ltp;
....
if ((ltp = bsearch(&p, lt, LT_SIZE, sizeof (Team_record), pcomp)) == NULL)
        printf ("No team has 44 points\n");
else  printf ("%s\n", ltp->name);
....
```

As with Cobol's **search all**, we would normally use **bsearch** on an array in which at most one element would match the value sought. The elements of the array would typically be records (**struct**s) in which one of the members acted as a unique identifying key. Typically, the search would find the record in order that other components might be amended or retrieved.

13.8. Date and time

Cobol's **accept** statement can be used to obtain the current date, day number, time or day of the week. C's facilities for dealing with dates and times are more complex and much more flexible than Cobol's. To use them, include the line

        #include <time.h>

If all you want to do is print the current date and time, and you are not too fussy about format, you can do so by declaring a variable (say *t*) of type **time_t** (**time_t** is defined in *<time.h>*):

        time_t t;

then, to print, use the statements

        t = **time** (**NULL**);
        printf ("%s", **ctime** (&t));

This will print a string of this kind:

        Wed Mar 02 16:32:09 1994

followed by a new-line character.

Date and time together are referred to as *calendar time*. Two different representations of calendar time are defined as types in *<time.h>*. One is **time_t**, which is an arithmetic type, generally of little use in its raw state, and the other is a structure type,

struct tm, which contains the components listed below. The values shown beside them are those corresponding to the above date and time:

int tm_year	94	(year less 1900)
int tm_mon	2	(0=January, 1=February, etc.)
int tm_mday	2	(day in month)
int tm_hour	16	(range 0 thru 23)
int tm_min	32	(range 0 thru 59)
int tm_sec	9	(range 0 thru 61. This is correct!)
int tm_wday	3	(0=Sunday, 1=Monday, etc.)
int tm_yday	60	(Days since 1 January)
int tm_isdst	0	(Daylight saving time. 0 = no; positive = yes; negative = don't know)

A variable of type **struct tm**, and its members, may be used by a program in any of the ways that variables of other **struct** types and their members may be used. You may, indeed, feel that if you have the current date available in this form, you can do all you want to do with it without recourse to any further standard conversion functions. The following diagram shows the standard functions declared in *<time.h>*:

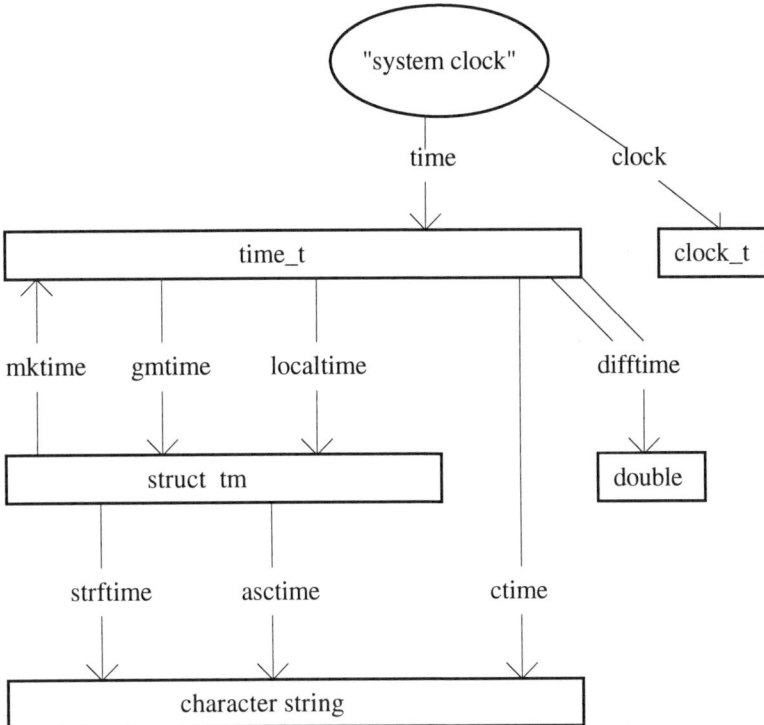

To obtain the current calendar time, the function **time** is called. It returns a value of type **time_t**, and takes one argument, of type **time_t***; if this pointer argument is not null, then the return value is also assigned to the object it points to. Commonly, a program will immediately convert the value returned by **time** into either a character string or a *broken-down time* value (i.e. a **struct tm** value). In the diagram the types are shown as boxes, and the names of standard functions appear on the arrows. For example, the standard function **gmtime** converts a value of type **time_t** to type **struct tm**, as does the standard function **localtime**.

Take care in using these functions - most of them receive or return *pointers to* the indicated types.

Here is a summary of what some of these functions do. Each description is headed by the declaration of the function as it appears in *<time.h>*.

clock_t clock (void);
> Returns the processor time used by the program since its invocation. To measure the time spent in a program, the function should be called at the start of the program and its return value subtracted from the values returned by subsequent calls. The arithmetic type **clock_t** is defined in *<time.h>*, as is the macro **CLOCKS_PER_SEC**, the value by which a **clock_t** value should be divided to determine the value in seconds.

double difftime (time_t time1, **time_t** time0);
> Returns the difference *time1 – time0*, expressed as a number of seconds.

struct tm* localtime (const time_t* timer);
> Converts the calendar time pointed to by *timer* into a broken-down time, expressed as local time. Returns a pointer to the broken-down time.

struct tm* gmtime (const time_t* timer);
> Converts the calendar time pointed to by *timer* into a broken-down time, expressed as Co-ordinated Universal Time (UTC). (Correct action by this function will depend on your system being set up correctly.) Returns a pointer to the broken-down time, or, if UTC is not available, returns a null pointer.

char* ctime (const time_t* timer);
> Converts the calendar time pointed to by *timer* to local time in the form of a string. The string has the format shown at the start of this section. The various elements in the string are all of fixed size - the weekday and the month are always 3 characters, the day within month always 2 characters, etc. Single spaces separate the elements. You can therefore rely on finding the same element in precisely the same position in the string. Returns a pointer to the string. Is equivalent to
>
> > **asctime (localtime** (timer))

char* asctime (const struct tm* timeptr);
> Converts the broken-down time in the structure pointed to by *timeptr* into a string in the same form as that produced by **ctime**. Returns a pointer to the string.

The two remaining functions, **strftime** and **mktime**, are more complex. **strftime** is similar to **sprintf** - under control of a format string, it generates a string of characters in an array, with the % symbol denoting insertion of values. With **strftime**, the inserted values are those of selected parts of a broken-down time. Here is a simple example which, for instance, on a Tuesday in March, will place in array *c* the string "Today is Tuesday and the month is March":

> **time_t** t;
> **char** c [S_C];
> ....
> **time**(&t);
> **strftime** (c, S_C – 1, "Today is %A and the month is %B", **localtime** (&t));

(The form of the **time** call is different here, but equivalent in effect to the one used before.) The first argument of **strftime** is a **char** array pointer, the second is the maximum number of characters (excluding the terminating null) to be put in the array, the third is the format string, and the fourth is a pointer to an object of type **struct tm** (which is what **localtime** returns). **strftime** returns the number of characters placed in the array; if more than the specified maximum are generated, it returns 0 and the array content is indeterminate. The full list of insertion symbols is:

%a	locale's abbreviated weekday name (see section 13.16 for *locale*)
%A	locale's full weekday name
%b	locale's abbreviated month name
%B	locale's full month name
%c	locale's date and time representation (probably as with *ctime*)
%d	day of month (01 - 31)
%H	24-hour clock hour (00-23)
%I	12-hour clock hour (01-12)
%j	day of year (001-366)
%m	month (01-12)
%M	minute (00-59)
%p	AM or PM (or locale's equivalent)
%S	second (00-61)
%U	week number (00-53): first Sunday of year is first day of week 1
%w	weekday (0-6): Sunday is 0
%W	week number (00-53): first Monday of year is first day of week 1
%x	locale's date representation
%X	locale's time representation
%y	year without century prefix (00-99)
%Y	year with century prefix (e.g. 1994)
%Z	time zone name, if available; otherwise, no characters
%%	%

The function **mktime** takes one argument, of type **struct tm***, converts the calendar time to type **time_t**, and returns the converted value (or –1 if the value cannot be represented), thus:

```
time_t t;
struct tm  tm1, tm2;
....
t = mktime (&tm1);
```

Such conversion can be useful in enabling a program to use **difftime** on calendar times originally represented as broken-down times, as in

difftime (mktime(&tm1), **mktime**(&tm2))

but **mktime** has another interesting use. As well as converting to type **time_t**, it "regularizes" the values in the broken-down time structure pointed to by its argument. If, for instance, we add 32 to **tm_day** in the structure *tm1*, and *tm1*'s contents previously represented a time on 3rd March, they will now represent the same time on 35th March. But if we now say

mktime (&tm1)

the date represented in *tm1* will be 4th April and the values of *tm1.tm_wday* and *tm1.tm_yday* will be suitably adjusted. This is a valuable feature, enabling a program to compute easily the calendar time corresponding to a specified interval before or after a given calendar time.

13.9. Wide characters

The type **char** is inexorably bound up with the idea of a *byte*. Almost invariably, the size of a **char** is 8 bits, giving 256 distinct character values.   But there are environments, notably those involving Asian languages, where more than 256 distinct characters have to be represented. The C Standard provides a special type for such environments - the type **wchar_t**, which is defined in <*stddef.h*> and also in <*stdlib.h*>. Where an implementor realistically supports this type (rather than just mapping it on to **char**), a **wchar_t** object consists of more bits than a **char** object. Like **char**, **wchar_t** is an integral type.

The encoding of characters in objects of type **wchar_t** is implementation-dependent, but the null character must always be encoded as 0, and the encodings of the members of the basic source character set (with the possible exception of new-line) must be the same in both **wchar_t** and **char**. (See section 12.2.3 for the basic source character set.)

A constant of type **wchar_t** is written in the same way as a character constant, except that the letter L is prepended. 'a' is a character constant, and thus of type **int**; L'a' is a constant of type **wchar_t**. Similarly, a string literal may have L prepended, making it an array with elements of type **wchar_t**. Precisely what should be written within the single or double quotes preceded by L is implementation-defined.

wchar_t objects can be used in similar ways to **char** objects - we can do arithmetic with them, we can compare them, we can have arrays and strings of them;   we can probably assume that type conversion treats them in the ways we would intuitively expect. It seems likely that implementors will implement this type by making it a synonym for another integral type - probably **short int** or **int**. A number of writers say that **wchar_t** "is always a synonym for one of the other integral types", but I have found no confirmation in the Standard. If you have to use wide characters, your implementor's documentation will be your best introduction.

13.10. Volatile types

An object of any type may be *qualified* by declaring it to be **const** or **volatile** or both. We have already seen what **const** means: the program must not change the value of a **const** object. The qualification **volatile** means something quite unrelated to **const**, and is mentioned here only because the language syntax suggests that they *are* related and normal English usage suggests that they are somehow opposites. In fact, an object may be both **const** and **volatile**.

A **volatile** object is one whose value may be changed by an agency other than the program. For example, declaration of an object as **volatile** would be appropriate where the object's value may be changed by an asynchronous interrupt function, or where the object corresponds to a memory-mapped input/output port. The reason for declaring such an object as **volatile** is to warn an optimizing compiler not to make assumptions about the object's value. If the **volatile** qualification were removed from the declaration of x in the following code, a compiler would be tempted to remove the test specified by the **if** statement:

```
extern volatile int  x;
....
x = 0;
....
....
if (x==0)  ....
....
```

An object declared as both **volatile** and **const** is one whose value may be changed by something external to the program, but not by the program itself.

13.11. Robustness

Professional Cobol programmers go to much trouble to make their programs robust. File-handling errors are trapped to declarative (**use**) procedures, arithmetic errors are detected by **size error**, and bound checking is applied to subscripts. When an error occurs, the program produces a report, tries to recover, and, in the worst cases, degrades gracefully, preserving the states of the files and giving intelligible messages to users.

We have already seen how file-handling can be made robust in C programs, but what about arithmetic errors? And what about the storage access violations which you have no doubt experienced in your early grapplings with arrays and pointers? Arithmetic overflow may either simply be ignored or result in program abortion, as the implementor chooses; the diagnostics in the case of abortion may be less than helpful. Storage access violations usually result in abortion. Has C any facility to enable a program to trap these errors and handle them sensibly, as a Cobol programmer might expect?

Well, in a way, it has. There is a *signal* facility which, in effect, allows you to write functions to handle particular kinds of exception conditions. This may sound hopeful, and Cobol-like, but the bad news is:

1. An implementation need not actually raise an exception condition, so it's up to your implementor to decide whether your function will ever be called.
2. Your function has no means of knowing where in the program the exception condition arose, or what variables may be involved.
3. Your function cannot safely access any files, or even output a message - "the behaviour is undefined if the signal handler calls any function in the standard library" (with a very small number of exceptions).
4. Your function cannot safely and portably refer to any object with static storage duration (except for assignment to a very special type of variable defined in *<signal.h>* - **volatile** *sig_atomic_t*).
5. If the exception condition relates to an arithmetic error, your function cannot **return** to continue program execution from the point where the error occurred. (It *can* do so for other types of error.)

Assuming it gets called at all, what *can* your function do? In truth, very little. It is allowed to call the **abort** function (whose actions before returning control to the environment are implementation-defined), which will not help your quest for robustness, or it can call the **exit** function. This function flushes file buffers and closes the program's files before returning control to the environment. Before doing either of these, it calls any functions "registered" by another function, **atexit** (i.e. any functions, pointers to which have previously been passed as arguments to **atexit**. Your function itself should not call **atexit**, since the latter is a standard library function). So one way to get special action on an exception condition is to pass suitable functions to **atexit**. The other thing your exception-handling function can do is call **longjmp**, a necessary abomination which enables you to return in an orderly manner to a previously designated point in your program.

It would be inappropriate here to go into further detail, but you will have gathered that building some degree of robustness into a C program is a complex business; it is certainly a far cry from just specifying a declarative procedure, and you will need to learn about quite a few esoteric language features in order to do it. It should be said, though, that *signal* has other, more appropriate, uses which are beyond the scope of this book.

13.12. Bitwise operators

Most programming languages above the assembly-language level treat data as being constructed from certain atomic types, like character, integer, real and boolean, with no facilities for explicitly operating on the underlying bit patterns. One of C's great strengths as a system programming language is that any *integral* type may be treated as a sequence of bits and may be manipulated by the kind of operator commonly available in assembly languages. Before these operators are applied, the operands undergo type conversion, either the "usual arithmetic conversions" or the "integral promotions" (see section 12.5.2). You will remember that the integral promotions apply to individual operands, regardless of others in the expression, and the usual arithmetic conversions apply to pairs of operands to convert them to the same type. The operands may, of course, be expressions.

There are six operators in all. One is the unary operator ~ (complement), which flips all bits in its single operand, the integral promotions having been applied. Each of the remaining operators takes two operands.

Three are logical bitwise operators. The usual arithmetic conversions are applied to both operands. The three operators are listed here in descending order of precedence. The rules on the right apply to each corresponding pair of bits.

&	(and)	$0 \& 0 = 0$	$0 \& 1 = 0$	$1 \& 0 = 0$	$1 \& 1 = 1$
^	(exclusive or)	$0 \wedge 0 = 0$	$0 \wedge 1 = 1$	$1 \wedge 0 = 1$	$1 \wedge 1 = 0$
|	(inclusive or)	$0 \| 0 = 0$	$0 \| 1 = 1$	$1 \| 0 = 1$	$1 \| 1 = 1$

Given the declarations

```
int  i = 5;
int  j = 9;
int  k = 13;
```

the expression

        i | k ^ i & j

is equivalent to

        i | (k ^ (i & j))

giving the result 13, because 0101&1001 = 0001; 1101^0001 = 1100; 0101|1100 = 1101 (high order 0s are unchanged throughout).

The remaining two operators, which have equal precedence, are << (left shift) and >> (right shift). The integral promotions are applied to both operands. The result is the value of the first operand shifted by the number of bit positions specified by the second operand. (If the value of the second operand is negative, the result is undefined.) The << operator loses high order bits and generates 0-value low order bits. For example, the results of

           5 << 2   *and*   −6 << 3

are 20 and −48 respectively. The >> operator loses low order bits; if the type of the
first operand is unsigned, or if it is signed and the initial value is non-negative, then 0-
value high order bits are generated; if it is signed and the value is negative, the result is
implementation-defined. In other words, the Standard leaves it to the implementor to
decide whether a right shift of a signed operand is a logical shift or an arithmetic shift.

Like other operators we have seen, the bitwise binary operators (not of course the unary
operator ~) have corresponding assignment operators: &=, ^=, |=, <<= and >>=. For
instance, the expression

           a <<= b

is equivalent to

           a = a << (b)

If you are writing complex expressions which involve the bitwise operators, look
carefully at the precedence table in Appendix 1. The complement operator (~), being
unary, associates right to left; all the others associate left to right.

13.13. Hexadecimal notation

A 16-bit unit of storage may contain

           1010011110011110

Depending on the type of object(s) mapped on to the unit, this may be interpreted as a
signed integer or an unsigned integer of some type, or two characters, or one wide
character, or part of a floating-point value, or a sequence of bit-fields, and so on. A
program is sometimes concerned with the representation itself, rather than the value
represented. For instance, a program may want to "collate" from a word the top eight
bits, using the & operator. This requires the use of a word in which all bits are 0 except
the top eight bits, which are 1. It would be tedious to write the bit pattern of the word
as 0s and 1s. *Hexadecimal* notation helps the programmer to specify the pattern more
easily: for a 16-bit word, the value is written as *ff00*, and for a 32-bit word as
ff000000.

You are probably already familiar with hexadecimal notation - it represents a string of
bits by grouping the bits in fours, and expressing each group as a digit corresponding to
its numeric value, 10 through 15 being represented by the letters *a* through *f.* The bit
string at the start of this section would be written as *a79e* in hexadecimal. Programs
which print the contents of storage locations for diagnostic purposes commonly do so in
hexadecimal; the reader of the printed output finds this more acceptable than a string
of 0s and 1s would be.

Grouping the bits in fours is convenient for many current machine architectures; long ago, grouping in threes was suitable for certain machines, giving *octal* notation. C has always provided for octal notation, but all you need to know about octal is that it can be a nuisance because an integer constant written as a sequence of digits starting with 0 (zero) is interpreted as an octal, rather than a decimal, constant.

A hexadecimal integer constant begins with the characters *0x*; and the digits following are taken as a number base 16. The declaration

>   **int** hi = 0x1b;

initializes *hi* to the value 27 (i.e. 1*16 + 11*1). A character constant too may be expressed in hexadecimal, as in

>   **char** hc = '\x41';

which initializes *hc* to the value 65 (decimal), which in ASCII is the letter 'A'. Of course, if we really mean 'A', we should say so; the hexadecimal form should be used when the program requires the bit pattern rather than the character 'A'. Otherwise the program will not be portable. But an important use for hexadecimal is in specifying characters which have no graphical representation or standard escape sequence; these should be defined as macros so that they can easily be changed when the program is taken to another environment, e.g.:

>   #define ACK '\x06'

Hexadecimal escape sequences may also be used in string literals. The literal "\x41\x42" is the same, in an ASCII environment, as "AB". For safety, do not mix hexadecimal escape sequences with ordinary characters in a string literal.

In all cases, the hexadecimal digits following the letter *x* form a hexadecimal number, not a left-justified sequence of bit patterns. In other words, 0x3 or '\x3' is equivalent to 0x03 or '\x03', *not* to 0x30 or '\x30'.

For output of values in hexadecimal representation, calls of **printf**, **sprintf** and **fprintf** may contain %x in their format strings. The corresponding argument is treated as being of type **unsigned int**. As with %d, %hx applies to a **short**, and %lx to a **long**, argument (see section 12.2.1), and field width and precision may be specified (see section 6.1). For input of values in hexadecimal notation, calls of **sscanf** and similar functions may contain %x to match a string of hexadecimal digits; the corresponding argument is treated as a pointer to **unsigned int**. With the use of %hx or %lx, the argument is treated as a pointer to **unsigned short int** or **unsigned long int**. Substitution of *o* for *x* in the above gives corresponding facilities for octal representation.

If you prefer to write hexadecimal numbers using the traditional upper-case A through F instead of lower-case, you can do so; for the **printf** family of functions, use of *X* instead of *x* after a % in a format string produces upper-case output.

13.14. Bit-fields

Within a **struct** or a **union**, we can specify the sizes of particular integer objects. We may say something like:

> **unsigned int** goals_for :5;
> **signed int** goal_diff :6;
> **int** percent_wins :7;

These declarations declare *bit-fields* which have these characteristics:

> *goals_for*: a 5-bit object; range of values 0 through 31.
> *goal_diff*: a 6-bit object; range of values −32 (or −31) through 31.
> *percent_wins*: a 7-bit object, which the implementor may choose to regard as **signed** or **unsigned**. (Remember that the implementor has a similar choice for plain **char** objects - see section 12.2.3.)

So, for portability, it is best not to declare a bit-field as plain **int**.

In most contexts, bit-fields may be used in the same way as **int**s or **unsigned int**s; they undergo integral promotions in the same way as **char**s and **short int**s. But they are subject to the following restrictions:

1. They may be declared *only within a **struct** or a **union*** and are therefore referenced by dot or arrow notation (see chapter 10).
2. The number of bits in a bit-field must not be greater than the number in an **int**.
3. Bit-fields do not have "addresses", because they do not necessarily begin or end on byte boundaries. You cannot therefore apply the unary & (address of) operator to a bit-field identifier. Nor can you have a pointer to a bit-field, so you cannot have arrays of bit-fields and you cannot pass values to bit-fields through function arguments (e.g. **sscanf** cannot set the value of a bit-field through an argument).
4. The **sizeof** operator cannot be applied to a bit-field identifier, because a bit-field need not be an integral number of bytes.

The Standard says that bit-fields are packed into addressable storage units (let's call them *words*, which is what they often are), but it leaves the implementor to decide whether a word is packed from the low order end to the high order or *vice versa*, and whether bit-fields may overlap word boundaries. Suppose the above declarations are to be mapped by a compiler on to store with 16-bit words. The packing may begin

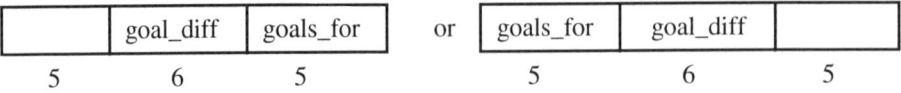

and the implementor decides whether *percent_wins*: (a) uses the remaining 5 bits of the word and 2 bits of the next word, or (b) is entirely mapped to the next word. Such decisions may affect the size of the structure or union in which the bit-fields are contained. So, though programs which use bit-fields are portable in terms of their references to the bit-fields, the structures themselves (if written to a file, say) are not.

If you know how your implementor maps bit-fields on to storage, you can explicitly control the boundaries of successive bit-fields by declaring unnamed bit-fields, as in

> **int** :3;

A special case is

> **int** :0;

which forces allocation of the next bit-field to the next word.

In system programming, bit-fields are useful in mapping data received from an external source; the mapping of course will not be portable. In application programming, bit-fields can be used to save space, where many small values have to be stored; but they need to be treated with care, and the saving may be outweighed by the increased program complexity and possibly increased running time.

13.15. Mathematical functions

One of C's distinct advantages over pre-1989 Cobol is the availability of library functions which realize many of the more common mathematical functions, such as trigonometric functions and the computation of logarithms. One function, **pow** *(x,y)*, returns the value of *x* raised to the power of *y*, which makes up for C's lack of an equivalent operator to Cobol's ******. (The function could have been named *power*, but this is C - why make it easy for the programmer?) Appendix 3 includes prototypes of all these functions. To use them, include

> #include <math.h>

You will probably also need

> #include <errno.h>

All the mathematical functions return a value of type **double** and take arguments of type **double**, though a few take additional arguments of other types. The mathematical functions have a robustness uncharacteristic of the language as a whole. They check for both *domain errors* and *range errors*.

A *domain error* occurs if an argument supplied to a function is outside the domain over which the mathematical function is defined. For example, you can't compute the square root of a negative value. The function **sqrt** returns the non-negative square root of its argument; if it is called with a negative argument value, a domain error occurs. For each function, the Standard specifies domain errors for which the implementation must check; the implementor may define further domain errors. In general, when a domain error occurs, a function returns an implementation-defined value and also sets **errno** (defined in *<errno.h>*) equal to the value of the macro **EDOM** (also defined in *<errno.h>*), an integer value.

A *range error* occurs if the result of a function cannot be represented as a **double** value, due to arithmetic overflow or underflow. On overflow, a function returns the value of the macro **HUGE_VAL** (or the negation of that value), and the value of the macro **ERANGE** is stored in **errno**. (**HUGE_VAL** and **ERANGE** are defined in *<errno.h>*.) On underflow, a function returns zero; whether or not **ERANGE** is stored in **errno** is implementation-defined.

At the start of program execution, the value of **errno** is zero, but it is never set to zero by any library function; clearing it is the responsibility of the program.

13.16. Locales

Cobol's flexibility in providing for different local conventions - editing pictures for currency values and environment features like **currency sign, decimal point, alphabet** and **program collating sequence** - was for many years regarded as being far in advance of anything provided in other popular languages. Those who have worked with Cobol are probably aware of how limited these features really are. C's new *locale* facility provides much greater flexibility; when taken up seriously by implementors, it will be a significant feature of the language. The appropriate header is *<locale.h>*.

The basic idea is that the implementor provides information about various aspects of different locales (i.e. national or language environments). A complete locale definition (the phrase is mine, not the Standard's), or a specified part or aspect of a locale definition may be set as current, or may be queried, by calling the function **setlocale**. At the start of execution of any program, the current locale is the default "C" locale.

The Standard provides only a framework, including the following aspects:

Collating sequence: A function **strcoll** behaves like **strcmp**, but uses the current locale's collating sequence. This will necessarily be a slow process, so another function **strxfrm** can be used to convert a string into one for which **strcmp** will give the correct locale ordering.

Character testing functions: Those functions in *<ctype.h>* which test characters are affected by the current locale.

Formatting of monetary values and numbers: A new type, **struct lcon**, is defined in *<locale.h>*. Its members are various pieces of information (18 in all) required to specify a locale's format.

Formatting of dates and times: Things like weekday names, month names and time representation are affected by the current locale. (These are among the things generated by the format string of the function **strftime** - see section 13.8.)

This is new territory. Since most of it is implementation-dependent, it is best explored with your implementor's documentation; but don't be too surprised if you find that your implementor provides only one locale - the default "C" locale!

14

More about Files

14.1. Introduction

This chapter explores other file-related aspects of C. It describes binary files and their processing; it also introduces what passes for random access in C and suggests that you explore your implementor's facilities for accessing files through system calls.

Except in section 14.2 and where otherwise stated, phrases like "the name of the file" are used in the Cobol sense of "the name by which the file is known within the program"; in C terms, this is the name of an object of type **FILE*** (see section 5.1). Wherever the identifier *f* is used, assume that it has been declared as

    FILE* f;

14.2. Deleting and renaming files

In specifying arguments to the following functions, we use the names by which files are known to the operating environment (the system names), not those by which the input-output functions access them. The system names are the true names of the files, not the names of objects of type **FILE***.

The arguments of **remove** and **rename** are of type **char***. The call

      remove ("cd1.dat")

deletes the file *cd1.dat*. (If the file is currently open, the effect is implementation-defined.) **remove** returns an integer: 0 if the operation succeeds, and non-zero if it fails. The call

      rename ("old.d", "new.d")

changes the name of the file *old.d* to *new.d*. (If *new.d* is the name of an existing file, the effect is implementation-defined.) **rename** returns an integer: 0 if the operation succeeds, and non-zero if it fails (e.g. *old.d* cannot be found, or *old.d* is currently open).

14.3. Buffering

Transfer of data in either direction between a file and main storage usually takes place in units called *blocks*. An area of main storage into which blocks are read, or from which they are written, is referred to as a *buffer*. Blocks and buffers are usually invisible to an application program; the program behaves as though it is accessing the file directly. Both Cobol and C give some control over the buffering strategy employed in relation to a particular file. Cobol's **reserve ... areas** enables a program to control the number of buffers used for a file, in order to smooth out efficiently file access time and processing time; its **block contains** enables a program to control the sizes of the blocks in a file.

We have been using files, as we normally would, without considering blocking and buffering. This is because the implementor defines defaults for the type of buffering used and the buffer size. It is best to use the defaults unless there is a good reason not to. But a program may override the defaults for any file by specifying the buffer size and the type of buffering to be used. There are three types of buffering, defined by these integral macros in <*stdio.h*>:

- **_IONBF**: no buffering. Transmit data "as soon as possible". Commonly, this mode may be used for output to an interactive device.
- **_IOLBF**: line buffering. Transmit data when a new-line character is encountered. Commonly, this mode may be used for input from a keyboard.
- **_IOFBF**: full buffering. For output, transmit data when the buffer is full; for input, transmit data until the buffer is full. In the case of output, **fclose** causes any untransmitted data in the buffer to be transmitted to the file; the same effect can be obtained without closing the file by calling the function **fflush**, which takes one argument, of type **FILE***. Commonly, full buffering is used for internal files. It is the default mode for files which the system knows not to be mapped to interactive devices.

After a file has been opened, and before anything else is done with it, a program may specify the buffering mode and the buffer size by calling the function **setvbuf**. The call

> **setvbuf** (f, **NULL, _IOLBF, BUFSIZ**)

specifies line buffering mode for file *f* and an implementor's default as the buffer size. (**BUFSIZ** is a macro defined in <*stdio.h*>; it will be at least 256.) The call

> **setvbuf** (f, **NULL, _IOFBF**, 4096)

specifies full buffering for file *f*, with buffer size 4096. If the second argument is not **NULL**, it is of type **char*** and points to an array to be used as the buffer, instead of having the system allocate its own buffer. Since "the contents of the array at any time are indeterminate", this last facility is not intended to enable an application program to use the buffer contents; its main purpose is to allow the program to control buffer allocation when memory is in short supply.

14.4. Binary files

So far we have used only text files. The only other type specifically defined in the Standard is a *binary file*. Like a text file, a binary file is a sequence of characters from the system's point of view, but it differs from a text file in these respects:

1. The values of objects in a program are written to a binary file without any conversion. For example, floating values may be written directly in their internal form, and the contents of arrays and structures may be written. It is guaranteed that, on any given implementation, the values read back from such a file will be identical to those written. The only exception is that some null characters may be added to the end of the file; consult your implementor's documentation.
2. Since the values written are the binary patterns held in main storage, it would usually be misguided to assign a binary file to a keyboard or a monitor or a printer.
3. Since different implementations store the same data types in different ways, it will not in general be possible to write a binary file under one implementation and read it under another. Like files containing **comp** items in Cobol, binary files are not portable; though, of course, functions may be written to convert them.
4. With a binary file, the system does not recognize any special characters. No system conversion whatever is applied. This is particularly relevant in an environment where, with a text file, the two-character sequence Carriage Return, Line Feed would be seen by a C program as a single new-line character.

Naturally, when we read a binary file, we will have to know the sequence of types it contains. It would be no good writing an integer followed by a double and later reading them as a double followed by an integer, or reading an array of a different length from the one written.

A word of warning. Even under a single implementation, the values of pointers written to a file will generally be meaningless when read back on another occasion. This is true, of course, whether or not the pointers are within structures or arrays.

A file is designated as a binary file by appending the letter b to the second argument string of the call of **fopen**. The following statements open the binary file "a.d" as an input file, and a new binary file "b.d" as an output file:

```
FILE* f1, f2;
....
....
f1 = fopen ("a.d", "rb");
f2 = fopen ("b.d", "wb");
```

A binary file is usually written by calls of **fwrite** and read by calls of **fread**. We have seen both functions used for text files, where the object read or written was an array of **char** (see section 5.8.1). The members of the array may, in general, be of any type. As a simple example, if we define a type

```
typedef struct  {
     double  d [10];
     int  i [4];
     char  c;
} S;
```

and an array of objects of that type:

```
S  arr [50];
```

then the array can be written to file *f* by the call

fwrite (arr, **sizeof** (S), 50, f)

which returns the number of elements successfully written. (This will be less than 50 only if a write error occurs.) The same data can be read back from the file to the same array by

fread (arr, **sizeof** (S), 50, f)

which returns the number of elements successfully read. (This may be less than 50 if a read error or the end of the file is encountered.)

Be careful when the *elements* of the array are character strings or structures including character strings. Again, a simple example will suffice. Given the declaration

```
char*  carr [] = {
     "Birkbeck College,",
     "Malet Street,",
     "London.",
     "WC1E  7HX"
};
```

you might be tempted to write the College address to a file by writing the array *carr*. Presumably, after writing

fwrite (carr,

you would stop short, for at that point you would be forced to remember that the size of each element is **sizeof** (**char***), and thus four *pointers* would be written to the file (and they would be useless when read back later by another program). The actual postal address could be written by

```
for (i=0;  i<4;  i++)
     fwrite (carr[i],  sizeof (char),  strlen(carr[i])+1,  f);
```

but this would make things difficult for a program which later read the file, for it would not know the lengths of the individual lines; it would have to read a sufficiently large chunk of data and then search for the terminating nulls which we were careful to write at the ends of lines. It would then have to deal with any excess data read after the end of the postal address, which might be cut off in the middle of some other type of object. It is generally unwise to write variable-length arrays to a binary file unless you precede them by an integral value giving their length.

The object in which such a value is stored before writing is unlikely to be in an array. It is likely to be a discrete object of some integral type. This brings us to a slight problem with the Standard's wording in its specifications of **fwrite** and **fread**. In both cases it refers to "the *array* pointed to by" the first argument. However, the first parameter is of type **void***, and careful reading of the rest of the Standard suggests that it should be perfectly permissible to pass, as the first argument, a pointer to any type of object; of course, when the first argument is a pointer to a discrete object, the appropriate size should be passed as the second argument, and 1 as the third (number of members). This works successfully with the implementations I have used, and there is no reason to believe that it would cause trouble with any other implementation. Code like the following should cause no problems:

```
double  d;
....

....
fwrite (&d, sizeof (double), 1, f);
```

Given our earlier declaration of *carr*, we can therefore write each line of the postal address, preceded by an integer giving its length (including the terminating null character):

```
int  s, i;
....
for (i=0; i<4; i++)  {
        s = strlen (carr[i]) + 1;
        fwrite (&s, sizeof (int), 1, f);
        fwrite (carr[i], sizeof (char), s, f);
}
```

Assuming that LINEMAX is the maximum number of characters in an address line, the same or another program can read the postal address back and store the four lines in an array:

```
char  c[4] [LINEMAX+1];
int  s, i;
....

....
for (i=0; i<4; i++)  {
        fread (&s, sizeof (int), 1, f);
        fread (c[i], sizeof (char), s, f);
}
```

This technique of preceding a variable number of elements by a count is not of course restricted to character strings; it may be used for variable-length arrays whose elements are of any type.

Things like postal addresses are obviously best stored in text files rather than binary files, but the above example is a useful illustration of the use of **fwrite** and **fread**. It is not intended as a recommended method; how you store data of this kind in a binary file will depend on such factors as how a program can most conveniently use data when retrieved from the file, and how important it is to save space in the file. The postal address in the example might be stored in a binary file as a fixed number of characters, using the maximum line length for each line; alternatively, the lines might be variable-length, each terminated by Carriage Return, Line Feed instead of a null character; an **int** might be written giving the length of the complete postal address, and then the whole address written by one **fwrite** call. There are other possibilities too.

In essence, all that **fwrite** and **fread** do is to transfer a number of bytes to or from a file. The number of bytes transferred is the product of the second and third arguments. For example, under an implementation with 8-bit **char**s and 16-bit **int**s, it is possible, though rarely useful, to write the contents of an array of 5 **int**s and read the same bytes back into an array of 10 **char**s. But erroneous reading of 5 **char**s instead of 5 **int**s will affect more than the result of the **fread** call concerned; all subsequent reads from the file, though correct in themselves, will be reading 5 bytes behind the bytes they should be reading. Fortunately, the prototypes of **fwrite** and **fread** specify the same kinds of parameters; if you look back at the last two program extracts in this section, you will see that the arguments of the **fread** calls match those of the corresponding **fwrite** calls. The simplest and safest way to read a binary file is to ensure that

- the sequence of **fread** calls reflects the sequence of **fwrite** calls in the program that wrote the file;
- the first argument of each **fread** call is a pointer of the same type as in the corresponding **fwrite** call;
- the second and third arguments have the same values as those of the corresponding **fwrite** call.

14.5. Random access

Not surprisingly given C's Unix association, the only method of file organization is sequential. This section explores C's attempts to superimpose some rudimentary random access facilities on sequential files.

In C, every file is a sequence of bytes. In a *text file*, the bytes are expected to represent characters; certain characters may have special significance to the system, and the actual contents of a text file may be different from the sequence of characters seen by a C program. In a *binary file*, the bytes are simply bit-patterns, and several consecutive bytes may represent the value of a single object; with one minor exception at the end of a file, there is no difference between the actual contents of a binary file and what a C program sees as its contents. If a program writes b bytes to a binary file, starting at a position p bytes from the start of the file, the next write operation is guaranteed to start at the position $(p+b)$ bytes from the start of the file. No such guarantee is given for a text file.

In Cobol, a file is a collection of records, and is accessed one record at a time. The logical structure of a file (its **organization**) may be sequential, relative or indexed, and a record may be accessed sequentially, randomly or dynamically. In the case of an indexed file, one or more embedded keys may be used to identify records for access purposes. In C, a file has no structure other than sequence and the division of a text file into lines; even this division may be ignored by programs using a file. C therefore has no equivalent of Cobol's record key, alternate record key or relative record number. How then can C claim to provide random access?

What some C programmers call "random access" is nothing more than a very poor alternative to the **start** statement in Cobol sequential access. C has a *file position indicator* which is automatically updated as a program progresses through a file. For a text file, the precise form of the indicator is undefined; all a program can do is ask for its current value, and later use that value to reset the indicator to the current point in the file. For a binary file, the indicator value is an ordinal byte number relative to the start of the file; if a binary file is written in fixed-length units, the value of the indicator corresponding to any unit can be computed. In the case of a large file, the value of the indicator may exceed the capacity of a **long int**; so, for program storage of indicator values, *<stdio.h>* defines a special type, **fpos_t**. We now look at these facilities in a little more detail.

Assume the declaration

     fpos_t pos;

Where *f* is a text file or a binary file, the call

     fgetpos (f, &pos)

will assign the current value of the file position indicator to *pos*. The value is usable only as an argument of **fsetpos**:

     fsetpos (f, &pos)

resets the file position indicator to the value of *pos*, thus resetting the current file position. Both functions return an **int**: 0 on success, non-zero on failure.

Of course, a program may make many calls of **fgetpos** and store the values in different **fpos_t** variables, or perhaps in an array of such variables. With diligence, you can write a program which constructs its own index to a file.

Where *f* is a text file or a binary file, the call

     rewind (f)

which returns no value, sets the file position indicator for *f* to the start of the file.

The other pair of functions, **ftell** and **fseek**, are of practical use *only for binary files*. (For text files, their facilities merely duplicate those of **fgetpos**, **fsetpos** and **rewind**.) **ftell** returns a **long int** value. After execution of

```
long int  k;
....

....
k = ftell(f);
```

the value of *k* will be the current value of the file position indicator for *f*. (A return value of −1 indicates failure.) For a binary file, this is the number of bytes from the start of the file. A later call

fseek (f, k, **SEEK_SET**)

will reset the file position indicator (and thus the current file position) to the original position. **fseek** returns an **int**: 0 for success, non-zero for failure. Its prototype is

int fseek (FILE* stream, **long int** offset, **int** whence);

This function resets the file position indicator for file *stream*. *offset* is used as a distance measured in bytes (a positive value means forward, a negative value backward) from the point in the file specified by *whence*. *whence* may be one of three integral constants defined in *<stdio.h>*:

SEEK_SET: the start of the file
SEEK_CUR: the current value of the file position indicator
SEEK_END: the end of the file

(Because a binary file may have additional characters appended, use of **SEEK_END** is not guaranteed by the Standard to work correctly on all implementations!) A successful call of **fseek** clears the end-of-file indicator if set.

Here are some calls of **fseek**, showing how they affect the file position indicator (*fpi*):

Call	*Effect*
fseek (f, 100, **SEEK_CUR**)	(fpi += 100)
fseek (f, −50, **SEEK_CUR**)	(fpi −= 50)
fseek (f, 1000, **SEEK_SET**)	(fpi = 1000)
fseek (f, 0, **SEEK_END**)	(fpi set to end of file)
fseek (f, −80, **SEEK_END**)	(fpi set to 80 bytes before end of file)

This facility enables you to write functions which use a binary file to simulate approximately the facilities of a Cobol relative file (but only with fixed-length record storage).

14.6. Extending existing files

You will recall from section 5.3 that a text file may be opened in what Cobol calls **extend** mode by specifying "a" (append) as the second argument of **fopen**. Similarly, to open a binary file in append mode, we specify "ab" (append binary) as the second argument. In either case, the effect is that all subsequent output to the file is "forced to the then current end-of-file, regardless of intervening calls to the **fseek** function".

(Oddly, there is no mention of **fsetpos**.) This is what we would expect, but, as we saw in section 14.4, an implementor may add null characters to the end of a binary file. When we open such a file in append mode, what happens? The Standard says: "In some implementations, opening a binary file with append mode may initially position the file position indicator ... beyond the last data written, because of null character padding". So you may find some extra null characters in a binary file which has been extended; given the nature of a binary file, this may be a serious hazard.

14.7. Updating a file

So far, we have seen how C provides three of the four open modes of Cobol:

Cobol	*C text file*	*C binary file*
open input	**fopen** (...., "r")	**fopen** (...., "rb")
open output	**fopen** (...., "w")	**fopen** (...., "wb")
open extend	**fopen** (...., "a")	**fopen** (...., "ab")

but we have not seen the C provision corresponding to Cobol's **open i-o**. In C, when we want to update a file, we choose one of the above forms of **fopen** call, and append a '+' to the second argument string. For a text file the forms are "r+", "w+" and "a+", and for a binary file they are "rb+", "wb+" and "ab+".

The '+' has the effect of allowing all input and output operations, with the restriction that all output goes to the end of the file in the cases of "a+" and "ab+". Otherwise, the only difference is in what happens when the file is opened:

"r+", "rb+":   The file must already exist at the time of opening.

"a+", "ab+":   If the file does not already exist, a new file is created.

"w+", "wb+":   Creates a new file. If the file already exists, its present content is lost.

Having opened a file in any of these update modes, a program can move freely around the file, reading and writing as required. If the mode is not "a+" or "ab+" and the file position indicator is not at the end of the file, output to the file of b bytes of data overwrites the next b bytes in the file (or perhaps fewer at the end of the file). Thus, though a program may laboriously use a C file to simulate a Cobol file, by calculating "record" positions or by keeping a table of "record" positions in the file, it cannot change the length of a "record" or insert a new "record" between existing "records". To do such ordinary things, the program would have to copy the complete file, making the changes where appropriate.

An input operation cannot be followed by an output operation, nor an output operation by an input operation, unless there is an intervening call of **fsetpos**, **fseek**, **rewind** or **fflush**. (The only exception is after an input operation detects end of file.) You may feel that the Standard should have made the implementor responsible for the whole business of buffer management in these cases, but will just have to accept the limitation.

14.8. Temporary files

Temporary files are always binary files. The function **tmpfile** takes no arguments and returns a value of type **FILE*** (or a null pointer if a temporary file cannot be created). As with **fopen**, we can assign the value returned to a variable and use that variable to denote the file.

The effect of calling **tmpfile** is to create a file and open it in "wb+" mode. The file is temporary in the sense that it will be deleted automatically when it is closed or on normal program termination. (The implementor defines whether or not such a file is deleted on abnormal termination.) Temporary files are useful when a program, as part of its internal working, wants to store intermediate data in files; they avoid the need to devise system names, and they prevent the file storage becoming cluttered with files which are of no further use.

14.9. Operating system facilities

If you are an experienced Cobol programmer, your reaction to this chapter may have been resigned amusement (if you've met Unix people before) or exasperation (if you haven't). Apologists for standard C are in the habit of extolling its "well-stocked library of functions for manipulating external files" (to quote just one of them); but now you have seen the reality. The reality is no more than physically sequential files (in the sense that you can't change the length of an item in a file or insert a new item between two existing items) and the ability to move the file position indicator to a particular character position in the file. That is all you have in standard C.

One reason for your reaction may be your knowledge that your machine has file management software which makes available all the file handling facilities you need, and that there is no way of using that software through standard C. Take comfort - all is not lost. Your C implementor may well provide *non-standard* types and functions which give C the file-handling functionality of Cobol. The general picture is that the implementor may provide *#include* files and additional library facilities which enable you to call system functions resembling the file-accessing statements of Cobol. For example, in one particular implementation of C, you can use the Record Management Services of VMS on a DEC VAX mainframe to achieve much greater flexibility in file handling than even Cobol would give you.

Use of these extended facilities will of course make your program non-portable, so you will design your program in such a way that their use is concentrated in a few modules which can reasonably easily be replaced when the program is taken to a new environment which offers the same functionality.

15

A Language for Professionals?

Earlier chapters have taken you through most of the features of C. This last chapter considers the language as a whole and attempts a brief assessment.

The original purpose of C was admirably fulfilled. Over a large range of hardware, C achieves the low-level control and efficiency which are usually associated with assembly languages; at the same time, it provides the control structures and the data structuring and modularization facilities of a third-generation language. It is of particular value as a target language for automatically-generated programs. Programmers who have worked extensively in machine code or assembly languages will need no convincing that C has made an outstanding contribution to programming. The current trend, however, is to regard C as a general-purpose language. Indeed, in 1978, the originators of C described it as such: both the Preface and the Introduction of Kernighan and Ritchie's classic book (*The C Programming Language*) began with the words "C is a general-purpose programming language". The authors claimed that

> 'although it has been called a "system programming language" because it is useful for writing operating systems, it has been used *equally well* to write major numerical, text-processing, and data-base programs'

(the italics are mine). Similar overselling of C has continued ever since.

The nineteen-sixties saw a quest for a single universal language in which programs for all application areas could be written at a "third-generation" level. The resulting languages, Algol 68 and PL/1, were large and complex and needed big powerful machines. It is easy to see why C was attractive when it appeared in the following decade. Here was a relatively simple language, easily compiled and making minimal hardware demands. Subject to the omission of features like multiprogramming and parallelism, it was also claimed to be general-purpose and "more convenient and effective for many tasks than supposedly more powerful languages" (Kernighan and Ritchie again). This seeming magic was achieved by the simplest of means. The designers said, in effect: "We give you a small basic language and a library facility. Anything (like input, output, string manipulation or mathematical functions) that isn't in the language can be provided by your implementor or by yourself, in the form of library functions. Quite a lot of the functions you want may be written entirely in C and will therefore be portable to other implementations." The data types and computational capabilities of the basic language were based on a generalization of the PDP-11 architecture and applicable to a good range of other architectures. The language was therefore a kind of portable assembler, but immeasurably more convenient to program in than any real assembly language, thanks to its expressions, its control structures and its data structuring features.

Application programs routinely use input, output, and many other facilities that are excluded from the basic language, and thus make heavy use of library functions. It was clearly desirable that these essential facilities should be the same in all implementations. As a result, the Standard specifies not only the basic language but also a multitude of facilities which must be provided by the library. It specifies a standard language *and* a standard library. From the programmer's viewpoint, it is this combination of basic language and library that constitutes the standard C language. (*Minor note:* For use in such contexts as programming embedded systems and operating systems work, the Standard allows *freestanding implementations*, in which the only standard library components are the contents of the headers <float.h>, <limits.h>, <stdarg.h> and <stddef.h>. A freestanding implementation is of no value for writing a normal application program.)

And here the apparently self-evident needs to be stated. Suppose you are designing a language, and you feel that a particular facility would be useful in the language's application area. You may do one of three things:

- do not provide the facility, on the ground that programmers can obtain the required functionality by using other language features to devise their own procedures or functions. For instance, a language may not provide a facility for exponentiation.
- build the facility into the basic language by introducing appropriate types, statements and/or operators. For instance, Cobol provides the exponentiation operator **.
- provide a standard function (or macro). For instance, C provides a function, **pow**, for exponentiation.

If you choose to provide the facility, there are arguments for and against each of the last two options, arguments that need not be reiterated here. The essential point is that, whichever of the two options you choose, *you are specifying part of the language*. If programmers want to use a particular facility, they have to learn the appropriate syntax and semantics; either they learn about particular types, statements and/or operators, or they learn about the appropriate standard library functions. From a programmer's viewpoint, the **fgets** function is as much part of the C language as the **read** statement is part of the Cobol language.

The authors of most C textbooks seem to lack an appreciation of this simple point. Their message is that "C is a small, lean language", "easy to learn", and you can conveniently do nearly anything with it. Yet almost invariably their very first programming example has to use a library function, which of course is not part of the "small, lean language", and their later programs are often awash with calls of library functions. Either C is a small language (without the library), *relatively* easy *for experienced programmers* to learn, in which you can't conveniently do any serious application programming at all, or it is a big language (C and the standard library), tiresome to learn, but convenient for a reasonable range of applications. If you really want to go outside system programming and do the things that Kernighan and Ritchie say you can do "equally well" (i.e. "major numerical, text-processing and data-base programs"), you'll have to learn about the library, or else write your own primitive functions. For each library function of interest, you'll have to know its idiosyncratic name, the ordering of its parameters, the significance of its return values, and the name of the appropriate header.

Suppose you want to copy a string (safely). Do you remember that the function is called **strncpy**? Do you remember its parameters and their ordering? Do you remember what it returns? Do you remember what header you should include in order to use it? This is the price you pay for the "small, lean language" (with no *string* type), of which Kernighan and Ritchie say, with only slight exaggeration: "A programmer can reasonably expect to know and understand and indeed regularly use the entire language". The trouble is that you have to know so much more.

None of this is intended as an attack on C or its philosophy. It is, rather, an attack on the exaggerated claims so often made for the language. Yes, C is general-purpose, but only in the sense in which an assembly language is general-purpose - you have to work hard to do things which can be done with ease in more specialized third-generation languages. We often hear the answer: "C is a language for professionals; give them the primitives and they can cope". But amateurs, not professionals, are the people who learn to use just one tool and apply it to every problem, regardless of its suitability. The true professional uses the most suitable tools for a given job. There are things you'd rather do in C than in any other language; there are things you'd rather do in Cobol than in any other language; and the same can be said of Icon, Ada, and other languages. Historically, of course, if you were stuck with Unix, you wouldn't have much choice - C might be the only language you had. But there is no virtue in that necessity, and it is a necessity that is fast disappearing.

Unfortunately, eclectic programmers may not be allowed to choose the most appropriate language for a job. Particularly in the PC world, effective use of a language by a professional often requires not just knowledge of the language itself but also mastery of the multiplicity of options supplied by the implementor, a language-specific software development environment, and language-specific add-on software aids. Moving to a new language today can involve a high investment in learning. Many software houses and user software departments quite reasonably insist that their in-house expertise be concentrated on one language rather than spread thinly over several. Because of its flexibility, C has been an obvious choice in such places, even if the choice results in greater program complexity in application areas where C is inappropriate. But the really hard work for professionals working in C is the enormous programming and testing effort required if their programs are to be robust and reliable.

Oddly enough, several authors give the impression that C's permissiveness actually makes it a language suitable for professionals. One writer puts it like this: "A professional forester would use a chain-saw to cut down trees quickly, aware of the dangers of touching the blade when the machine is running; C programmers work in a similar way". C, these writers state or imply, is no language for learners or amateurs - it's a professional's tool. Part of the "basic philosophy" of C, according to Kernighan and Ritchie, is that "programmers know what they are doing"; other writers echo this by saying that C "trusts the programmer". As a programmer, I *may* find this attractive; as a programming manager or as a user of the program, I certainly do not. Do I want to risk having some random data corrupted by the programmer's undetected misuse of an array? Do I want a program in which adding one to a very large number turns it unnoticed into a very small number? Do I want a run-time error to crash the system? Do I want to be the victim of the programmer's chain-saw?

Professional programmers often have to write secure, robust programs; they have to be able to detect errors and, when errors occur, retain control, save vital data, and degrade the application gracefully. They need all the help they can get from the language, and they get precious little from C. The "protective environment", at which some C programmers scoff, is in fact more important to the professional than to the amateur.

But distaste for the hype surrounding C should not blind us to the very real merits of the language. Once its quirks have been mastered, it is remarkably pleasant to work in. You may have found already that experience of C's detailed computation and control features - things like the generality of expressions and of the **for** statement, and the extended assignment operators - has made you impatient with more pedestrian languages. Certainly there are programmers who misuse these features to produce obscure code - "elegance" and "conciseness" are too often synonyms for unintelligibility - but at least the temptations are not as great as in APL. Sensibly written, C code can be well-modularized, readable and maintainable, and it is the responsibility of management to ensure that coding standards exist and are enforced.

One advantage of learning C, if you have come from Cobol (or Fortran), is that you may now have met for the first time two basic concepts that have been around as long as programming itself - recursion and pointers. Cobol suffers greatly from their absence, and when you have used them in real programs you will wonder how you ever got along without them. They are essential items in every professional programmer's toolbag.

Another advantage is that you will find it relatively easy to move from C to object-oriented programming. C++ may not be the best of the object-oriented languages, but it appears to be the most widely used. Learning it is a formidable task for those with no experience of C.

Despite all the reservations expressed in this book, I enjoy programming in C. I hope you will too.

Appendix 1

Operator Precedence and Associativity

In the following table, operators are listed in descending precedence; all operators between one horizontal line and the next have the same precedence. Each of the symbols −, +, * and & appears twice in the table, once as a unary operator (all the unary operators are at the second-highest level of precedence), and once as a binary operator. The operator shown as "(type)" is the cast operator.

Associativity	Operators
Left to right	( ) [ ] -> .
Right to left	! ~ ++ -- + − (type) * & sizeof
Left to right	* / %
Left to right	+ −
Left to right	<< >>
Left to right	< > <= >=
Left to right	== !=
Left to right	&
Left to right	^
Left to right	|
Left to right	&&
Left to right	||
Right to left	?:
Right to left	= *= /= %= += -= <<= >>= &= ^= |=
Left to right	,

A reminder:

Precedence determines the order in which operators in an expression are applied. The higher the precedence, the earlier the operator is applied. For example

> x = a + b * −c && d

is equivalent to the fully parenthesized expression

> (x = ((a + (b * (−c))) && d))

Associativity determines the direction in which operators of equal precedence are applied, either *right to left* (* is a unary operator here):

> *++p   *equivalent to*   *(++p)

or *left to right* (* is a binary operator here):

> 15 / 2 * 3   *equivalent to*   (15 / 2) * 3

Notice that right to left evaluation of the last expression would give a quite different result (2 instead of 21).

Appendix 2

Reserved Identifiers

The keywords of the language are:

auto	double	int	struct
break	else	long	switch
case	enum	register	typedef
char	extern	return	union
const	float	short	unsigned
continue	for	signed	void
default	goto	sizeof	volatile
do	if	static	while

This list appears to compare favourably with the long list of Cobol reserved words. Regrettably, the C Standard also reserves many other identifiers.

General restrictions

The keywords listed above cannot be used in any context other than with their standard meaning, except as macro names. Other identifiers reserved in all contexts are:
- identifiers that begin with two underscores or with one underscore and an upper-case letter.
- names of macros defined in standard library headers, when these headers are *#include*d.

The second of these groups is natural enough; but note that the restriction presumably forbids you to *#undef* the name and then use it for something else.

Another reasonable, and obvious, restriction is that identifiers made available to a program by inclusion of a standard header file cannot be reused at source file level to mean something else; the included header, of course, becomes in effect part of the source file.

Restrictions on external names

The remaining reserved identifiers are related to the standard library functions and their possible future expansion. In any source program, identifiers in the following classes are reserved in relation to their use as *external names* (i.e. as identifiers which are visible outside the source file). The Standard prohibits their reuse, regardless of which standard library headers the program includes.

- All identifiers with external linkage in all standard library headers. This includes **errno**, **setjmp** and **va_end**, besides the identifiers of all functions, types and macros made available through standard headers.
- Macro names beginning with the letter E and a digit, or E and an upper-case letter, or LC_ and an upper-case letter, or SIG and an upper-case letter, or SIG_ and an upper-case letter.
- Function names beginning with *is, to, str, mem* or *wcs*, where any of these is followed by a lower-case letter.
- Names of all existing *<math.h>* functions suffixed by *f* or *l*.

Your compiler may not enforce these reservations, but failure to observe them may give your program trouble in the future.

Some of these restrictions will be irksome - you can unthinkingly name a function *top* or *strength* or a macro END_OF_FILE. You should not deliberately reuse a standard identifier to mean something else, but there is always the possibility of doing so accidentally. Here, for once, the silly names of most of the standard library functions are a blessing - no sensible programmer would unwittingly reuse a name like *strncmp*.

But be careful. Using a compiler which shall be nameless, I defined a function called *read*, confident that no standard C function would have such a straightforward name. I was right, but disaster ensued because the system wrongly confused my *read* with the Unix system call of the same name. I do not use that compiler now.

Remember, though, that these problems will arise only if you use the identifiers as *external names*, and not with the identifiers of objects or functions you declare as **static**. To reiterate the recommendation given in sections 11.5.1 and 11.5.2: all source-file level declarations of objects and functions should include the word **static** unless you positively intend them to be referred to in other source files. Not only does this minimize the reserved identifier problem; it also improves program modularity.

Appendix 3

Library Summary

The standard library consists of many function definitions and fifteen headers. A header typically contains prototypes for a particular group of library functions, together with associated type and macro definitions. Your C program will normally **#include** the headers for the things it wants to use. The headers, of course, become part of your program for compilation. Inclusion of headers therefore means that your program contains the appropriate type and macro definitions, as well as the function prototypes, which give the compiler enough information to check that the program's use of the functions is consistent with the function definitions. The functions themselves do not become part of the executable program until the linkage stage, after the program has been compiled. (*Minor note:* Implementors are allowed to implement a function as a macro, but must also implement it as a function, since programs must be able to get a pointer to a function.)

It is not always easy to remember which header should be **#include**d for a particular function, macro or type, or the order of the parameters for a particular function. This Appendix is intended to help you look these things up quickly. All items in the standard library are listed in alphabetical order in the third column. The first column gives the appropriate header name. In the case of a function, the full prototype is given, with the function's return type occupying the second column.

You will notice that **NULL** is defined in more than one header. In order to make use of **NULL**, your program must include any one or more of these headers. The same is true of the types **size_t** and **wchar_t**.

This list is not a substitute for the fuller information given elsewhere in this book and by your implementor's documentation. But very often you will remember what a function does and what its parameters are, but not the order of the parameters. To help, I have tried to use meaningful names for the parameters where appropriate.

Header	Type	Name	Notes
stdio.h		**_IOFBF**	*constants for third argument*
stdio.h		**_IOLBF**	*of **setvbuf** (Sect 14.3)*
stdio.h		**_IONBF**	
stdlib.h	void	**abort (void)**	*(raises SIGABRT)*
stdlib.h	int	**abs (int** i)	*absolute (unsigned) value*
math.h	double	**acos (double** x)	*arc cosine of x*
time.h	char*	**asctime (** **const struct tm*** timeptr)	*(Sect 13.8)*
math.h	double	**asin (double** x)	*arc sine of x*
assert.h	void	**assert (int** expression)	*(Sect 3.7)*
math.h	double	**atan (double** x)	*arc tangent of x*
math.h	double	**atan2 (double** y, **double** x)	*arc tangent of y/x*
stdlib.h	int	**atexit (void (*func)(void))**	*(Sect 13.11)*
stdlib.h	double	**atof (const char*** string)	*converts chars to **double***
stdlib.h	int	**atoi (const char*** string)	*converts chars to **int***
stdlib.h	long int	**atol (const char*** string)	*converts chars to **long int***
stdlib.h	void*	**bsearch (** **const void*** key, **const void*** base, **size_t** no_elements, **size_t** element_size, **int** (*comp)(**const void***, **const void***))	*(Sect 13.7)*
stdio.h		**BUFSIZ**	*(Sect 14.3)*

stdlib.h	void*	**calloc (**
		    size_t no_elements,
		    size_t element_size)
			(Sect 9.3)

math.h	double	**ceil (double** x)	*ceiling of x*
limits.h		**CHAR_BIT**	*no. of bits per **char***
limits.h		**CHAR_MAX**	*max **char** value*
limits.h		**CHAR_MIN**	*min **char** value*
stdio.h	void	**clearerr (FILE*** file_p)	*(Sect 5.6)*
time.h	clock_t	**clock (void)**	*(Sect 13.8)*
time.h		**clock_t**	*arith type capable of representing time*
time.h		**CLOCKS_PER_SEC**	*(Sect 13.8)*
math.h	double	**cos (double** x)	*cosine of x*
math.h	double	**cosh (double** x)	*hyperbolic cosine of x*
time.h	char*	**ctime (** **const time_t*** timer)	*(Sect 13.8)*
float.h		**DBL_DIG**	*characteristics of objects of*
float.h		**DBL_EPSILON**	*type **double***
float.h		**DBL_MANT_DIG**	
float.h		**DBL_MAX**	
float.h		**DBL_MAX_10_EXP**	
float.h		**DBL_MAX_EXP**	
float.h		**DBL_MIN**	
float.h		**DBL_MIN_10_EXP**	
float.h		**DBL_MIN_EXP**	
time.h	double	**difftime (time_t** later, **time_t** earlier)	*(Sect 13.8)*
stdlib.h	div_t	**div (int** num, **int** denom)	*quotient and rem division*
stdlib.h		**div_t**	*struct type returned by **div**; members are **quot** and **rem***

errno.h		**EDOM**	*domain error (Sect 13.15)*
stdio.h		**EOF**	*end of file (Sect 5.4)*
errno.h		**ERANGE**	*range error (Sect 13.15)*
errno.h	int	**errno**	*set by some library functions to identify errors*
stdlib.h	void	**exit** (**int** status)	*terminates execution*
stdlib.h		**EXIT_FAILURE**	*arguments for **exit** function*
stdlib.h		**EXIT_SUCCESS**	
math.h	double	**exp** (**double** x)	*exponential function of x*
math.h	double	**fabs** (**double** x)	*absolute (unsigned) value*
stdio.h	int	**fclose** (**FILE*** file_p)	*(Sect 5.3)*
stdio.h	int	**feof** (**FILE*** file_p)	*(Sect 5.6)*
stdio.h	int	**ferror** (**FILE*** file_p)	*(Sect 5.6)*
stdio.h	int	**fflush** (**FILE*** file_p)	*(Sect 14.3)*
stdio.h	int	**fgetc** (**FILE*** file_p)	*(Sect 5.4)*
stdio.h	int	**fgetpos** (**FILE*** file_p, **fpos_t*** position)	*(Sect 14.5)*
stdio.h	char*	**fgets** (**char*** into, **int** length, **FILE*** file_p)	*(Sect 5.6)*
stdio.h		**FILE**	*(Sect 5.1)*
stdio.h		**FILENAME_MAX**	*max length of system file name + 1*
math.h	double	**floor** (**double** x)	*floor of x*
float.h		**FLT_DIG**	*characteristics of objects of type **float***
float.h		**FLT_EPSILON**	
float.h		**FLT_MANT_DIG**	

float.h		**FLT_MAX**	*characteristics of objects of*
float.h		**FLT_MAX_10_EXP**	*type **float***
float.h		**FLT_MAX_EXP**	
float.h		**FLT_MIN**	
float.h		**FLT_MIN_10_EXP**	
float.h		**FLT_MIN_EXP**	
float.h		**FLT_ROUNDS**	
math.h	double	**fmod (double** x, **double** y)	*remainder of x/y*
stdio.h	FILE*	**fopen (const char*** file, **const char*** mode)	*(Sect 5.3)*
stdio.h		**FOPEN_MAX**	*max no of files open simultaneously, including **std** files*
stdio.h		**fpos_t**	*(Sect 14.5)*
stdio.h	int	**fprintf (FILE*** file_p, **const char*** format, **...**)	*like **printf**, but names file*
stdio.h	int	**fputc (int** character, **FILE*** file_p)	*(Sect 5.4)*
stdio.h	int	**fputs (const char*** from, **FILE*** file_p)	*(Sect 5.5)*
stdio.h	size_t	**fread (void*** into, **size_t** element_size, **size_t** no_elements, **FILE*** file_p)	*(Sect 5.7, 14.4)*
stdlib.h	void	**free (void*)**	*(Sect 9.3)*
stdio.h	FILE*	**freopen (** **const char*** file, **const char*** mode, **FILE*** file_p)	*reallocates name to another file and opens*
math.h	double	**frexp (double** x, **int*** exponent)	*breaks x into normalized fraction and integral power of 2*

stdio.h	int	**fscanf** (**FILE*** file_p,
		  const char* format,
		  ...)
			like ***sscanf***, *but takes data
			  directly from a file*

stdio.h	int	**fseek** (**FILE*** file_p,
		  long int offset,
		  int whence)
			(Sect 14.5)

stdio.h	int	**fsetpos** (**FILE*** file_p, **const fpos_t*** position)	*(Sect 14.5)*
stdio.h	long int	**ftell** (**FILE*** file_p)	*(Sect 14.5)*

stdio.h	size_t	**fwrite** (**const void*** from,
		  size_t element_size,
		  size_t no_elements,
		  FILE* file_p)
			(Sect 5.7, 14.4)

stdio.h	int	**getc** (**FILE*** file_p)	*like* ***fgetc***, *but may be macro*
stdio.h	int	**getchar** (**void**)	*as* ***getc*** *for file* ***stdin***
stdlib.h	char*	**getenv** (**const char*** name)	*searches environment list for name*
stdio.h	char*	**gets** (**char*** into)	*dangerous version of* ***fgets*** *for file* ***stdin***
time.h	struct tm*	**gmtime** (**const time_t*** timer)	*(Sect 13.8)*
math.h	double	**HUGE_VAL**	*(Sect 13.15)*
limits.h		**INT_MAX**	*max* ***int*** *value*
limits.h		**INT_MIN**	*min* ***int*** *value*
ctype.h	int	**isalnum** (**int** ch)	ch *alphabetic or numeric?*
ctype.h	int	**isalpha** (**int** ch)	ch *alphabetic?*
ctype.h	int	**iscntrl** (**int** ch)	ch *a control character?*
ctype.h	int	**isdigit** (**int** ch)	ch *a decimal digit?*
ctype.h	int	**isgraph** (**int** ch)	ch *non-space printing char?*

ctype.h	int	**islower** (**int** ch)	ch *a lower-case letter?*
ctype.h	int	**isprint** (**int** ch)	ch *a printing character?*
ctype.h	int	**ispunct** (**int** ch)	ch *a punctuation character?*
ctype.h	int	**isspace** (**int** ch)	ch *a space character?*
ctype.h	int	**isupper** (**int** ch)	ch *an upper-case letter?*
ctype.h	int	**isxdigit** (**int** ch)	ch *a hexadecimal digit?*
setjmp.h		**jmp_buf**	*an array type for holding environment information*
stdio.h		**L_tmpnam**	*max length of temp file name + 1*
stdlib.h	long int	**labs** (**long int** i)	*absolute (unsigned) value*
locale.h		**LC_ALL**	*constant values for first*
locale.h		**LC_COLLATE**	*argument of* **setlocale**
locale.h		**LC_CTYPE**	*(Sect 13.16)*
locale.h		**LC_MONETARY**	
locale.h		**LC_NUMERIC**	
locale.h		**LC_TIME**	
float.h		**LDBL_DIG**	*characteristics of objects of*
float.h		**LDBL_EPSILON**	*type* **long double**
float.h		**LDBL_MANT_DIG**	
float.h		**LDBL_MAX**	
float.h		**LDBL_MAX_10_EXP**	
float.h		**LDBL_MAX_EXP**	
float.h		**LDBL_MIN**	
float.h		**LDBL_MIN_10_EXP**	
float.h		**LDBL_MIN_EXP**	
math.h	double	**ldexp** (**double** x, **int** p)	*returns* $x*2^p$
stdlib.h	ldiv_t	**ldiv** (**long int** num, **long int** denom)	*quotient and rem division*
stdlib.h		**ldiv_t**	*struct type returned by* **ldiv**

locale.h	struct lconv*	**localeconv** (**void**)	*sets structure for current locale*
time.h	struct tm*	**localtime** (**const time_t*** timer)	*(Sect 13.8)*
math.h	double	**log** (**double** x)	*natural log of x*
math.h	double	**log10** (**double** x)	*base-ten log of x*
limits.h		**LONG_MAX**	*max **long int** value*
limits.h		**LONG_MIN**	*min **long int** value*
setjmp.h	void	**longjmp** (**jmp_buf** env, **int** val)	
stdlib.h	void*	**malloc** (**size_t** size)	*(Sect 9.3)*
stdlib.h		**MB_CUR_MAX**	*for multibyte characters*
limits.h		**MB_LEN_MAX**	*max bytes in multibyte char*
stdlib.h	int	**mblen** (**const char*** chars, **size_t** max)	*length of multibyte character*

stdlib.h	size_t	**mbstowcs** (
		     wchar_t* to,
		     const char* from,
		     size_t max)	

stdlib.h	int	**mbtowc** (
		     wchar_t* to,
		     const char* from,
		     size_t max)	

string.h	void*	**memchr** (
		     const void* s,
		     int ch,
		     size_t n)
			locates first occurrence of
			 ch *in first* n *characters*
			 of s

string.h	int	**memcmp** (
		     const void* s1,
		     const void* s2,
		     size_t n)
			compares first n *characters*
			 of s1 *and* s2

string.h	void*	**memcpy** (**void*** to, **const void*** from, **size_t** size)	*(Sect 4.4)*
string.h	void*	**memmove** (**void*** to, **const void*** from, **size_t** size)	*(Sect 4.4)*
string.h	void*	**memset** (**void*** to, **int** ch, **size_t** size)	*(Sect 4.4)*
time.h	time_t	**mktime** (**struct tm*** tm)	*(Sect 13.8)*
math.h	double	**modf** (**double** x, **double*** int_part)	*breaks x into integral and fractional parts*
assert.h		**NDEBUG**	*(Sect 13.3)*
locale.h		**NULL**	*null pointer constant*
stddef.h		**NULL**	
stdio.h		**NULL**	
stdlib.h		**NULL**	
string.h		**NULL**	
time.h		**NULL**	
stddef.h	int	**offsetof** (struct_type, member_name)	*a macro: offset of member from start of struct*
stdio.h	void	**perror** (**const char*** string)	*maps **errno** to message*
math.h	double	**pow** (**double** x, **double** y)	*returns x^y*
stdio.h	int	**printf** (**const char*** format, **...**)	*(Chapter 2, etc.)*
stddef.h		**ptrdiff_t**	*type for pointer difference values*
stdio.h	int	**putc** (**int** ch, **FILE*** file_p)	*(Sect 5.4)*
stdio.h	int	**putchar** (**int** ch)	*as **putc**, for file **stdout***
stdio.h	int	**puts** (**const char*** string)	*writes string to **stdout**, with new-line character appended*

stdlib.h	void	**qsort** (
		    const void* base,
		    size_t no_elements,
		    size_t element_size,
		    int (*comp) (**const void***,
		        const void*))
			(Sect 13.6)

signal.h	int	**raise** (**int** signal)	
stdlib.h	int	**rand** (**void**)	*returns random number*
stdlib.h		**RAND_MAX**	*max value returned by* **rand**
stdlib.h	void*	**realloc** (**void*** item, **size_t** new_size)	*(Sect 9.3)*
stdio.h	int	**remove** (**const char*** file)	*(Sect 14.2)*
stdio.h	int	**rename** (**const char*** old, **const char*** new)	*(Sect 14.2)*
stdio.h	void	**rewind** (**FILE*** file_p)	*(Sect 14.5)*
stdio.h	int	**scanf** (**const char*** format, **...**)	*uses* **stdin**
limits.h		**SCHAR_MAX**	*max* **signed char** *value*
limits.h		**SCHAR_MIN**	*min* **signed char** *value*
stdio.h		**SEEK_CUR**	*(Sect 14.5)*
stdio.h		**SEEK_END**	*(Sect 14.5)*
stdio.h		**SEEK_SET**	*(Sect 14.5)*
stdio.h	void	**setbuf** (**FILE*** file_p, **char*** buffer)	*default form of* **setvbuf**
setjmp.h	int	**setjmp** (**jmp_buf** env)	*saves environment*
locale.h	char*	**setlocale** (**int** category, **const char*** locale)	*(Sect 13.16)*

stdio.h	void	**setvbuf** (**FILE*** file_p, **char*** buffer, **int** mode, **size_t** size)	*(Sect 14.3)*
limits.h		**SHRT_MAX**	*max **short int** value*
limits.h		**SHRT_MIN**	*min **short int** value*
signal.h		**sig_atomic_t**	*(Sect 13.11)*
signal.h	void(*)(int)	**signal** (**int** signal, **void (*func)(int)**)	
signal.h		**SIG_DFL**	*constants for use in signal*
signal.h		**SIG_ERR**	*handling*
signal.h		**SIG_IGN**	
signal.h		**SIGABRT**	
signal.h		**SIGFPE**	
signal.h		**SIGILL**	
signal.h		**SIGINT**	
signal.h		**SIGSEGV**	
signal.h		**SIGTERM**	
math.h	double	**sin** (**double** x)	*sine of x*
math.h	double	**sinh** (**double** x)	*hyperbolic sine of x*
stddef.h		**size_t**	*unsigned integral type of*
stdio.h		**size_t**	*result of **sizeof** operator*
stdlib.h		**size_t**	
string.h		**size_t**	
time.h		**size_t**	
stdio.h	int	**sprintf** (**char*** array, **const char*** format, ...)	*(Sect 6.1)*
math.h	double	**sqrt** (**double** x)	*non-negative square root of x*
stdlib.h	void	**srand** (**unsigned int** seed)	*set seed for **rand***
stdio.h	int	**sscanf** (**const char*** string, **const char*** format, ...)	*(Sect 6.2)*

stdio.h		**stderr**	*names, of type* **FILE***, *for*
stdio.h		**stdin**	*standard error, input and*
stdio.h		**stdout**	*output files, respectively*
string.h	char*	**strcat (char*** to, **const char*** from)	*as* **strncat**, *but without length*
string.h	char*	**strchr (const char*** string, **int** ch)	*(Sect 4.7)*
string.h	int	**strcmp (const char*** string1, **const char*** string2)	*(Sect 4.6)*
string.h	int	**strcoll (const char*** string1, **const char*** string2)	*(Sect 13.16)*
string.h	char*	**strcpy (char*** to, **const char*** from)	*as* **strncpy** *but without length*
string.h	size_t	**strcspn (** **const char*** string1, **const char*** string2)	*max no of initial chars in* string1 *which are not in* string2
string.h	char*	**strerror (int** error_no)	*maps* error_no *to a string*
time.h	size_t	**strftime (char*** array, **size_t** max_chars, **const char*** format, **const struct tm*** tptr)	*(Sect 13.8)*
string.h	size_t	**strlen (const char*** string)	*(Sect 4.2)*
string.h	char*	**strncat (char*** to, **const char*** from, **size_t** length)	*(Sect 4.5)*
string.h	int	**strncmp (** **const char*** string1, **const char*** string2, **size_t** length)	*as* **strcmp**, *with max length*
string.h	char*	**strncpy (char*** to, **const char*** from, **size_t** length)	*(Sect 4.4)*

string.h	char*	**strpbrk** (
		  const char* string1,
		  const char* string2)
			pointer to 1st char in string1
			  which is also in string2

string.h	char*	**strrchr** (**const char*** string,
		  int ch)
			pointer to last occurrence in
			  string *of character* ch

string.h	size_t	**strspn** (**const char*** string1,
		  const char* string2)
			max no of initial chars in
			  string1 *which are in*
			  string2

string.h	char*	**strstr** (**const char*** string, **const char*** substring)	*(Sect 4.7)*
stdlib.h	double	**strtod** (**const char*** string, **char**** endpointer)	*converts chars to* **double**
string.h	char*	**strtok** (**char*** string1, **const char*** string2)	*breaks* string1 *into tokens*

stdlib.h	long int	**strtol** (**const char*** string,
		  char** endpointer,
		  int base)
			converts chars to **long int**

stdlib.h	unsigned
	long int
		strtoul (**const char*** string,
		  char** endpointer,
		  int base)
			converts chars to **unsigned**
			  long int

locale.h		**struct lconv**	*(Sect 13.16)*
time.h		**struct tm**	*(Sect 13.8)*

string.h	size_t	**strxfrm** (**char*** to,
		  const char* from,
		  size_t maxchars)
			(Sect 13.16)

stdlib.h	int	**system** (
		  const char* command)
			calls host system to execute
			  command

math.h	double	**tan** (**double** x)	*tangent of* x
math.h	double	**tanh** (**double** x)	*hyperbolic tangent of* x
time.h	time_t	**time** (**time_t*** timer)	*(Sect 13.8)*
time.h		**time_t**	*(Sect 13.8)*

stdio.h		**TMP_MAX**	*no of unique temp file names*
stdio.h	FILE*	**tmpfile** (**void**)	*(Sect 14.8)*
stdio.h	char*	**tmpnam** (**char*** string)	*generates a file name*
ctype.h	int	**tolower** (**int** ch)	*(Sect 3.3)*
ctype.h	int	**toupper** (**int** ch)	*converts to upper-case*
limits.h		**UCHAR_MAX**	*max* **unsigned char** *value*
limits.h		**UINT_MAX**	*max* **unsigned int** *value*
limits.h		**ULONG_MAX**	*max* **unsigned long int** *value*

stdio.h	int	**ungetc** (**int** ch,
		   FILE* name)
			*pushes character back onto
			   input stream*

limits.h		**USHRT_MAX**	*max* **unsigned short int** *value*
stdarg.h	*type*	**va_arg** (**va_list** argp, *type*)	*(Sect 13.1)*
stdarg.h	void	**va_end** (**va_list** argp)	*(Sect 13.1)*
stdarg.h		**va_list**	*(Sect 13.1)*
stdarg.h	void	**va_start** (**va_list** argp, *parameter_n*)	*(Sect 13.1)*

stdio.h	int	**vfprintf** (**FILE*** file_p,
		   const char* format,
		   va_list arg)
			as **fprintf***, but uses* **va_list**

stdio.h	int	**vprintf** (**const char*** format, **va_list** arg)	*as* **printf***, but uses* **va_list**

stdio.h	int	**vsprintf** (**char*** array,
		   const char* format,
		   va_list arg)
			as **sprintf***, but uses* **va_list**

stddef.h stdlib.h		**wchar_t** **wchar_t**	*type for wide characters*

stdlib.h size_t **wcstombs** (**char*** to,
       const wchar_t* from,
       size_t max)

stdlib.h int   **wctomb** (**char*** to,
       wchar_t from)

Appendix 4

Index of Cobol Features

In their early grapplings with C, Cobol programmers often say "I know how to do this in Cobol, but how do I do it in C?". This index to the Cobol features mentioned in the book should help you find the relevant features of C.

Index

Note: *Appendix 3 lists alphabetically all the functions, macros and types defined in the standard library, and refers to the main text where appropriate.   This index omits standard library items that are not treated in the main text.*